THE B.A.B.Y. BOOK: BEST ADVICE FOR BABY & YOU

The Essential Parent's Hospital Guide to Postpartum Care From Delivery to Discharge... and Beyond!

PARENT'S GUIDE – REVISED 2ND EDITION
KAREN L. BREWER, BSN, RNC-MNN

The B.A.B.Y. Book: Best Advice for Baby & You © Copyright 2023 by Karen L. Brewer.

All rights reserved. No part of this publication may be reproduced, distributed or transmitted in any form or by any means, including photocopying, recording, or other electronic or mechanical methods, without the prior written permission of the publisher, except in the case of brief quotations embodied in critical reviews and certain other noncommercial uses permitted by copyright law. Please do not participate in or encourage the piracy of copyrighted materials in violation of the author's rights. Purchase only authorized additions.

Willful copyright infringement can result in criminal penalties, including imprisonment of up to five years and fines of up to $250,000 per offense. Copyright infringement can also result in civil judgments.

Adherence to all applicable laws and regulations, including international, federal, state and local governing professional licensing, business practices, advertising, and all other aspects of doing business in the US, Canada or any other jurisdiction is the sole responsibility of the reader and consumer.

Although the author and publisher have made every effort to ensure that the information in this book was correct at press time, the author and publisher do not assume and hereby disclaim any liability to any party for any loss, damage, or disruption caused by errors or omissions, whether such errors or omissions result from negligence, accident, or any other cause.

Neither the author nor the publisher assumes any responsibility or liability whatsoever on behalf of the consumer or reader of this material. Any perceived slight of any individual or organization is purely unintentional.

For more information, email: mombabyrnc@gmail.com

ISBN: 978-1-961473-00-3 Paperback
ISBN: 978-1-961473-01-0 eBook ePUB
ISBN: 978-1-961473-02-7 eBook AZW or AZW3 (Amazon)
ISBN: 978-1-961473-03-4 eBook IBA (iBooks Apple)

Important Disclaimer

This book is about routine care. There may be some issues or diagnoses that you may come across with your care or your baby's care, which may not be addressed in this book. This is where the obstetrician or pediatrician comes into play. They should discuss with you and educate you on any "out of the ordinary" situations and how the care will be administered.

Although I am a nurse by profession, all the information in this book is for educational purposes only. This book does not constitute medical advice or establish a patient-nurse relationship through your use of this information. Although I strive to supply accurate information and suggestions in this book, it's in no way a substitute for medical advice, and you should not rely solely on this information.

Download Your Free Checklists

READ THIS FIRST

To say "Thank You" for purchasing my book, I wanted to give you something back in return.

Below is the link to download several checklists and selected quantities of valuable information to help you get ready for the "BIG DAY!!" This includes:

- Before the "Big Day" Checklist... things to do the last trimester to get yourself ready...

- Hospital Bag Checklist... know what to pack what you'll need, and not need (with explanation sheet)...

- Baby Necessities (and What Not to Buy)... so you spend your money wisely...

- Nursery Registry Checklist... list of things you need to put in your baby registry at your favorite store or website... and more!

This way you have a more informative set of checklists *specific* to you, my group of parent readers. I may even have more surprises to add to the list!!

Download here: https://www.mombabyrn.com/checklists

Reviews

"I have to tell you a story first before I share my review of your book. About a week ago, before I read your book, my 19-year-old daughter asked me my opinion about bathing a baby. I asked what she meant, and she said there is this covering on babies that some people think should not be washed off. I thought, hmm... perhaps Karen mentions this in her book, and I will let you know. How awesome that when I read your book, the answer was on pages 141 and 142 under the baby's first bath!

I believe you have done an outstanding job in service to moms on what they can expect or may experience. It was a pleasure reading it, and I wish I had it myself back when I had our daughter. . . . You addressed so many issues that are important, and very obviously, your specialty and expertise shone through. . . . I really enjoyed reading it, and I thought the way you added some humor and warmth was very well done!"

Michelle DeLizio Podlesni, RN
President of National Nurses in Business Association
Founder and Author of *"UNconventional Nurse®*
Going from Burnout to Bliss!"

"Here is my review: I could have written about it all night.

I was a Labor and Delivery Nurse for years and worked postpartum. I was also cross-trained in the operating room and taught birthing classes. I read "The B.A.B.Y. Book (Best Advice for Baby & You)", and I thought I would find something to be incorrect or just not covered. I was wrong! This book covers everything a parent needs to know when anticipating the birth of their first baby.

As a nurse, I appreciate how thoughtful Karen was in writing this book. Many patients are often caught off guard by possible complications and medications to expect to take while delivering and recovering. I taught birthing classes, and I know for sure this book goes further in depth.

What really blew me away was Karen's thoughtfulness about the entire experience of the parents and their new baby. This is proven by the amount of detail she goes into for the care of the new infant. She takes time to even mention overstimulating the baby.

Karen is correct, "Everything we do as nurses or practitioners are to make sure you and your new baby have a great start to your new life ahead." A great start is by reading this book which covers everything necessary, is easy to read, and easy to understand."

Lydia Cook, RN
Owner and CEO of *Lydia Cook Coaching, LLC*

Dedication

First and foremost, I would like to give God the glory, for through Him, I would not be here today sharing my nursing knowledge with parents and nurses alike. He gave me hope, courage, strength, passion, compassion, and fortitude to carve my path in the world—an empathetic soul who found her calling, lending a hand and helping to heal others. He continues to work through me to help teach in an entirely new course, pen to paper, still helping to guide parents and nurses along the way. The love of healing and caring is as strong as the love of research and teaching. My wish is to continue teaching until I can teach no more. Thanks be to God for allowing me this special time on Earth.

This book is very dear to my heart, and I would not be where I am today without *three* very special "angels"— who have been given back to God:

To my parents, Jim Rinehart and Goldie Simmons Rinehart Frost—if not for you two, I would not be where I am today. You brought me into this world and taught me that I could do anything I put my mind to, and I did just that. Thank you for believing in me, loving me, and trusting I would do well with my life.

To my stepmother, Ella Culbertson Pippenger Rinehart— You helped raise me in those adolescent years and into young adulthood. Instilling in me to be independent, disciplined, and hard-working, which had paid off ten-fold.

Thanks to all of you, I am who I am today— a wife, mother, nurse, author, content writer, and entrepreneur. I hope I have made you all proud, my Heavenly angels.

Love to you all,
Karen

Table of Contents

Introduction 1
Preface 4
Mother's Care 7
Immediate Post-Delivery 8
   Fundal Massage 8
   Intravenous (IV) Fluids 9
   Rehydration 11
   Getting Out of Bed/Back into Bed 11
   Continued Postpartum Nursing Care 14
Vaginal Deliveries 16
   Perineal Care 16
      Vaginal swelling 17
      Hemorrhoids 17
      Hematomas 18
      Episiotomies/vaginal lacerations/stitches 19
      Cleansing bottle/Hygenique® sprayer or sitz bath 20
      Topical pads and medications 21
      Perineal pads/panties 22
   Moving Around in Bed/Moving Up in Bed 22
Urgent/Emergent Issues During Labor and/or Delivery 24
   Cord Prolapse 24
   Breech Presentation 25
   Placenta Previa 25
   Shoulder Dystocia 26
   Fetal Distress (Fetal Intolerance to Labor) 28

Cesarean Section Deliveries **29**
 What to Expect During Your Initial Recovery *31*
  Intravenous (IV) lines *32*
  Intravenous (IV) fluids *33*
  Intravenous (IV) meds *33*
  PCA pump. *36*
  Ice chips/sips of water *37*
  Eating after surgery *38*
  Sitting up in bed *39*
  Incentive spirometers *40*
  Dangling and getting out of bed. *41*
  Foley catheters *42*
  Perineal care *44*
  Ambulating in the halls. *45*
  Use of the rocking chair. *48*
  Chewing gum *49*
 Incisional Care/Issues *49*
  Oozing or bleeding from the site. *50*
  Cleaning your incision *50*
  Numbness at the incision site *51*
  Burning on or around the site. *52*
  Bruising around the site *53*
  Pain more on one side *53*
  Pain from additional surgical procedures *54*
 Some Incision Do's and Don'ts. *55*
  Some of the "don'ts". *55*
  Bracing your incision. *56*
  Moving your body up in bed *56*
  Turning over in bed *57*
Pain Management. **58**
 Vaginal Pain Relief. *62*
 Cesarean Section Pain Relief *64*
  Intravenous (IV) pain relief. *66*
  PCA pain relief (see under IV meds above) *67*
  Oral pain medications *68*

    How to take oral pain medications *69*
    Weaning off oral narcotic pain meds. *70*
    Physician's ordering style for oral pain meds *72*
    Reasons for recommended oral pain meds *73*
    Women with a history of opioid use *75*
  Pain Management Conclusion *75*

Voiding (Urinating) **77**

Bleeding/Clots/Hemorrhaging **80**

Other Medications/Supplements **84**
  Colace® (docusate sodium) or Peri-Colace® (w/added laxative) *84*
  MiraLAX®/Milk of Magnesia®/Ducolax®. *85*
  Tums®/Gas-X®/Phasyme®/Mylicon®/Mylanta®—and Others *86*
  Prenatal Vitamins *87*
  Iron Tablets (ferrous sulfate). *88*

Vaccinations **90**
  Hepatitis B. *90*
  MMR (Measles, Mumps, Rubella) *90*
  Tdap (Tetanus, Diphtheria, and Pertussis) *92*
  Influenza Vaccine. *95*
  Pneumococcal Vaccine *97*

Lab Work **98**
  CBC (Complete Blood Count) *98*
  ABO & Rh Factor Incompatibilities. *99*
  Group B Beta Strep (+ or -). *101*
  Hepatitis B, Syphilis, Gonorrhea, HIV (or AIDS) *102*

To Mothers Using Illicit Drugs and/or Having Limited/No Prenatal Care . . **103**

Q&A on Other Post-Delivery Concerns **107**

Post-Hospital Complications / Emergencies **124**

Baby's Care 127

Beginning with Recovery **128**

Detailed Recovery for the Baby. **131**
  Suctioning Out the Baby *131*
  Vital Signs *132*
  Baby's Other Recovery Needs *134*

    Apgar scores *134*
    Baby's measurements *135*
    Ballard scoring *136*
    Erythromycin eye ointment *137*
    Vitamin K *138*
    Hepatitis B vaccine *138*
    Blood sugars (blood glucose) *139*
    Baby's 1st bath *141*

Diapering Your Baby **145**

Some "Oddities" Found When Changing Diapers. **149**
    Small Number of Diapers *149*
    Pink-Tinged Spots on the Diaper *150*
    Sacral Dimples *150*
    Lots of Large Stools at the Beginning— and Then None *151*
    Swollen Genitals *152*
    Findings with Little Girl's "Parts" *152*
        Vaginal discharge *152*
        Smaller outer labia *152*
        Labial skin tags *153*
    Findings with Little Boy's "Parts" *153*
        Undescended testicles *153*
        Penile torsion *153*
        Hypospadias *154*
        Congenital chordee *154*
        Natural circumcision *155*

Changing Baby's Clothes **156**

Wrapping Baby in a Blanket **159**

Other Newborn Observations **160**
    Findings on the Head *160*
        Conehead (elongated head) *160*
        Caput succedaneum (swollen head) *161*
        Cephalohematoma (blood-filled, swollen head) *161*
        Sutures on the skull (ridges) *162*
        Fontanels ("the soft spot") *163*
        Bruising on the head or face *165*

Abrasions, scratches, and lacerations. 165
Findings on the Facial Features 166
    Eyes, ears, and face 167
Skin Color and Conditions 168
    Color differences 169
Surface Skin Conditions/Lesions. 177
    Certain skin conditions 177
    Birthmarks or lesions 179
Immature Body Systems. 182
    Eyes 182
    Liver. 183
    Nervous system 183
    Gastrointestinal system (gastric reflux). 184
Preterm or Premature Newborn. 186
    Respiratory (breathing) difficulties. 187
    Feeding difficulties 188
    Gastrointestinal (stomach/intestinal) issues 188
    Hypothermia (low body temperature) 189
    Hypoglycemia (low blood sugar) 189
    Cardiac (heart) issues 190
    Brain issues 191
    Blood issues 191
    Immune system 192
Q&A on Other Baby Concerns 193
Feeding Your Baby During Your Hospital Stay. 209
    Exclusive Breastfeeding is BEST…but It's <u>YOUR</u> Choice. 209
    "Ten Steps to Successful Breastfeeding". 211
    Starting to Breastfeed. 216
    Comfortable breastfeeding positioning 218
    Establishing Breastfeeding. 220
    Positions for feeding baby 221
    Nipple shape and size. 223
    Poor breast attachment 223
    Sore nipples 224
    Be proactive with your nipples 225

Instant gratification	*225*
Breast massaging	*226*
Expressing Colostrum	*226*
When your milk comes in	*227*
The engorgement period	*227*
Documenting feedings	*230*
Supplementation	*231*
Banked breast milk	*232*
Formula supplementation	*232*
Supplemental Nursing System (SNS)	*233*
Nipple Damage from Breastfeeding	*233*
Expressed colostrum or milk	*234*
Lanolin ointments/creams	*235*
Hydrogel pads	*235*
All-purpose nipple cream	*236*
Nipple shells	*236*
Breast Augmentation/Reduction	*237*
Flat or Inverted Nipples	*238*
Latch assist	*239*
Nipple shields	*239*
Breast pump	*240*
Pacifier Usage During Breastfeeding	*241*
Pumping Your Breasts	*245*
Starting to pump	*245*
Cleaning your pumping equipment	*246*
Baby's Not Wanting to Eat	*246*
Just too tired	*246*
Don't want to eat because… BARF!!	*247*
Burping your Baby	*248*
After the Feeding and Burping are Over…	*251*
Breastfeeding Conclusion	*252*
Q&A on Other Breastfeeding Concerns	**253**
So… You Choose to Formula Feed Your Baby	**264**
Preventing Milk Supply from Coming In	*265*
First Thing to Do Before Beginning to Feed	*266*

- Baby's Not Wanting to Eat 267
  - Just too tired 267
  - Don't want to eat because… BARF!! 268
  - Don't seem to like the taste of the formula 268
- Baby Having Difficulty Feeding from the Nipple. 269
  - Stroking the nipple down the tongue 270
  - Using chin support 270
  - Using cheek support 271
  - Working around an intense gag reflex 271
- Forgetting to Breathe While Sucking on the Nipple. 272
- Sucking Very Hard, Thus Sucking Down the Formula 273
- Overfeeding Your Baby Formula 274
- Burping Your Baby 276
- After the Feeding and Burping are Over… 279

Q&A on Bottle Feeding Concerns **280**

Circumcisions (The "Boys Only" Club) **284**
- Care of the Circumcision Site 288
  - Plastibell 288
  - Mogen or Gomco clamps 289
  - Drainage or oozing from the site 290
  - Watching for the 1st post-circumcision void 291
  - Crying or sleeping… which one is it going to be?? 292

Other Topics of Discussion **294**
- Sudden Infant Death Syndrome (SIDS) 294
  - Physical factors 295
  - Environmental factors 295
  - Infant risk factors 296
  - Maternal risk factors 297
  - Prevention 297
- Co-Sleeping 299
  - Benefits of co-sleeping 299
  - Cons to co-sleeping 299
- Bed-Sharing 300
- Rooming-In During Your Hospital Stay 301
- Anxiety Around the Baby 304

Your Discharge from the Hospital **306**
    Birth Certificate/Affidavit *306*
    Paternity Testing *307*
    Car Seat Check. *308*
    Screenings for the Baby *311*
        Bilirubin levels. *311*
        Critical congenital heart defects (CCHD) testing *312*
        Hearing screening *313*
        PKU (phenylketonuria) testing/state testing *314*
        Blood testing/typing. *315*
The "OTHER" Topics. **317**
    Visitors, Visitors, Visitors. *317*
    Sick Visitors *320*
    Inexcusably Pushy Visitors. *323*
    Passing the Baby Around "Like a Football" *326*
    Social Media. *328*
    Generational Pictures. *329*
    Hospital Gifts *330*
    A Note to the Fathers/Significant Others. *330*
It's the "Little Things…" **333**
Last… But Not Least **335**
Conclusion **336**
Acknowledgments. **339**
About the Author **341**
References **343**

Introduction

The anticipation and waiting are over!! You are in the home stretch and are either ready to deliver or have just delivered your brand-new bundle(s) of joy. You have been reading books, scouring the internet, and/or getting advice and info from your family and friends. For first-time parents, you have feelings of excitement and anxiety about the new baby. Will the baby be born okay? Will I be a good mother/father? Am I ready for this? Then— after the baby comes, you become anxious about "every little thing." Is the baby too hot or too cold? Getting enough to eat? Am I doing everything right? Am I doing anything right?

Relief, joy, and worry overwhelm you. The first few days after delivery become a blur, and you cannot remember anything. You panic!!! Your nurses have educated and instructed you on caring for yourself and your baby— and maybe went over things once or twice. Now you can't remember something your nurse taught you. Unfortunately, you may only remember less than half *(<50%)* of everything your nurse went over during your stay— maybe more like 25%. As the saying goes, "In one ear and out the other." That's not a lot of retention, but just remember how wild, crazy, and overwhelming the past few days have been for you! By the time you go home, you'll wonder, "What just happened??" It was all a blur. Thus, begins the worry…

I tell my patients three things:

- *Do not* hesitate to ask questions
- *Do not* worry about asking them more than once
- *Do not* apologize for asking them!!

This includes *ALL* Moms and Dads, not just the newbies. Sometimes you forget things from one child to the next, especially the "little details," and that's okay to ask questions again. Your nurse should not make you feel guilty for any of these things, and if they try to— *don't let them!*

You're getting inundated with *so* much information quickly that you cannot comprehend it all. It is so difficult to do when you are totally exhausted— so you forget *a lot*. So ask lots of questions, and don't worry if you already asked them before— *that's okay*. No question is a stupid question— no matter how many times you might ask it!! We, as nurses, want you to be well-educated and comfortable with everything before you leave to go home, whether it's your postpartum care or your baby's care.

Teaching patients and significant others how to care for themselves *(and I do mean the guys, too)* and how to care for the baby is *so* important. It is probably *the* most important task I performed as a postpartum nurse. Yes, I carefully assessed and checked all my patients and made sure they were pain-free *(or as close as possible)*. I also dealt with any problems and/or challenges during their stay. But— I spent much of my time teaching the family about mom and baby care— or reminding and/or re-educating the experienced parents. Sometimes the smallest details would be forgotten. So— I have taken the time to provide a more comprehensive reference guide to help with questions or concerns you might have before— or after you are discharged from the hospital.

> ~Education is the shared commitment between dedicated teachers, motivated students, and enthusiastic parents with high expectations.
>
> ~~ Bob Beauprez

Preface

With over 20 years of in-hospital mother-baby experience, I have loved and continue to love teaching patients how to care for themselves and their new babies. But one of the things I noticed during my career is parents have many questions, some of which have nothing to do with routine care but are about— "little things." At least, what *I* thought were "little things" could genuinely concern parents. Even veteran parents who have not encountered something specific with themselves or previous babies. Those concerns and questions gave me the idea to write this book. I started researching online to see if I could find something out there that has been written for parents to help address these concerns and questions. In looking for a book or guide like this one 5 years ago, I found there was *nothing out there*, and still— even now when I updated this second version of this book.

There are self-help books for breastfeeding, postpartum depression, pregnancy, baby care, etc. Still, nothing specifically about mom and baby care during their hospital stay and for things that might pop up shortly after returning home. At least I didn't find any— fast forward 5 years, and there still isn't a book written in as much detail as this one here. The only exception was buying several other books— or piecemeal information from several books or guides which might have helped resolve their questions. That would cost some additional money. And who wants to spend a lot of money on multiple books when other things would be more important to spend your money on? There is *now* the new baby you must be financially responsible for— and we all know they are *EXPENSIVE!* Let's spend our money wisely, shall we?

Even though patients are educated in the hospital— or at least, *I hope* they are— sometimes the "little things" are forgotten. Things that should be taught to every patient but *never* are. Nonetheless, nursing care can be varied. Some nurses don't thoroughly explain things, only briefly summarize specific issues and move on. Some don't like to do the teaching at all and try to only provide direct patient care, thus cheating parents of a well-rounded educational experience. And not all nurses can give patients their undivided attention all the time due to time constraints or other more time-consuming patient issues. *(**Unfortunately, emergencies and problems to do come up that must take precedence.)* There's also the looming issue of nursing shortages nationwide and worldwide. From just a couple years ago to now, in 2023, nurses are leaving hospitals in droves. So, the light bulb came on— that *"aha"* moment when I realized patients might benefit from a book that would help address those questions or concerns with themselves and their babies. So I set out on a long journey to provide patients and their significant others with a guide in book form to cover every topic I could think of. This way, if something does get missed by your nurses, you then have this guide to refer back to and fill in the blanks for you.

Now— not all the information is evidenced-based because there may *not have* been a study on a particular situation or matter. Although a lot of data does come from evidenced-based practice. Some studies are used to educate medical professionals throughout their careers. Some info comes from reference books, journals, and websites.

And— some of it comes from good old-fashioned nursing judgment and practice. Wherever the information comes from, you can be assured it's researched, documented, and referenced for accuracy— and/or became part of my practice as a nurse in the hospital setting.

Mother's Care

Care of the mother after birth is crucial to her well-being. This assists her in healing after delivery and allows her to care for the baby *(or babies)* and family. From the delivery, the mother focuses on the baby and what life will be like in the days, months, and years ahead. How will the new baby fit in? How will I be able to cope? Many thoughts race through parents' minds on how much impact this new little being has on their family. It's essential to focus on the baby and their daily needs, but mothers must be aware of how much their focus must be on themselves too. When teaching various aspects of post-delivery care, one of the main topics I emphasized regularly is: *"You must take care of yourself... in order to take care of your baby."* With this thought in mind, let's move on to caring for Mom. We will focus on both vaginal and cesarean deliveries regarding recovery and care.

Immediate Post-Delivery

Immediately after delivery, you will begin the recovery phase of your postpartum care. Your blood pressure, pulse, respiration, and temperature will be monitored repeatedly. You will be given various medications and intravenous *(IV)* fluids to aid your recovery. You will also be monitored for response to your body's ability to start moving normally *(post-epidural, spinal, or general anesthetic)*— allowing you to start caring for yourself. You may be given additional medications, such as antibiotics if you have an infection or Pitocin® to help your uterus along with muscle contraction. Uterotonics *(i.e., Methergine®, Hemabate®, Cytotec®, additional Pitocin®)* are given to aid in uterine muscle contraction if you have postpartum hemorrhaging. Other medications may also be given to you depending on your individual "plan of care." Still, for the sake of this guide, we will focus on routine postpartum care.

Fundal Massage

This is the part that all patients really hate when it is being administered. Your nurse supports the uterus from the bottom, right above the pelvic bone, finds the top of your uterus at about your belly button, and pushes down from the top. Then she *SQUEEZES AND RUBS IT REALLY HARD!!!* Suppose you're lucky enough to have had an epidural or spinal that has not worn off entirely. In that case, this is maybe only slightly uncomfortable. However, if you aren't so lucky… *WOW!!* You may want to punch out your nurse for hurting you so badly! I assure you that your nurse is not a sadist. She is ensuring that after your delivery, your uterus is contracting effectively to close off the blood vessels where the placenta was attached. Also, any blood clots that might have formed after the baby was delivered are completely removed.

Clots in the uterus that aren't removed increase the potential for later developing a postpartum hemorrhage. It's also essential any placental fragments are removed as well. Generally, your doctor will inspect the placenta after removal to make sure of this. Still, even the very smallest fragment might be missed. Remaining tissue can also cause a postpartum infection— and we absolutely *do not* want to go there! Just be reassured this intense fundal massage is generally during your recovery phase only, usually the first two hours.

After the recovery, your nurse should only check to ensure your uterus stays firm and in the right location. She does not need to massage anywhere near as hard as is done during recovery *(**Unless you have one who really is a sadist, then I feel for you.)* If she finds it is not firm, be aware that the heavy fundal massage *will be* commencing again until such time it is firm. So, while you may think your wonderful delivery nurse has *now* become "Evil Incarnate," you will be thankful she is doing what is necessary to ensure you recover well. Brace yourself; it really is a *"necessary evil!"*

Intravenous (IV) Fluids

You will begin receiving intravenous *(IV)* fluids either right before you deliver, during a scheduled cesarean section, or when you go to the hospital for induction or are in labor. Either way, this is to help get you and keep you hydrated during the labor/delivery process. You lose fluids throughout either process, so it helps to rehydrate after your delivery is complete. Lactated ringers and D5LR *(Dextrose 5% & Lactated Ringers)* are the most commonly used IV solutions.

How long you will continue receiving these fluids after your delivery and recovery depends completely on if you have a vaginal or cesarean section. For vaginal deliveries, IV fluids will usually be removed after recovery is completed and you have been up to void without difficulties. For cesarean sections, IV fluids generally will be continued past the recovery period until approximately 12 hours or so. This depends on the institution and if you can take water orally without any nausea and vomiting. You also need to drink enough water to help keep you hydrated without further use of additional IV fluids.

You may have the IV fluids *restarted* if you have any signs, symptoms, or complications, such as:

- Dizziness/passing out during your 1st trip to the bathroom
- Fever
- Nausea and vomiting
- Increased blood loss/hemorrhaging and/or clots
- Decreased blood pressure
- Very low urine output

You will be removed from the fluids again once the crisis has resolved and you have recovered from whatever situation required additional fluids.

For mothers who are Rh-negative and your baby's labs come back showing Rh-positive, we can leave the IV site open and saline locked until you receive Rhophylac®. This can be administered in this site, so you don't have to get a shot in the gluteus maximus *(bottom)* again. *YAY!!* However, if your hospital only has RhoGAM available then I'm sorry— it will be a shot in the tush. *Booo!!*

Rehydration

After you have delivered, it is essential you get rehydrated with plenty of fluids. Suppose you have had or will have a vaginal delivery. In that case, your nurse will likely finish giving you IV fluids when she determines you have been thoroughly rehydrated. She will also strongly suggest you drink plenty of water to keep you hydrated, which helps aid in recovery. This does not mean drinking soda, tea, coffee, etc., to get the job done, although these may be had in moderation. Your body currently is made up of upwards of 72.5%-75% water compared to the 60% men and non-pregnant or non-newly delivered women. Therefore, water is the preferred way to get rehydrated without IV fluids.

Suppose you have had/will be having a cesarean section. In that case, you will be slowly introduced to ice chips, and if you tolerate those, then move on to taking sips of water. Once you tolerate sips, you will be advanced to drinking water. However, you will remain on IV fluids until you put out a significant amount of urine through the Foley catheter you have in place. Only then will you be removed from IV hydration and will continue drinking lots of water.

Getting Out of Bed/Back into Bed

Your nurse will check on you at various times during your recovery to check your Aldrete score:

- How awake you are
- How well you can breathe
- What your blood pressure looks like

- How good your oxygen saturation in your blood
- How much function you have in your arms and legs after your delivery

This is used to help determine if you have any after-effects of your anesthesia or can get out of bed without difficulty. You should recover relatively quickly if you have not had an epidural, spinal, or general anesthesia. However, if you have blood loss, some medications may affect you when you stand up and move around; your nurse will also repeatedly check how you feel as you move.

Whatever you do— *DO NOT* get out of bed for the first time without your nurse present! Nothing is worse than a patient who thinks, "I feel just fine. I can do this on my own." You can go from feeling just fine to "I'm going to pass out" in a heartbeat. So— make sure she's there!!! For cesarean deliveries, it may be several hours before your nurse will allow you to get up. Still, the same concept applies to you as well. I'll let you in on a little secret— nurses *really* don't like having to fill out an incident report if you have fallen— so, please, please, please— don't make them!! I batted 1.000 with this incredibly detailed suggestion, and not one of my patients had ever hit the floor on my watch— in all my 20+ years!! That's a record I kept as long as I worked on the maternity unit.

When your nurse is by the bedside, and you are ready to get up, position the head of the bed so it raises you to a sitting position. Bend your knees and place your feet flat on the bed. The closer you can comfortably manage to pull your feet toward your bottom— the better. Then place your hands flat on the bed next to your hips. Use your hands and feet to gently lift your bottom off the bed and move over toward the edge of the bed. *(**You may have to do this several times in* *small increments to get to the edge, and that's okay.)* Then rotate your hips to the side, place your elbow against the raised headboard and your other hand by your elbow, or grasp the handrail. Then swing your legs over the edge of the bed and push yourself to a sitting position. Now— *do not* immediately get up! Sit there for a minute or two to ensure you have your bearings and are not lightheaded, dizzy, ears ringing, vision blurring, etc.

Once you feel stable, plant your feet on the floor shoulder length apart, look straight ahead and not down to the floor, push off the bed, and then stand up. Again, wait at least 15-30 seconds to ensure you are stable before heading to the bathroom or walking around the room for the first time. If at any time you start to feel lightheaded, dizzy, ears ringing, or vision blurring— let your nurse know immediately! You can go from, "I am starting to feel…" to falling to the floor rather quickly. This way, she can get you back to bed quickly and safely. She may request assistance from other staff to help get you back to bed without incident, so don't be alarmed when she does.

The concept of properly getting out of bed is based on my observation of mechanics utilized by different nurses. During years of nursing, I have found both vaginal and cesarean delivery patients can decrease the potential pain they might cause themselves by following my method.

- *For vaginal delivery patients* - this technique eliminates "scooting" on your bottom area, which may be sore, swollen, and/or stitched up. Any way to decrease the amount of pain and discomfort in this area is always a plus.

- *For cesarean section patients* - this helps by utilizing your arms and legs to assist in maneuvering into a new position without placing additional strain on the incision site. If you "scoot" on your bottom, you will pull your incision site from the lower segment. When you "scoot" forward, it stretches the skin below your incision downward, causing pulling on the incision and unnecessary additional pain. This is because your vaginal skin is linked all the way up to your incision site. Also, any time you can keep from using your abdominal muscles to move around and get in or out of bed— this is "a good thing." *(**And, I might add, those muscles are not functioning for the time being.)*

Continued Postpartum Nursing Care

After completing your initial recovery, you will go into the postpartum care phase for the remainder of your hospital stay. Every four hours now, for the next 24 hours, you will have your vital signs checked. After the first 24 hours, you will be checked once every 12 hours until discharge. Your nurse will ask if you have any pain and medicate you. She will also ask if you have any questions or concerns, address them, and see if you need instructions on your or your baby's care. Then she will go over the paperwork requiring completion before you go home. Whenever you have questions or concerns you happen to think of when your nurse is absent, use your call light to contact her for assistance *or* write it down and ask when she returns.

If your nurse is unavailable at that time, usually, another nurse can fill in and take care of your needs in her absence. Please be patient with the staff getting someone there to assist you, as we previously discussed in the *"Preface"* regarding the ongoing shortage of nurses everywhere. Hopefully, this is not the case on your hospital unit, but it could be, so please be kind to the staff remaining and willing to still care for all the patients. Your nurse may have gone from caring for

3-4 patients to caring for 5-6 or more, which is extremely difficult. Those 5-6 patients could be 10-12 on a smaller hospital unit where your nurse may care for both mother and baby. *(**It is on the hospital unit I worked on. That is called couplet care.)* A postpartum nurse on a larger hospital unit may only care for the mothers, and nursery nurses will care for the babies. That may make the nurses have 10-12 mothers instead of couplets to care for. It is still a considerable number of patients to care for on *any* unit. All the more reason there is a need for a guide to help patients with any education the staff may not have the time to address. This guide will help bridge the gap between you and your nurses when time is scarce to accomplish all needed education.

Vaginal Deliveries

After your baby is delivered, you will be enamored with the new bundle of joy on your chest. While your attention is elsewhere, your doctor is busy repairing your vaginal area and cleaning you up. You will be checked for lacerations, tears, and any bleeding areas, and the appropriate repairs will be made. If you're lucky, there aren't any repairs to be made— you get to skip the step of the repairs and jump into the post-delivery clean-up phase.

Your nurse will follow behind, cleaning your perineum and removing all the drapes surrounding you once everything is completed on the doctor's end. She may put an ice pack on your perineum— if you might be swelling soon, remove your legs from the stirrups and replace the previously removed parts of the labor bed.

Once you have completed your recovery phase, you will get up to the bathroom for the first time after your delivery. Your nurse will assist you in getting up for the first time and then go over how to take care of your perineum once you have sat on the toilet. The following is what I went over with my patients on how to take care of themselves post-delivery.

Perineal Care

Care for your perineal area, which includes your vagina and rectal area, is very important to help eliminate the possibility of infection and to promote healing. Since the word "vagina" may be a medical term that makes the average person uncomfortable speaking, your nurse may use any of the various nicknames given to this general region.

I've heard "hoo-hoo" or "hoo-hah" used many times throughout my career. So, to lend a little humor to our teaching, I will utilize "hoo-hah" or "nether region" a few times during this lesson.

Vaginal swelling

After a vaginal delivery, you may have mild to severe swelling to your hoo-hah's outer and inner folds. These folds are called the labia majora and labia minora, respectively. Due to pelvic pressure placed on your hoo-hah before delivery and all the pressure from pushing the baby out during delivery, both the inner and outer folds of the labia can become swollen. This can become extremely uncomfortable to sit on your bottom. So, lie down on either side whenever you can and place a pillow between your legs. This can take a great deal of pressure off the area. Ice packs placed at the site soon after delivery will help with reducing the swelling and help numb the affected area, so ask for it if it is not offered to you. You can continue requesting ice packs for the next 24 hours to help with the swelling, and your nurse will also provide topical meds. *(**See "Topical pads and medications" below.)* When you *must* sit up, such as during eating or breastfeeding, you may want to lean slightly to one side or the other and wedge a small, thin pillow or soft blanket under the raised "butt" cheek. Unfortunately, you can do nothing for the pressure caused down there if you must laugh, cough, or sneeze. Brace yourself the best you can and hope it doesn't hurt too much.

Hemorrhoids

These are other things that can put additional pressure on your bottom. During pregnancy, they develop in some patients due to the pelvic pressure on the rectal veins, which causes blood to collect.

They may be mild to severe and may become quite uncomfortable. Straining to have a bowel movement due to constipation will also aggravate and possibly cause them to *"pop out."* Then the added pressure of pushing out a baby can also make them *"pop out"* of the rectum. Generally, they will go back up into the rectum after delivery as the swelling subsides. The same issues apply to hemorrhoids as it does to vaginal swelling regarding the pressure placed on them while sitting. The *"Topical pads and medications"* recommendations below can also help with them. Even if you do not feel like you have hemorrhoids, your nurse may find evidence of them.

Suppose the hemorrhoids do not recede back into the rectum. If you continue to have issues with hemorrhoids after discharge, and/or they continue to be a problem for you, follow up with your OB doctor and let them know. They may treat the issue or refer you to a specialist who can treat them.

Hematomas

This can be caused by a rupture or trauma to the blood vessels with no tears or lacerations on the outer tissue during delivery. Blood then leaks or flows into the tissues causing the hematoma. Most of the time, your body will reabsorb this collection of blood without any problem. If the blood continues escaping, and a hematoma forms and enlarges over time, this can become extremely painful. Generally, pain medications do not seem to relieve much pain, if at all. Suppose your nurse has determined you may have a hematoma through the continuous complaint of pain and getting absolutely no relief from medications. In that case, she should look at your nether region to check specifically for a hematoma to determine if this is true. If it is, the physician will need to evacuate the blood and repair the cause of the hematoma. This may cause additional soreness, but the pain relief should be remarkably better.

Episiotomies/vaginal lacerations/stitches

These are some of the issues that make *most* mothers tremble and quake during their recovery time. The very thought of having to go #2 puts the *"fear of God"* in them! The nether region is already sore, tender, or down-right painful, and to have a bowel movement any time soon is a *mortifying* thought! Our skin and hoo-hah can stretch, but some cannot stretch enough to avoid developing surface lacerations or tears in their nether region. Your doctor may perform/has performed an episiotomy to help provide additional room for the baby to come out. They will then repair that and any other necessary lacerations. An ice pack afterward can help numb the area and reduce any swelling you may have. *(**See "Topical pads and medications" below.)*

Here is another little tip for those with vaginal or possible rectal repairs. *(**Yes, some people will need repairs to the rectum too, if you have had what is called a 4th degree— a complete tear through the rectal wall.)* Sitting down on the toilet, chair, or bed may cause those stitches to feel like they will pull completely out due to the stretching of the skin when we sit down. A little technique I thought up years ago is to do— a Kegel. *(**You know? That exercise you've been taught to do or read about during your pregnancy?)* So, before you sit down, tighten up your vaginal and rectal muscles and *hold them,* then sit down and relax those muscles. By doing this, you are drawing the skin in a bit more so that when you sit down you don't feel like it will pull apart. Many mothers over the years told me this did help quite a bit.

Vaginal Deliveries

Cleansing bottle/Hygenique® sprayer or sitz bath

Hospitals have assorted items to aid you in cleaning your nether region after going to the bathroom. Some may have a Hygenique® *(wall sprayer)* that cleans you like a removable shower head. Or, they may have a portable Hygenique® sitz bath to place in the toilet to act as a bidet, which sprays your perineum after you have voided and/or stooled. Others may have just a clear, plastic cleansing bottle, called a peri-bottle, to add water and cleanse off with. Be careful *not* to use cold water, which may cause you to *jump* when spraying yourself and make you uncomfortable. But then again, if you have "hoo-hah" swelling, this might feel pretty good. Warm water is the best to use for comfort. But no matter your hospital's method, bottle, or sprayer, use it *every* time after you do your business!! *(**And don't forget— prepare it BEFORE you go to the bathroom, so it's ready to use when needed.)*

Delivery compromises you by putting you at risk for infection. Your nether region is now a portal *(entrance)* for infection. So *do not* skip this step, whether you have had vaginal or cesarean deliveries. While you are still sitting down, completely clean yourself off with water. Use the whole water bottle or spray over 10 seconds using the Hygenique® wand or sitz bath. This will ensure the area is thoroughly cleansed. Be sure to continue this process over the next several days— and for at least a week once you have returned home. This will allow any repairs to start closing up and be on the road to healing. *(**Better a lot than not enough!)* Once you are clean, then dry off with toilet paper. Gently *pat* dry if you had a vaginal delivery— *owww-weee!* After a cesarean section, these patients can dry off normally.

If you have issues with a burning sensation from your lacerations or stitches while urinating, use your peri-bottle or Hygenique® while you go. This will help to dilute the urine and lessen the burning sensation. (**This is another little suggestion that has been helpful to mothers over the years.)

Topical pads and medications

During your recovery, you may be given several possibilities of pads or topical medications. Dibucaine is a topical cream or gel that can be placed directly on your hoo-hah. This medication relieves itching and pain by numbing the area for you. Another one might be Dermaplast®, which is in the form of a spray. This has a numbing medication *(benzocaine),* but it also contains aloe and lanolin to help aid healing. Preparation H®, made of hydrocortisone, helps with burning, itching, and swelling. Generally used for hemorrhoids, it also helps reduce the swelling on your hoo-hah. You may also be given Tucks® *(witch hazel)* cleansing pads to place directly on your nether region. These have a cooling and soothing effect on your stitches and/or lacerations. Any or all of them are great alternatives for those who do not take or want to take oral pain medicine.

You may decide you only want the witch hazel pads, which is fine. You can add both creams and spray to the witch hazel pads if you choose. After you have finished your business, cleansed with water, and dried off, take two witch hazel pads and overlap them to make an extended pad for complete coverage. Place an approximately 1-inch length of Preparation H® *(hydrocortisone)* cream in the middle and smear it out. (**Fold the pads in half, rub them together to spread the cream out, then separating them will accomplish this.) Then add the dibucaine *(numbing)* cream *or* Dermaplast® spray to the Preparation H®. Stand with your legs spread apart, and gently tuck the pad against your hoo-hah and rectum *("butt" hole.)* Then bring your legs together, allowing your body folds to hold the pads in place. Pull up your *very sexy* granny panties the hospital provides for you, and you're done. Leave the pads and medication in place until the next time you use the restroom and clean the area, then replace them with new ones.

Perineal pads/panties

Your hospital will provide you with perineal *(feminine)* pads and disposable underwear or panties for your stay. Every time you use the restroom or shower, change your perineal pad and any topical pads you may have left in place. This will help in avoiding infection. Your disposable underwear or panties are meant for short-time usage, and when they get visibly soiled, be sure to toss them and get a new pair of them as well.

Moving Around in Bed/Moving Up in Bed

Since your vaginal and bottom area is sore, you need to take care not to cause unnecessary pain in that region. As we discussed earlier, scooting and sliding on your nether region will cause you pain, so here are a few pointers on how to avoid that.

When changing positions in bed, such as turning over to your side, draw your knees up and plant your feet on the bed. Next, lift your bottom off the bed and rotate your hips a little to the side you are turning over to. You may have to repeat this several times to get into the new position you want, but this will allow you to turn over into a side-lying position without causing additional pain. When you want to turn back over to your back or to the other side, repeat this step as many times as you need to get into the new position.

Now, if you slowly migrate toward the foot of the bed, you can use some of the same techniques to correct this. First, put the head of the bed all the way down so you're not going against gravity, and then *grab* hold of the upper bed rails toward the top. Next, draw your knees up far enough to easily push off the bed without your feet slipping back down. Once you're in position, you want to lift up your bottom from the bed while you pull with your upper arms and push with your feet. This technique helps eliminate undue pain in your vaginal area and helps to move you back up in a better position in bed.

Urgent/Emergent Issues During Labor and/or Delivery

This can be a scary, intense, and anxiety-filled time for parents during what they assumed would be a standard, uncomplicated vaginal delivery. Unfortunately, things *do* happen, and you must be prepared for anything that might change your labor plan. Issues and events can occur during labor, which can be unpredictable and must be handled quickly to avoid a serious or life-threatening event for the mother, baby, or both. Here are some circumstances which can quickly change the course of the delivery from a vaginal delivery to a cesarean section.

Cord Prolapse

This very dangerous event can happen during labor— if the water breaks when the baby is not fully engaged against the head of the cervix. If the baby is "floating" in amniotic fluid and the water breaks, the cord can slip past the baby's head then pass through the vagina and out. Suppose the baby's head begins to engage in the pelvis. In that case, the cord can then be compressed between the head and the vaginal wall and cut off its blood/oxygen supply, harming the baby's well-being.

If this were to occur, you would find a nurse placing her fingers into the vagina and climbing on your bed. She will be riding in the bed with you— while making a rapid trek with other delivery personnel to the operating room for cesarean delivery. Her fingers will remain in the vagina, keeping the baby's head up and away from the cord until the cesarean is performed and the baby is removed.

Breech Presentation

Most times, a breech presentation has been previously determined and monitored regularly during your OB appointments. Having a hand, foot, or buttocks touched by a nurse during a cervical exam, if you present to the unit in labor, is unusual. But babies can do acrobatic acts very quickly and turn into a breech presentation without anyone knowing that it happened before you came to the hospital. If a baby is breech, an OB doctor can attempt to turn the baby around during what is called an external cephalic version. They usually try this close to your due date.

This is usually performed in the hospital setting in the event there is a need for an emergency cesarean. If done between 37-39 weeks, the version has a success rate of approximately 65%. Only 6-7% of those babies return to the breech presentation before delivery. If performed successfully, the doctor can attempt induction or wait closer to the due date. Suppose the baby cannot successfully be turned back around or has distress during the procedure. In that case, a cesarean section is in order.

Specific criteria must be met for the procedure to be performed. Before attempting a version, your OB doctor will determine if you meet the requirements.

Placenta Previa

In one out of every 200 pregnancies, this event might occur. Placenta Previa is where the placenta partially or completely covers the cervical opening to the vagina. The placenta is a very highly vascularized *(lots of blood vessels)* part of the womb, which provides for the transfer of nourishment and oxygen to your baby. Suppose this is determined early in the pregnancy. In that case, the physician monitors it frequently by ultrasound to determine if the placenta has migrated away from the cervical opening. As the baby grows and the womb stretches, the placenta will usually begin to naturally migrate away from the opening of the cervix, eliminating the concerns for a cesarean section. If this does not happen, then a cesarean section will be scheduled and done for the safety of both mother and baby.

Suppose an obstetrician has not monitored this previously due to little or no prenatal care, and a woman goes into labor. In that case, this could prove fatal to both mother and baby. Usually, vaginal bleeding during pregnancy is the first indicator to a woman there is something wrong. She will usually present herself to a hospital to be checked and monitored. Suppose the bleeding is severe enough, and the previa is diagnosed by ultrasound. In that case, the doctor may perform an emergency cesarean section if deemed necessary at that time. But— if the bleeding starts slowing down or stopping, the doctor may continue carefully monitoring the mother in the hospital and delay delivery. This will be done if the baby is too early, which might cause them issues.

The longer a woman can remain safely pregnant, the better the baby's outcome. Still, an emergency cesarean will be performed without hesitation if this becomes life-threatening.

Shoulder Dystocia

Large babies, disproportionate or small pelvis, post-date babies, the mother's short stature, or a history of previous shoulder dystocia can place the mother and baby at risk for shoulder dystocia. A shoulder dystocia is when the baby's head has been delivered, but the shoulders cannot be easily delivered after. The shoulders are usually caught on the pubic bone *(symphysis)* and less commonly on the sacral promontory *(the superior aspect of the sacrum)*.

This is one of the most anxiety-provoking procedures during a vaginal delivery for doctors and nurses. If shoulder dystocia has occurred, several procedures can be administered to help deliver the baby successfully, but some are not without possible issues.

The *McRoberts maneuver* is the first to be used. This is where the nurse or other personnel pull the mother's legs back into her chest and rotate them outward. This flattens the sacral promontory *(the superior aspect of the sacrum)* and opens up the pubic symphysis— giving the pelvis more room to deliver the shoulders.

If the McRoberts maneuver is unsuccessful, suprapubic pressure would be next. This is where a nurse places their hands in a "cardiac resuscitation position" over the back of the fetal shoulder, then pushes downward and away. This attempts to rotate the baby's shoulder inward towards its chest, which can help to reduce the shoulder and allow it to present itself successfully.

Another maneuver can be performed, such as the doctor internally rotating the baby's forearm over the chest and out of the vagina, which helps to give more room for delivery of the other shoulder. But using this procedure comes with the risk of breaking the clavicle or forearm of the baby to facilitate delivery and/or causing nerve damage on the affected side.

Doctors will usually determine before delivery if you can deliver vaginally. This is because of the concern for fetal distress, injury, or death caused by getting "caught" in the pelvis and cutting off oxygen to the baby. Suppose your pelvis would not allow for a safe delivery, and/or you have a large baby on board. In that case, the obstetrician will suggest that a cesarean section be performed before you go into labor so this event does not occur.

Fetal Distress (Fetal Intolerance to Labor)

You may be going through your labor relatively smoothly until your baby shows signs of distress at some time during labor. This is when the baby's heart rate starts a downward trend during the contractions, and the baby has difficulty recovering from them. If this pattern continues during each contraction or the baby starts showing signs of not recovering from the contractions, the obstetrician may order a cesarean section to deliver the baby quickly. All induction medications, if used, are turned off. Medication, such as Terbutaline, is given to stop all contractions, and you will be prepped for surgery.

Cesarean Section Deliveries

This particular section is devoted to just cesarean section deliveries, which will affect the mother during their hospital stay and beyond. Cesarean section patients have more to deal with and additional needs and/or demands during their extended recovery period. Recuperating from *major surgery*, mothers must care for themselves and learn about and care for their babies. The recovery time is much longer with a cesarean section—10-12 weeks or more *(with some patients, it may be months.)* There's a minimum of at least 5-6 weeks before you really start feeling like you're "back to normal." Your body needs this time to fully recover from major surgery and heal. If you have had, are planning to have, or unexpectedly had a cesarean section, then you need to read all about it in this section.

Here your dreams of vaginal delivery and normal recovery have been dashed at the drop of a hat— caused by predetermined medical issues or urgent/emergent issues during labor. You may start experiencing feelings of inadequacy as a woman because you did not deliver the way nature intended. Well, let me tell you right now— that's completely *not true!!* Get that thought right out of your head now!! You have carried this baby in your body for nine months. Certain situations dictate you and your baby would be better off with cesarean delivery. Sometimes it may be sooner rather than later. Nothing more. So don't let doubts about your womanhood or fears of inadequacy come into play. Safety for you and your baby should be your number one priority. That is, above all else, *THE* most important thing.

We all know nothing is black and white in our world, so why would the delivery method be any different?? Honestly, I have "ridden both sides of *that* fence." My first two babies were born vaginally, but my youngest thought she needed to be different— she didn't tolerate labor. I would have a contraction, and her heart rate would get lower and lower and then would come back up as my contractions subsided. It was hard to determine what was happening then— did she have a tightened, pinched, or knotted cord? Was it due to positioning? We didn't know, so the safest way to eliminate the problem was to deliver her by cesarean section. Certainly, I wouldn't say I liked the idea of having a cesarean section, especially since I was completely dilated to 10 on the operating room table. Still, she wouldn't tolerate even the slightest vaginal push— sooo— cesarean section it was!

The decision was easy for me— my baby's safety came first. Since we had no clue the cause of the decreasing heart rate, I just gave the okay to change course— and to the O.R. we went. However, that decision can be hard when you anticipate having your baby normally instead of "abnormally." You may be quickly thrust into this decision due to an emergent situation or slowly acclimated to the idea during your prenatal visits due to breech presentation, too large of a baby, issues with your anatomy, etc. No matter how it happens, it was not in your game plan.

But really— what is most important to you?? Mine was to have a healthy baby without any post-delivery issues. It was not worth the risk of putting my child in danger or risking long-term effects on my baby's mental capacity due to lack of oxygen. (**Prolonged decelerations in the baby's heart rate are one of the baby's responses to lack of oxygen.)* I didn't feel guilty about my decision— my priority was a positive outcome for both of us. You shouldn't feel guilty or inadequate because you had a cesarean section. Just remember the goal— healthy mom/healthy baby.

Certain factors may predispose you to a cesarean section for the safe delivery of your baby or babies and possibly your safety. Here are a few of those factors:

- Multiple babies
- Maternal infection, which makes vaginal delivery risky
- Unexpected labor events *(discussed in the section before)*
- Large baby
- Mother's medical condition *(which may make a vaginal delivery risky)*

What to Expect During Your Initial Recovery

When ready for your 2-hour recovery, you will be returned to your labor nurse if she also does postpartum care or your new postpartum nurse for continued care. She will assist you with breastfeeding your baby if you are planning this since you cannot sit upright for a little while. She will also keep IV fluids running and medicate you through your IV line for pain, itching, nausea, and/or vomiting, and antibiotics if needed.

Suppose you had an epidural or spinal before surgery. In that case, you may be given Duramorph® *(morphine sulfate)* in your spinal catheter before being taken to the PACU *(post-anesthesia care unit)* after your surgery. Depending on the anesthesiologist's choice, this medication gives you long-term pain relief for 12-24 hours. Suppose you have general anesthesia during your surgery. In that case, you will be on a PCA *(patient-controlled analgesia)* pump during your recovery period and given pain medication until you can take oral pain medications.

Since you have had a cesarean section, your recovery time is longer than with a vaginal delivery. The initial recovery time is the same two hours, but you will be on IV fluids longer, not getting out of bed for several more hours, and need extra help with your care and your baby's care. So, we'll go over what you can expect during your postpartum recovery after completing your initial recovery care.

Intravenous (IV) lines

You will have had an IV line started before your labor-turned-cesarean section or your scheduled cesarean section. This IV line will help administer IV fluids before, during, and after your delivery and provide access to administer IV medications before, during, and/or after your delivery.

Generally, we will keep IV lines open and running after the delivery—or lock off the site once we stop your IV fluids. We will leave it in for a little longer until we receive results from the labs we ordered for the morning after your surgery. Labs coming back during or after your surgery showing infection, low hemoglobin, issues with your platelets, etc., then we already have IV access still in place. Now we don't have to stick you again! Also, if you are Rh negative and your baby's labs come back showing Rh positive, by having the IV site still open, you can receive Rhophylac®. This can be administered in this site, so you don't have to get a shot in the gluteus maximus *(bottom)* again.

After receiving all the post-delivery results, we will remove the IV site if there isn't any reason to keep the line open. I don't know about you, but I didn't want to stick people more than necessary. I tried to avoid removing the IV site instead of having to restart it if it was pulled too soon and we needed it back.

Intravenous (IV) fluids

When you have a cesarean section, you will have an IV running with fluids for approximately 12-24 hours, depending on how well you are getting/staying hydrated. This will also be the site to administer IV medications for several hours after delivery, so we want to keep this open and available during that timeframe. If you have other issues, you may be required to have the IV site/fluids running longer. So, there will be several things we take into consideration before we stop IV fluids.

First, we look at your hydration status and figure that by looking at your urine output. We have been pumping fluids into you since before delivery, but we must get those fluids back out, too. When you get to the point of rehydration, you will start giving back a decent amount of urine. Second, starting as quickly as possible, we offer you ice chips when you can take them without nausea/vomiting. Then we slowly move you toward taking sips of water and then on to drinking water. We can eliminate your IV fluids when you're drinking plenty of water, giving back plenty of urine, and not running a fever. So, we will flush the IV line with saline solution after detaching the IV tubing.

Intravenous (IV) meds

During your recovery period, you may be given several different medications: for pain, shivering, nausea and vomiting, or itching. With opioid pain relievers, the nursing staff will monitor you closely. The anesthesiologist providing your care will also briefly monitor for any side effects. This includes allergic or anaphylactic (life-threatening) reactions you may experience. Any or all of the drugs given will help to relieve your symptoms while you are in recovery:

- *Demerol® (meperidine hydrochloride)* - This medication is given to you for breakthrough pain and shivering. In PACU, you will be watched closely for respiratory depression *(slowing down or stopping breathing)* and heavy sedation *(puts you in a state of deep sleep and hard to arouse.)* Respiratory depression and sedation are a big concern since you simultaneously have other pain medications on board.

   You may have some breakthrough pain after returning to the recovery area following surgery, so this might be given to you for additional pain relief. You also may have a case of uncontrollable shivers, which is a common phenomenon after surgery. Demerol® is a medication that can help control these shivers for you.

- *Stadol® (butorphanol)* - Another pain medication that may be given to you for breakthrough pain after surgery. As with Demerol®, you will be monitored for respiratory depression and sedation during recovery. This drug is primarily used just for breakthrough pain relief.

- *Sublimaze® (fentanyl citrate)* - Fentanyl citrate is administered by IV injection or a PCA pump for IV pain management. Depending on the type of anesthesia used for your surgery determines what kinds of pain meds you can be given. You may receive small dosages for breakthrough pain after an epidural or spinal anesthetic. It may also be used in a PCA to be controlled by you when you need additional pain medication after general anesthesia surgery.

- *Morphine sulfate* - Used for pain relief, morphine can be used as IV medication given in a PCA pump after general surgery. You can pump the medication as needed during your recovery. Or, if you had Duramorph® *(morphine sulfate)* added to your epidural or spinal after your cesarean, small doses can be given for additional pain relief.

- *Toradol® (ketorolac)* - In most cases, Toradol® will be ordered for administration to you after your surgery. This medication is not a narcotic but is like taking "IV ibuprofen." Toradol® works well with any IV or epidural/spinal narcotic pain reliever to manage post-operative pain. *(**See the section below under "Cesarean Pain Management")*

- *Zofran® (ondansetron)* - After surgery, you may have some nausea and/or vomiting, which is common. Using preoperative and anesthesia medications along with the surgery itself may cause you to have nausea and/or vomiting afterward. Zofran® is one medication used to correct this issue.

- *Phenergan® (promethazine)* - This is another medication to combat nausea and/or vomiting— if you have it after surgery. Usually, Phenergan® is used as the first line of defense in medicating for nausea and/or vomiting. Zofran® is used if Phenergan® is ineffective or if you still have mild symptoms. However, it can have a sedating *(drowsy)* effect on you if it is used. Zofran® generally does not.

- *Benadryl® (diphenhydramine)* - One of the most common but irritating side effects of Duramorph® *(morphine sulfate)*— used for long-duration pain relief post-cesarean of 12-24 hours— is itching. This is *not* an allergy to Duramorph®, but it is still an aggravating side effect.

Generally, you may start itching first on your nose or around the nose and mouth. Then the itching may migrate downward and affect other areas of your body, or you may have a full-blown case everywhere. Everyone is different as to if and how much itching you might encounter.

PCA pump

In recovery, you may be started on a PCA pump to deliver pain medications during your recovery period. This is for patients with general anesthesia or allergies to spinal narcotics used for cesarean sections. Fentanyl citrate, Demerol® *(meperidine),* morphine sulfate discussed earlier, along with Dilaudid® *(hydromorphone)*, are all medications used for PCA pain relief.

The PCA *(patient-controlled analgesia)* pump allows you to give yourself a certain amount of pain medication ordered specifically for you if and when needed. This can be good for you by allowing you to control when you take the medication and not have to call for it, then wait until a nurse retrieves it and administers it to you. Even though you can control giving yourself the medication when you want, you cannot give yourself too much. The pump only allows you so much control because the machine has lockouts at certain amounts or intervals to limit how much medication is given within 6-8 minutes. When taking water and/or food without nausea or vomiting, the PCA pump can be shut off, and you can start taking oral pain medications. The PCA pump will then be removed if you tolerate food and water without issue.

The downside to having a PCA pump is that when you fall asleep for extended periods, you may wake up and have too much pain, which the pump cannot control. Suppose you have an issue with pain control and cannot take water or food without nausea or vomiting. In that case, you must stay on this medication until you can get past that. If you are having continued pain without relief, let your nurse know. The anesthesiologist can change the order for additional IV push pain medications or change your lockout amount and/or interval on the PCA machine.

Ice chips/sips of water

During recovery, your nurse will start you off with some ice chips to wet your mouth, as it will be very dry after surgery. Over a 30- to 60-minute period, you may continue to suck on ice chips off and on to ensure you are tolerating those before moving to sips of water. Once you are ready, your nurse will switch you to taking sips of water— and I mean *sips*. If you try and guzzle down the water too fast, it usually comes back up shortly after that. I don't think you want to be throwing up after having major surgery, but if you insist— go right ahead. Many have thought this wouldn't happen to them, and they did it anyway, only to find out I knew what I was talking about.

Why your body wants to regurgitate up nice, refreshing ice-cold water is not something you would think it would do, but it does. You have an empty stomach which doesn't react well to ice-cold water, so it decides to get rid of it. Not something you want after surgery on your abdomen, which would cause you to have pain, and I know you don't want additional pain. So, take it slow and easy to get your body used to it, then you can advance to the next best thing— clear liquids!

Eating after surgery

When you begin passing gas, which shows us you are ready to start eating, you can start having clear liquids before advancing to more solid foods. This would include chicken broth, Jell-O, apple juice, frozen flavored ice, Sprite, or 7up. When you are ready for the clear liquids, I only recommend you start with the broth and maybe the ice first. You may not want to tackle the flavored and sugary things like apple juice and Jell-O, which might not sit well on your stomach. Once you tolerate clear liquids, you can be advanced to a regular postpartum diet.

When you start with regular solid foods, be wary about what you eat. The hospital food is usually safe with everything given to you because it will be healthier for your needs. With that said, some hospitals allow mothers to choose what they want from the menu of food provided each day. You should avoid greasy offerings *(fried foods)* and fast foods *(for their minimal nutritional value)* your husband or visitors might bring in for you. Your body is healing from surgery, so you want to provide good, nutritional foods to help with that healing.

I strongly suggest you stay away from the Sprite or 7up for a few days at least. The carbonation causes additional gas, and you will already have a large build-up after surgery because the gut slows down or stops moving anything through. That includes the gas build-up in your gastrointestinal tract *(stomach and intestines)*. Until you pass gas regularly, I recommend you don't drink any until then, and only in moderation. *(**See the section below on "Ambulating in the halls.")* Also, avoid any vegetables or beans that might cause additional gas build-up *(i.e., beans, cauliflower, cabbage, brussels sprouts, broccoli, sometimes onions, etc.)* Even though vegetables and beans are good for you, they can cause additional discomfort from gas build-up, at least until you pass gas frequently and in large quantities. By following these recommendations, you will have a more pleasant recovery experience.

Sitting up in bed

When you leave the operating room and are moved to the PACU *(post-anesthesia care unit)* for your initial recovery, you are lying flat on the gurney or regular hospital bed. You will continue resting and recovering in this position for about an hour. If you are still on a gurney, you will shortly be moved onto a regular hospital bed. Once in this bed, your nurse will slowly advance you to a sitting position.

Not everyone does this the same way, but I found it best to move the head of the bed up only three or four inches first and see how you tolerate it. Then keep moving it again three or four inches every 20-30 mins at a stretch. This way, you slowly acclimate to the change in your position. Suppose you move up too quickly after the surgery. In that case, you may become lightheaded, dizzy, nauseous, and/or vomit. This can be caused by several factors.

First, the surgery causes the body to become weak and feels fatigued, like you had a really hard workout. Then total exhaustion kicks in. This is a normal occurrence after surgery, also part of the natural healing process. It would be very unusual if you didn't feel this way. Second, anesthesia medications can affect your blood pressure by causing it to drop *(hypotension)* and which also causes body fatigue. Then third, there's also the breathing factor involved. You tend to have shallow breathing when you have pain after surgery. This decreases the oxygen in your blood, decreasing how much oxygen is getting to all of your cells. These, and some other potential causes *(i.e., infection, fatigue coming into surgery, dehydration, etc.),* are to blame for this.

So, to eliminate this from happening, try moving the head of the bed up a little at a time, then rest, then move it again, then rest, and so on. This will make the transition to sitting up so much easier.

Incentive spirometers

A respiratory therapist should set you up with an incentive spirometer and demonstrate its use if you were under general anesthesia *(put to sleep)* during your surgery. If the respiratory therapist is unavailable, your nurse can show you how to use it.

This device is used to help you remove the remaining anesthesia from your lungs and to prevent the development of pneumonia. It will help to open up your lungs fully and help you cough out the remaining anesthesia. You will use this device every hour while you are awake and when you awaken after sleeping. This will continue until you are up and walking around.

The downside of using this device is that opening up the lungs will force you to cough repeatedly. This will not feel particularly good on your incision, so supporting your abdomen well will help prevent some or all of any additional pain. *(**See the section below under "Some Incision Do's and Don'ts" for bracing your incision.)*

Dangling and getting out of bed

Position your bed so that the head is raised when you are ready to sit on the side of the bed and then get up. Bend your knees and place your feet flat on the bed. The closer you can comfortably manage to pull them up toward your bottom —the better. Then place your hands flat on the bed next to your hips. Use your hands and feet to gently lift your bottom off the bed and move *towards* the edge. You may have to do this several times to get closer to the edge, and that's okay.

By the time you get to the edge of the bed, your legs should start to hang over the edge. Once you have done this, put more weight on your side closest to the edge and slowly rotate on your hip. Next, put your elbow against the raised head of the bed and your other hand by your elbow or grasp the handrail. Then swing your legs over the edge of the bed slowly and push yourself to a sitting position using your hand and elbow.

Once you are sitting on the side of the bed, sit there for a few minutes to get acclimated to sitting in that position. Let your feet dangle off the side of the bed, and move your legs around while you are dangling. Wait to see if you get lightheaded, dizzy, ears ringing, vision blurring, or starting to have some nausea. If you start having any of these symptoms, you can lie back down in bed. Sometimes you will have some of these symptoms because you haven't moved this much since the surgery and need to try it out first before you start to stand up.

When all is well, and you have none of the symptoms or very mild ones, you can move a little forward and place your feet shoulder-width apart on the floor. Look straight ahead and not down towards the floor, then use your hands on the bed to help push yourself up into a standing position. Remember to use all your arms and legs during this maneuver to avoid undue stress on the incision site. If you have forgotten why, go back to the *"Getting Out of Bed/Back into Bed"* in the *"Immediate Post-Delivery"* section above. There— now you have gotten yourself out of bed. To get yourself back into bed, just do everything in reverse.

Foley catheters

You will be sporting one of these Foley catheters until you at least get you up and moving. This is because you will be somewhat immobile from surgery and unable to get up and empty your bladder for several hours afterward. Some people complain about them because they are uncomfortable, and they can be. But in general, we try and remove them as quickly as possible anyway, so the sooner we get you up and moving, the sooner we can remove them.

We will closely monitor how well you are giving back all those fluids we've been pumping into you, plus any excess fluid from swelling your body is trying to get rid of. It's not unheard of to lose quite a lot of fluid during the surgical process, so we need to replenish it and start getting urine back once you rehydrate. We also look at and smell your urine because urine can tell us several things. It's still too dark, so not getting hydrated. It's cloudy, which could mean an infection of some kind. It has an unpleasant, abnormal odor, again, possible infection.

Now, there is something else to watch for while you still have the catheter on board. If, at any time, you start feeling like "I need to go pee," like your bladder is filling up, then *let* your nurse know. Sometimes after surgeries, the catheter tip in your bladder gets displaced, causing it to "butt up" against the side wall of your bladder and not allowing the urine to drain out. At the same time, the balloon which holds the catheter in your bladder blocks off the other drain hole. If it can't drain, your bladder will fill up. It can then contribute to lower abdominal pain at the incision site. This is due to the pressure from the filling bladder pushing on it— from the inside. If this is happening to you, let your nurse know so she can fix that for you.

Your nurse can milk the tubing to draw out the urine by lifting the tubing up high. Then it is lowered back down and lifted again, then repeated until there is no more urine to drain. (**This may take several minutes to empty a full bladder. It sometimes took me 10-15 minutes.) Once she's finished you should have immediate relief.

When the catheter could be removed, I gave my patients the option of having it for the night or getting it out sooner. Suppose they really want the catheter out as quickly as possible. In that case, they must be capable of walking to the bathroom and tolerate being out of bed without difficulty. They must also have good output and no fever. Some wanted that *"darn thing out,"* so let's do what we needed to make it happen. Others didn't mind having it and like not getting up every 1-2 hours to void— as they have for the past few months. So, we could leave it in until morning— then it *must come out*.

Once the catheter is removed and you are taught hoo-hah care, you will be given about 4-6 hours to pee. If you cannot pee on your own, your nurse must empty the bladder for you. She does this by reinserting a one-time catheter briefly to do just that. Most of the time, this is unnecessary, as patients can urinate without much difficulty. But sometimes it doesn't work— and here are some reasons why:

First, there is trauma to the ureters, urethra, and bladder. Those little ol' tubes get traumatized when the catheter is placed. The tubes pull urine out of the bladder and then push it out of the body, and if traumatized, they don't function very well. This is due to the bladder being manipulated during surgery, then pushed/shoved out of the way to get the baby out. It is now "frozen" and unable to do what it's intended to do— empty your bladder. When that happens, it needs to take time to "wake up" and start working like before surgery, but sometimes it takes longer than we want, hence the need to empty the bladder for you.

Second, if the bladder gets overdistended *(overly full)*, it can displace the uterus. As discussed earlier, this can increase the chance of postpartum bleeding/clotting and/or hemorrhaging. *(**See the section on "Voiding")*

And if you are still unable to pee after being emptied out, your nurse will place a short-term Foley catheter, and you will be further evaluated. However, as stated before, this happens very "few and far between." It just doesn't happen very often.

Perineal care

Your perineal care will be much the same as it would be for a vaginal delivery. After urinating, use your plastic cleansing bottle, Hygenique sprayer *(attached to the bathroom wall)*, or sitz bath *(placed in the toilet)* to cleanse thoroughly and remove any dried or fresh blood from your hoo-hah. If you have not used a Hygenique® sprayer or sitz bath, ensure your nurse shows you how to set it up and use it. As stated in the vaginal care section above, delivery compromises you by putting you at risk for infection. Your nether region is a portal *(entrance)* for infection, so whether you had a vaginal or cesarean delivery, *do not* skip this step. While you are still sitting down, completely cleanse yourself off with water. Cleanse off with a full bottle of water or for over 10 seconds with the Hygenique® wand or sitz bath to make sure the area is thoroughly cleaned off. Once you are finished, then dry off with toilet paper normally. Continue to do this every time you use the toilet for as long as you are bleeding.

As discussed in the vaginal delivery section above, the weight and pressure of the baby's head deep in the pelvis can cause hemorrhoids. This can be very painful for some women. Be sure to ask your nurse to get a physician's order for some Preparation H® *(hydrocortisone cream)* if you have hemorrhoids and they're causing discomfort. Just because you had a cesarean section doesn't mean you must be uncomfortable sitting on your bottom, too!

Ambulating in the halls

This is *necessary* when it comes to recovering from a cesarean section. When you get up and start walking around on your own, you will also need to start walking around the unit. This is very important for your recovery, so *do not* avoid this during your stay. And if you are up walking around, back and forth in the room— Does. Not. Count! You need at least one lap around the maternity unit or half a lap if it's a large unit, approximately 5-10 mins of steady walking. Your nurse should instruct you how much, but if she doesn't, do what's suggested above. I cannot count how many times I asked my patients if they walked in the halls and how much, and I get the answer, "Well, I walked around the room." And my sweet but a bit sarcastic reply to this would be, "I didn't ask you if you were walking around the room. I asked if you had been walking in the halls." Most of the time, their answer was they had not walked in the halls at all. To this, I would reply, "Then I will tell you again why it is important to walk in the halls and not just in the room…" and so I will now communicate to you the reasons and benefits, as I did with my other patients.

The first benefit of early ambulation is the reduction or elimination of blood clots forming in your legs. Deep vein thrombosis, or DVTs, is a very significant post-surgical complication to avoid. These clots can travel to your heart, lungs, or brain. After any major surgery and some minor ones, a patient is at risk for developing blood clots in their legs. Therefore, ambulation is key in the prevention of this potentially *deadly* complication. By ambulating in the halls, that long-distance walking helps with venous circulation in the legs. Anytime the circulation is decreased, blood can pool in the lower extremities and increase the chance for the blood to clot. During the early recovery period, until you can ambulate, you will wear pneumatic sequential compression cuffs *(a mechanical pump that massages your legs)*. These cuffs keep the blood circulating in your legs until you can get up and walk around. Once you have the green light to walk, keeping that circulation going by walking at least two to three times daily in the hallways. Remember— this is *so* important.

Another benefit is improved patient outcomes and recovery. Studies show that early and frequent ambulation helps patients recover quicker and requires shorter hospital stays. By ambulating, you are accelerating your recovery by moving around more frequently. Ambulating helps enable you to care for yourself and your baby, thus making your transition from hospital to home easier.

Last— ambulation helps to get motility *(movement)* going again in your bowels. When you have abdominal surgery, the trauma to your intestines from being moved around causes them to "go to sleep." They shut down and stop any movement in your bowel, including pushing through the gas. When this happens, the gas can build up and start causing you sharp abdominal pains— and pain medications *will not* have *any* effect on this. By getting up and ambulating in the halls, you will get the motility in your bowel going and start passing some of that gas. Do this at least two to three times a day for about 10-15 minutes each.

Now, you may build up more gas than you get rid of, which can happen even if you pass some gas. If you are, and you're walking in the halls like you should, be sure to let your nurse know if it is getting uncomfortable for you. She can give you something to aid in passing more gas.

When patients passed very little or no gas and became uncomfortable, I started them off with a more holistic method than jumping right into medication. My concoction was a cup of warm prune juice *followed* by a cup of *caffeinated* coffee or hot tea. Now, you may think…*eeewww!! Prune juice!!* I can honestly say warm prune juice *does not* taste bad. I've even had a few nay-sayers turn up their noses at that, only to find out it wasn't as bad as they thought. And in all my years, only a handful refused to try it— and they were *very* "picky" eaters.

Now— the reason for using warm prune juice and hot tea/coffee is simple. Prune juice is a natural laxative. *(**Now you know why all those old folks eat them prunes and drink that juice!)* Tea or coffee *with caffeine*— is a natural stimulant. And— both of them being warm to hot help to stimulate as well. Woo-hoo— there is a method to my madness!! In all the years I have given this two-fisted concoction, I can honestly say it worked well for them. —*AND* they didn't have to use a Dulcolax suppository to complete the job. I can't tell you the last time I had to give a patient one when I was still working on the unit. It worked that well.

Your nurse should ask you if you are passing gas, and you must be honest. Tell her if it's just a little or a whole lot. You may be passing what you think is a lot of gas, but sometimes you may be building up more gas than you are getting rid of. And don't be embarrassed to do so in front of her, or anyone else, for that matter. If you do not want to pass gas in front of anyone, ask them to leave the room briefly. You mustn't hold on to the gas and not let it release. You are recovering from major surgery and have issues that need to be resolved, and bowel function is one of them. *So, let 'r rip, tater chip!!*

I remember having a patient who refused to pass gas, even in front of her husband. She had a lot of pain because of gas buildup. I couldn't get her to pass it until I had her husband step in and give her the "go-ahead" to pass it in front of him, and she wouldn't feel any better until she did. I even told her if she didn't want to pass it in front of anyone, even her husband, then tell them to go outside until she passed what she could, and then they could all come back in. Unfortunately, she didn't want to interrupt her visitor's time there with her, so she didn't ask them to leave. Her husband and I had to convince her passing the gas was more important than talking to her visitors. Her priorities were not leading her in the right direction, so we helped her get those priorities straight.

Use of the rocking chair

This is another useful tool to get gas to move through your system, if available at your hospital. The back-and-forth rocking helps to keep you in motion so the gas bubbles can move around. You can use the rocking chair when you're just sitting around the room or if you cannot ambulate due to assorted reasons or complications. If a rocking chair is unavailable, you can mimic rocking in a chair while sitting up. That will work in a pinch.

Chewing gum

Chewing gum after surgery can decrease the time you start passing gas, improving the return of bowel function. Research has found that gum causes the digestive juices to start flowing, which in turn aids in returning bowel function. Suppose you cannot start eating soon after surgery due to nausea/vomiting or other complications. In that case, this may be a temporary alternative to feeding your irritable stomach. Be sure to ask your nurse for some, and if the hospital doesn't provide gum, have your significant other get some down in the gift shop or have someone bring some in for you.

Incisional Care/Issues

When you have a cesarean section, the surgery takes approximately 30-40 minutes from start to finish. Several layers are cut through to get to the uterus and remove the baby, so several layers are sewn back up. The outer layer of skin is either sewn, stapled, or a combination of sewing/gluing. Your doctor may also put several strips of tape called steri-strips on the site. Generally, the suture used today is absorbable, so removal is not required. Staples on the outer skin will be removed just before you go home or a few days after surgery in the doctor's office. Steri-strips will be placed along the incision site. These strips generally begin to "fall off" within 5-7 days. If longer, your doctor will have you remove them yourself. It can be any of these methods, depending on your physician's preference.

First, we're going to go over the care of your incision. Approximately 6-12 hours after surgery, the pressure bandage is removed. The incision site is inspected to see any active bleeding, oozing, redness, swelling, bruising, or gaps in the incision. It is also important to leave the dressing off to allow for air circulation to the wound, allowing it to heal. Your nurse may place a peri-pad across the site without taping it down but letting your underwear hold it into place, which is okay. Air can still get to the site for healing. It can also allow monitoring for any oozing or color of drainage and how much. Also, putting the pad across the site can protect it from bumping up against things like the sink or counter. For most women, the sink edge would hit right about where the incision is on the abdomen. Having the pad there helps to protect it.

Oozing or bleeding from the site

If you have drainage showing on your peri-pad, let your nurse know so she can see if it is normal amounts of drainage or if it warrants further assessment and/or care. Do not be too alarmed if you do have some drainage. Sometimes a pocket of fluid close to the surface of the incision will push its way through. This can be normal, but if unsure, check with your nurse. Make sure you change your pad each time you shower or cleanse your incision so you are not placing a soiled pad back over the site. We don't want any infections.

Cleaning your incision

When you shower for the first time after your surgery, *do not be* afraid to clean your incision— in fact, we want you to. This keeps bacteria from setting up residence and infecting your wound. After showering your body and/or hair, put some soap on your hands, lightly rub across the incision completely, and rinse. Once your shower is finished, towel-dry yourself as normal, but lightly pat dry your incision. When you finish drying, feel along your incision site. If it is still damp, take a hair dryer on a cool, low setting and completely dry the site.

You may need more frequent incisional care depending on the time of year *(summer vs. winter)* and if your belly tissue hangs down enough to cover up your incision. When it's hot, and you sweat, the extra flap of belly tissue— called a pannus— can allow for moisture to collect in your incision area. That trapped moisture and warm body allow bacteria to grow and flourish, which we all know is not good for your incision. When sitting around your room, periodically take your hands and gently lift up your pannus to allow air to circulate around your incision and help keep it dry. Also, clean the incision site more frequently. Once you return home, be sure to continue this care while your incision is healing. Contact your doctor as soon as possible if the incision is reddened, has unusual drainage, has an unpleasant odor, or is warm or hot to the touch. *(Warmer than usual.)* If you cannot see the site yourself, even with a mirror, have a family member check it for you.

Numbness at the incision site

For most patients, the area on and around the incision site will be numb for some time. This is normal, as the surgery has severed nerves along the incision site. It will feel numb to the touch and may have some pain sensitivity long after the wound heals. Generally, the sensation will take several months or even years to return to normal. As the nerves regenerate, the feeling along the site will begin returning.

To help with inflammation and/or pain, you may use an ice pack periodically during your recovery period. If your nurse does not offer this to you, ask. (**See the information below under "Burning on or around the site" on how long and how often to use an ice pack.)*

Burning on or around the site

For some patients, there is no numbness or very little, but the feeling will be as if your skin has been sunburnt, and you do not want to have anything touching it. I know this does happen, and some nurses may not know why you are having this kind of irritation or even figure it out. But, I can tell you it is real— because I experienced it myself. Again, it depends on how the nerves are severed and which sensation you will have, but numbness is the most typical feeling.

If you have a burning, irritating sensation on or around your incision site, you may do a few things to help get some relief. First off is placing the sanitary pad across the site. It will help keep your clothes from rubbing up against it and again help protect the site if you bump up against it. Second, placing an ice pack periodically across the site might give you some relief. Do this for about 20 minutes, maybe 4-6 times daily, and more if you want. Whatever helps to give you relief. But *do not* continually have an ice pack on there for longer than 20 minutes at a time. You can cause skin burns, frostbite, and damage deeper under the skin down to the tissues and cells.

During your recovery in the hospital, your nurse may offer either or both of these to you. If she doesn't, it doesn't hurt to ask for one or the other— or both. Ice to the incision can help with not only inflammation, it can also help with pain as well. Whatever method you use initially, be sure and wrap the ice pack with a towel or washcloth to prevent burns, frostbite, tissue damage, etc. Then after two or three days, or when you go home, place warm packs wrapped with a towel or washcloth, like a cold pack, on the site periodically. This will also help with getting the circulation going, which in turn helps promote healing.

Bruising around the site

When inspecting your incision within the first few days after surgery, you may notice bruising on or around the site. Any time there is surgical manipulation of the skin, there is a potential for bruising. So, do not be surprised to see this. However, you may see a lot more bruising than you may expect, and there may be swelling, especially on the lower segment of the incision site. *Do not* be alarmed if you do. There is a perfectly normal explanation for this as well.

When your doctor cuts through the layers of skin, tissue, fat, etc., they reach the bladder. To eliminate possibly nicking or cutting into the bladder, they move the bladder out of the way by placing a bladder blade over the top. The surgical nurse or tech then holds the blade and pulls it down toward your hoo-hah. Because of the slick surfaces from blood and fluid, sometimes the bladder blade will slip out of place and rake over the tissues, causing added trauma to the area. This additional trauma will cause bruising and swelling to those tissues, which will resolve over the next week or so.

Pain more on one side

There may also be some additional pain on one side of your incision site, more so on one side or the other. This can be painful twinges, tight pulling, or tugging sensations. This is due to which side of the OR table the doctor stands on to perform your surgery. If your doctor is right-handed, they will stand on your right side during the procedure. If a southpaw, then the left side. The doctor will pull and tug harder on the side closest to them, and each layer's sutures will be tied off on their side. Both issues will contribute to the additional pain to that side of your incision. And— you may have twinges of pain on that same side long after you heal. This is due to the adhesions *(internal scar tissue)* forming, over time, more on the affected side. *(**This is also true, from personal experience, as I still periodically feel this on my right side after 20+ years..)*

This pain you may feel can briefly take your breath away. It can happen from laughing, coughing, or just twisting your body. Don't be surprised if it does. As long as the pain subsides, roughly within 60 seconds or less, you can be reassured it is most likely caused by this phenomenon. If it lasts longer and continues to cause you pain, let your nurse know, as there may be another cause for your pain— besides adhesions from the surgery.

Pain from additional surgical procedures

There are other reasons you may have additional pain from your cesarean section surgery. When your tubes are tied during your cesarean, the doctor is in your abdomen longer, manipulating your internal organs more. They are checking to ensure the procedure is complete, they have not missed anything, and there are still no bleeding areas. The extra manipulation causes additional trauma in and around your abdomen and muscles, leading to more pain.

Another reason might be if you had previous cesarean sections or abdominal surgeries, you may have an overabundance of adhesions *(internal scar tissue)*. It would be necessary to "break up" or release the adhesions from other organs and tissues in the surrounding area. Again, more internal manipulation. This also would contribute to the additional pain from your surgery.

Some Incision Do's and Don'ts

Since you just had major surgery, there are a few things you need to be cautious of during your recovery time. It's easy to forget, especially if you have never had surgery, that you cannot move around as easily as you have before. Getting in and out of bed or even turning over when you sleep takes a little forethought before you engage in your task. This also goes for bending, reaching, stretching, or twisting. Any or all of these methods of moving around can cause pain and, in some cases, extreme pain. So, we will review the proper mechanics of moving during your recovery.

Some of the "don'ts"

Reaching, stretching, and twisting while sitting or standing can cause incisional pain. We generally take for granted that we can still move any which way, even after surgery. But in reality, you may cause yourself additional pain— and nobody wants to have additional pain. So, *think* before you move. "Will my movement cause me pain?" *or*

"How can I best move to avoid additional pain?" Just be mindful of what you do and how you do it, and your recovery will go smoother.

Lifting your legs off the bed when lying down or bending at the waist when trying to sit up can also cause pain. When you do this, you are engaging your tummy muscles in and around your incision site. Some of those muscles have been severed during the surgery, so lifting your legs and engaging those muscles to work will cause you undue pain over time, so refrain from doing this. For instance, you may think you are helping your nurse by lifting your legs when she is putting on/taking off your pneumatic pressure cuffs— but let *her* do the leg lifting for you. Just give her the "dead leg" by completely relaxing your leg muscles.

Bracing your incision

Three other issues may arise during your recovery: laughing, coughing, and sneezing. *Oh, NO!!* The last thing you want to think about is having any one or all of these problems cause additional pain. Patients are still told to place a pillow over their incision and brace it with their hands to alleviate abdominal movement, thus avoiding more pain. I found this method non-beneficial as I adopted a better method many years ago.

A colleague suggested this method, and I find it is better than the one still being used. If you must laugh, cough, or sneeze, cross your forearms over your belly, curl around your abdomen, and try grasping your sides with your fingers or fingertips, then tighten your hold. Doing this will place more counter-pressure against your abdomen by using your stiff shoulders and forearms than just using your hands. This will give you more control by giving what I call a "brick wall effect." Your abdomen will not move nearly as much, if at all, and may cause you little or no pain.

Moving your body up in bed

Sometimes when you are sitting up in bed or changing positions while sleeping, your body slowly migrates toward the foot of the bed. The more this happens, the more you start to slump in bed when sitting up, which puts more pressure on your incision. When this happens, there is a simple way to move back up in bed without putting any undo pain or pressure on your incision site.

First, put the head of the bed all the way down, then grab hold of the upper bed rails toward the top. Next, draw your knees up far enough to easily push off the bed with your feet without your feet slipping back down. Once you're in position, you want to lift up your bottom from the bed while you pull with your upper arms and push with your feet. This technique helps eliminate undue stress and pain at your incision site and moves you back up in a better position in bed. But *make sure* you move the head of the bed completely down before you do anything else. Otherwise, you will go against gravity and may cause more soreness or pain if you do not.

Turning over in bed

Changing positions in bed, from back to side *or* side to side, is done much like when you get in and out of bed. *(**See the earlier section "Getting Out of Bed" under" Immediate Post-Delivery" to refresh your memory.)* You *do not* want to twist at the waist to roll over. You want to draw your knees up and plant your feet on the bed as close to your bottom as you can. Lift your hips up and rotate your hips a little, say three to four inches, then set your "butt" back down. After rotating your hips, scoot your shoulders back the opposite way just a little. Repeat the process in small increments until you get into the position you want to lay in next. This will put very little strain on your incision and lessen the chance of causing pain in your abdomen. And don't forget to put a pillow between your legs for comfort when lying on your side.

Pain Management

Be prepared to read several pages on this topic because it's a very important section to make your recovery the best it can be— for you and your baby. This topic is where I can empathize with patients and their pain management, which will be the same issue for both types of deliveries. However, I will separate some of the information into vaginal and cesarean deliveries, for the pain management will generally differ for each.

Your nurse will ask you, "How would you rate your pain?" *or* "How would you rate your pain, on a scale of 0-10, with 10 being the highest?" Some patients seem to have a great deal of difficulty with this pain scale, in that they may be laughing and joking or talking to others and seem just fine but will rate their pain as— a 7 or 8. A patient's pain is subjective. We cannot feel their pain, so we must rely on their pain rating to determine how well the pain is being managed. But when the pain does not reflect how the patient acts, we must diligently get an accurate number. As nurses, we must ensure the patient understands the pain scale, allowing us to obtain a more accurate score and medicate accordingly.

One of the fabulous nurses I work with has a cute little analogy she uses when explaining the pain scale to patients. "If your pain is a zero, then you have no pain. If your pain is a 5, you might feel like crying, but if your pain is a 10, you *will* feel like "*OH... MY... GOD... JUST KILL ME NOW!!! Because I now have my arm cut off without any anesthesia!!*"

Before giving a pain score to your nurse, move around a little in bed, lifting your hips off the bed or acting like you'll get out of bed, just for a few seconds to gauge the pain better. If you haven't been moving around, usually your pain is not as high as it is when you do. This helps to give a more accurate pain score for your pain. Say you have recently been up moving about but are resting/sitting again. Use the pain rating when you were up and moving. An accurate pain rating will give you a better idea of how intense it is and if you require pain medication to manage it. If you have mild to moderate pain, you may only need a small dose of pain meds to help you get relief. A higher dosage and possibly higher concentration of meds may be in order if it's moderate to severe.

Sometimes, you may want to be proactive with your pain management— which is very *okay*. You will have uterine cramping as your uterus is working on getting smaller and smaller after delivery. Those cramps may be mild enough from a first delivery; you may only feel a small amount of cramping but do not require any medications, and that's fine. If it starts to intensify, you can request some at that time. But if you've had 2 or more babies, your cramping will continue to increase in intensity. By the time 3 or more babies had come along, I had moms feel like they were "…going through labor all over again." Yes, it has been described as that, so prepare for it to happen! If it doesn't, you can count yourself lucky— but be prepared on the next go-around. *(**Again, file it away in your brain for future reference.)*

Breastfeeding will also cause your uterus to contract as well. It's your body's natural way of triggering the oxytocin in your brain to cause contractions in the uterine muscle. This assists with the decrease of heavy bleeding and clots and helps your uterus to get back in the pelvis to its pre-pregnant state. So, it is a good thing, even though it "doesn't feel too *whoopee.*" Just be reassured this will only be intense and will lessen in severity over a very short time.

When the cramping is just starting, most of the time, it starts off mildly and then quickly and steadily increases in intensity. I did instruct my moms that taking ibuprofen ahead of time might help decrease the severity or help them stay "on top of the pain" before it increases. Some will want to have the ibuprofen given to them when it's time, and they can have it, so they can hopefully stay on top of it. A warm blanket or heating pad can also help decrease the cramping, but that and ibuprofen are all that can be given. *(**This is one of the issues that can affect both vaginal and cesarean deliveries equally.)*

There will also be general muscle aches and muscle soreness after either type of delivery. For vaginal deliveries, you may have muscle aches/soreness from all the pushing and pulling during delivery. You put your arms, shoulders, abdomen, face, back, and legs into an extensive workout during the pushing phase, so why wouldn't you be sore all over?! You will be experiencing, on or about the 2nd day after delivery, the "feeling like you've been hit by a Mack truck!" *Or*, you might feel you had the most extensive workout in the gym, only you had it in the delivery room. For a cesarean section, you will be pulled and tugged around. Muscles and organs are moved around during the surgery. Therefore, this is where most of your soreness will come from.

You may also have back pain, which may be caused by two different things or both. First, suppose you have an epidural or spinal before delivery. In that case, you might have soreness at the injection site from the medication used to numb the area. This medication can cause bruising to the tissues, therefore, soreness around the site. You will also have soreness from the insertion of the epidural needle, causing more soreness at the site. Then second, you may have pain in your back muscles, particularly the lower half. This can be caused by the simple fact you no longer have the baby's weight in front, so you're realigning your posture to compensate for the change in weight distribution. During your pregnancy, this would have been a gradual change in posture, whereas now, it is a sudden change. That sudden change puts a great deal of strain on those muscles, causing backache. Makes sense? Good— moving on!

For those who will be *or* are breastfeeding, be reassured any pain medications given during your recovery process are *okay* for breastfeeding. We certainly would not be offering any of these medications to you to take if they were not. They have been studied by the American Academy of Pediatrics (AAP) and the National Institute for Health (NIH) and determined to be safe for breastfeeding. They are categorized as far as how much, if any, effect they have on babies.

The drugs given to breastfeeding moms ranged from Non-Steroidal Anti-Inflammatory Drugs *(NSAIDs) (i.e., acetaminophen, ibuprofen, naproxen, ketorolac, etc.)* to antibiotics. They have been found to have no effect on breastmilk production or effect on breastfed babies. Narcotics *(i.e., oxycodone, hydrocodone, hydromorphone, morphine, fentanyl, etc.)* used for cesarean sections and vaginal deliveries, respectively, were found to have little or no effect on their babies within the first few days after delivery. This was possibly due to the little or no quantity of the narcotic being passed through the colostrum. Once the milk came in, babies *may* have become more sleepy and harder to arouse with the higher amounts present in the breast milk. Still, the strength of the prescription was also of a higher dosage. *(**20 mcg per dose versus 10 mcg per dose.)* Those were also found with babies whose mothers were taking narcotic medications for longer than 10 days, which is the usual length of time medication is prescribed for discharge prescriptions.

While unsure of other institutions' dosages of prescription narcotics for postpartum cesarean sections, the one I worked in utilizes lower dosages of narcotics for effective pain relief. This is 10 mcg *(i.e., 5 mcg of oxycodone per tablet.)* So, you can rest assured that taking pain medications, even narcotics, is safe for short-term therapy during your recovery period. They can be taken without causing babies too much drowsiness or making it difficult to arouse them for feedings. And don't forgo controlling your comfort and good pain relief for fear of it causing ill effects on your breastfed baby. Remember, you must take care of yourself, too, and narcotics are only for the short term.

Now, for the differentiation of pain relievers between vaginal and cesarean sections. First, we'll look at the vaginal pain medications and their indications, then move on to those given for cesarean sections.

Vaginal Pain Relief

Generally, patients giving birth the old-fashioned way will have pain in 1-4 primary areas. First will be, of course, vaginal pain. Any one or a combination of several can cause pain to be mild to severe. Due to trauma of the nether region *(i.e., swelling, lacerations, tears, episiotomies, and stitches)*, medications can range from plain Tylenol® *(acetaminophen)* to Percocet® *(oxycodone w/ acetaminophen.)* The other areas: the back, muscles, and uterus, would be taken care of with ibuprofen, which we discussed above.

- *Mild pain (1-3)* - Mostly, plain Tylenol® *(acetaminophen)* can be used for mild pain relief or by patients who do not want *any* narcotics. These are usually available in PRN form— *as needed only*. Still, you can take them regularly if that is what you want, so it will give you more continued pain relief.

Suppose you are not getting "good" pain relief and *still* do not want to take narcotics. In that case, you can ask your nurse if your doctor can order a higher dosage of Tylenol for the short term. The maximum you can have daily would be 3,000 mg, but it can go up to 4,000 mg for the short term. Before 2011 you used to be able to take a maximum of 4,000 mg daily, but it has since been reduced to 3,000 mg to lessen the amounts your liver must filter out.

- *Moderate pain (4-6)* - These medications listed, such as Norco® or Vicodin® *(hydrocodone w/acetaminophen)*, Ultram® *(tramadol)*, and Tylenol® #3 *(codeine w/acetaminophen)*, may be used for moderate to severe pain. Norco® is routinely used for vaginal area pain in our hospitals. It is only available to the patient *as needed* unless your obstetrician orders it routinely.

Depending on how much pain you are in, you *do* have the option to take this routinely. It can generally be taken every 4 hours— for a brief period *(i.e., during your hospital stay)*—and then taken as needed when the pain begins to subside. Either way, it will depend on how you feel and how much pain medication is needed. The doctors do not schedule these meds, only order on an "as needed" basis unless otherwise indicated, such as when having some more extensive vaginal repairs done.

- *Severe pain (7-10)* - These medications are ordered for those who have very extensive and deep vaginal repairs done. If a patient has received a "3rd or 4th-degree" repair, doctors will generally order Norco® first to start. They will also order Percocet® *(oxycodone w/acetaminophen)*, if needed, for pain relief, as this type of surgical repair goes into or through the rectal muscle wall. This is an extensive repair, and patients will *most assuredly* feel the intensity of it. We have been known to call these kinds of repairs *"vaginal c-sections."* You are in so much pain you do not even want to sit down on anything— toilet, bed, or chair!! *OUCH, OUCH... OUCH, OUCH, OUCH!! Not at all comfortable!!!*

So, to sum it up, ibuprofen would be used for muscle aches and uterine cramping. Acetaminophen for mild to moderate pain, Norco® or Vicodin® for moderate to severe vaginal pain, and Percocet® for severe vaginal pain. You should have prescriptions given to you for any or all medications you were receiving during your hospital stay for when you are discharged from the hospital.

Cesarean Section Pain Relief

This is a different ball of wax when it comes to pain relief. You are having major surgery. Your lower abdomen is cut open, and your baby is removed. Everything is put back into place and/or reattached, so your pain will naturally be more intense. Cesarean surgery is *major surgery*, so you must know getting good pain relief is essential. Below we will go over different types of pain relief, when to start taking narcotic pain meds, how to wean yourself off them effectively, and why the need for narcotic pain meds.

- *Mild pain (1-3)* - Very few post-cesarean patients will be in this category. These will be the women who have a *very high* threshold for pain and do not require much in the way of medications. I have seen some only take ibuprofen and do just fine, but these are a rare few. If I found they needed more pain relief and didn't want to take any narcotics, I suggested at least some acetaminophen to help with it. Both ibuprofen and acetaminophen work very well together for overall mild pain relief.

- *Moderate pain (4-6)* - Most women fell into this category from past experience caring for post-cesarean section patients. Using a narcotic pain reliever with ibuprofen and taking and weaning off the meds described below under *"How to Take Oral Medications"* worked well at controlling pain for these women. Usually, I suggested the patient take these medications on a routine basis for at least two to three days and then start to wean off. This way, they had continued pain relief and could move around more easily. They also rested more comfortably, which was especially needed since the patient had major surgery and had to get up and move while caring for herself and her newborn.

- *Severe Pain (7-10)* - Not many women fall into this category, but some do. These women have a very low threshold for pain; getting the patient's pain under control is challenging. Additional narcotic pain meds may be ordered, on top of the narcotic they already have, to get better pain management for them.

When a patient falls under this category, there may be extenuating circumstances that may be contributing to their pain. The patient may not be walking in the halls to help relieve gas building up in the abdomen. Thus they are very distended and have gas-cramping pain. They may also move around incorrectly when getting in or out of bed. Reaching, stretching,

Cesarean Section Pain Relief

and twisting is not good. Laughing, coughing, and often sneezing without supporting their abdomen are also bad. They may also have an overdistended bladder that pushes up against the incision from the inside. Another simple reason could be the bed's "knees," or lower end, are so high that the patient's upper thighs push up against the incision site. *Or the patient had gone way too long without pain meds before the pain got out of control.*

There may also be patients who had the unrealistic idea of being *pain-free* after the surgery, so they may consider any pain they had as severe. They may also not accurately grasp the pain scale, so they give a higher number than it really may be. The nurse should be mindful to fully describe the pain scale again to these patients. They may score the pain too high for what they may be feeling or appear to the nurse to be feeling based off of body language and facial expressions.

The last reason may be very concerning, as it may be due to the surgery itself. There may be some blood oozing from one of the many abdomen areas where the doctor might have a missed "bleeder," which wasn't tied off or cauterized. This can cause abdominal pain as the "free-floating" blood collects in the abdomen. If this is determined, additional surgery would be needed to correct this problem. *(**This is usually very rare but can happen.)*

Intravenous (IV) pain relief

First, you will usually start out with either an epidural or spinal. You may be given Duramorph® *(morphine sulfate)* in the OR before you leave. This is long-acting morphine, usually lasting approximately 12-24 hours for continued narcotic pain relief. During that timeframe, if you have any breakthrough pain, your nurse will be able to give any one of several IV pain meds to get you over the hump. Usually, they are low dosages of fentanyl, Demerol® *(meperidine)*, or additional morphine to aid the Duramorph®, but may also be others. Toradol® *(ketorolac)* is a non-steroidal anti-inflammatory drug *(NSAID)*, which is like taking *"IV ibuprofen."* This works well in combination with your narcotic to give you good overall pain control. If you are allergic to morphine or any narcotics ordered, the anesthesiologist will find another medication they can use.

PCA pain relief (see under IV meds above)

After having a general anesthetic in surgery, you will be set up with a PCA pump *(patient-controlled analgesia)* and a medication you can have. These would be Morphine®, Demerol®, Dilaudid®, or fentanyl. This is where you administer the pain medication to yourself, and the dosage amount will be controlled so you cannot give yourself too much. One of the problems with PCAs is if you fall asleep and your pain starts to climb, you may get behind on the pain relief, making it a little harder to keep the pain under control. But with a PCA, you can switch to an oral narcotic sooner— as soon as you tolerate oral hydration and/or other clear liquids.

If you are allergic to some or many IV or oral narcotics, the doctor will give you what you can have. Unfortunately, you may not get very good pain relief during your recovery. Some people are allergic to some— or *a lot*— of pain medications, making it hard to find alternative ones to help control their pain. I feel bad for patients who cannot take the appropriate pain medication(s) to get good pain relief. Alternative non-medication therapies, such as visualization, hot or cold packs, breathing techniques, meditation, etc., might have to be substituted or utilized in their particular cases.

Oral pain medications

When you can take oral medications, then Percocet® *(oxycodone w/ acetaminophen)* is generally the drug of choice for an abdominal surgery of this kind, at least with our physicians. This medication is usually given in conjunction with Motrin® *(ibuprofen)*. These two medications work *very well* for overall pain relief from the cesarean section. Percocet® is given for the actual surgical pain. In contrast, ibuprofen is given for generalized pain such as muscle aches, soreness, and cramping. Some facilities may order Ultram® *(tramadol)*, which is a narcotic-like medication for moderate to severe pain relief.

Depending on your institution, you may be given Vicodin® *(hydrocodone w/acetaminophen)*, or Norco®, for your incisional pain management. These narcotics tend to give less pain relief than Percocet® but may be your hospital's course of treatment for cesarean pain. Most hospitals I have researched give Percocet® for post-cesareans.

One thing your nurse may forget to give you unless it is routinely ordered is Colace® or Peri-Colace® to go with your narcotic pain meds. Narcotics cause constipation. In fact, it is one of the biggest issues when taking them. Therefore, getting it to accompany your narcotic pain meds is important. If it is not given to you, *ask* for it. You will be the one to deal with the bowel/gas buildup issues, which will not help you control your pain if these problems add to it.

How to take oral pain medications

When I told my cesarean patients how to manage their pain, I suggested taking the pain medicine for at least 2-3 days— and when they could have it. This would be the length of their hospital stay. That means around the clock:

- 1-2 tablets every 4 hours for oxycodone or hydrocodone (this includes 325 mg of acetaminophen per tablet)
- Every 8 hours for 800 mg of ibuprofen OR
- Every 4 hours for 400 mg of ibuprofen

Start with 2 tablets of your narcotic *(w/added acetaminophen)* and 800 mg of ibuprofen. I did wake patients to give pain medication unless they requested otherwise. This way, the patient had continuous pain relief and stayed under control. I would, however, alter the time a little to be when the baby was to feed, when vitals were due, or to not wake them at all. This way, it remained the patient's choice. But, if their pain would not stay under control, I recommended they routinely switch to every 4 hours. Therefore, I would wake them up to keep them on top of the pain. *(**The timeframe rarely changes on the ibuprofen for our patients, but your doctor may order it every 4-6 hours with the appropriate dosages accordingly.)*

If a patient slept through their dosage time and didn't take pain meds, their pain immediately went from a comfortable 2-3 up to 5-8 when they attempted to move around or get out of bed. When pain jumps up like that, it affects you in several ways:

- You now *don't* want to move around and do things you need to do, like walk to the bathroom, attend to your baby, walk the halls, etc. Moving around and being active are important for recovery.
- Your pain is no longer controlled, and you will play *"catch up"* with it. This may take several dosages of meds to get it back under control.

- The pain itself may cause you to get nauseated and, heaven forbid, vomit. Not a good thing to cause yourself when you've had surgery. Now you're vomiting, and the pain is getting even worse for you. Not good!

- You might encounter not being comfortable enough to sleep. If you can't sleep or heal, every problem you currently have can worsen. See how one little thing can have a snowball effect??

These reasons are why I strongly recommend carefully considering pain management when recovering from a cesarean section. *(** You may be given Roxicodone, which is without acetaminophen. If you do, be sure to ask for the acetaminophen to accompany it or ask for the order to be changed to oxycodone, where it's included.)*

Weaning off oral narcotic pain meds

When weaning off your narcotic pain meds, I suggested this to most of my patients— and now to you. First, continue to take the ibuprofen throughout the whole pain management process. This will be the last pain medication you will use at the end. Now for the narcotic: Take 2 tablets around the clock for the first few days. *(**If you weigh less than 125 lbs. or are supersensitive to narcotics, you may need only one tablet.)* You can best determine when the time is right based on your pain. When you get to the point you are moving around, and the time comes when your pain medicine is due, but you do not feel you need any pain meds at all— or very little— then cut the dosage in half. Now start taking one tablet every 4 hours instead of 2. If your pain at the end of these 4 hours starts jumping back up and you find out you might have cut down the dosage too quickly, you jump back up to 2 tablets and start the process again. If not, and your pain is still under control after 4 hours, then continue to take the new dosage of your narcotic for a while.

The next step is the last in the tapering process. Now when you again get to the 4-hour mark and do not feel like you need to take any pain meds at all, this is when you start stretching out the time you take the next dose. Take your next dose only when you are *just* starting to feel some pain but it's still low on the pain scale. Then you continue that process over the next few days. This is how you will successfully wean off these narcotics— and feel better in your healing process!

Lastly, you can do the same with ibuprofen once you are off the narcotics. Same process, but maybe even a shorter amount of time. *See*— education is the key to this issue and anything else you might encounter along the way. If you know how to take the medications properly, you can rest easy knowing that narcotic addiction will not be an issue.

Some patients may only want one Percocet® tablet and do fairly well with just one. They don't want to take a second Percocet® if they only have moderate pain. I have even combined that one Percocet® with taking another dose of 325 mg acetaminophen tablet to go with it. This way, they still get at least *half* the narcotic dosage and the *total* dosage of acetaminophen. Of course, they can take the different dosages of Percocet® and acetaminophen. And then take it with the ordered ibuprofen dosage for good overall pain relief. Then they use the same principle of weaning off these meds as discussed above.

Not all patients rate pain the same way— and that's normal. Some patients have a higher pain threshold than the average person and do not require taking meds the same— and I respect that. Therefore, I didn't force pain meds on any of my patients. I just educated them on what would be best for their recovery. If I noticed that they were refusing pain meds but were not handling their pain well, I would suggest taking a dose or two to get comfortable and get some much-needed sleep.

Some people *do* have a very high pain tolerance. So, for those patients who *refuse* to take narcotics during their recovery and can tolerate not having them, here's what you can do. If you prefer, you may take plain acetaminophen *(Tylenol®)* along with ibuprofen *(Motrin®)*. If your physician did not order the plain acetaminophen for you to take, ask your nurse to see if it can be ordered for you. This way, you will still benefit from both acetaminophen and ibuprofen during your recovery.

Physician's ordering style for oral pain meds

Now, with cesarean sections, pain management is a little bit different. Some physicians order the patient's pain meds to be given around the clock and then change the order at a later time. Other physicians may only order your pain medications PRN— there's that acronym *again,* meaning *as needed.* Either way, you will have narcotic orders for surgical pain management.

Generally, like in our hospitals, narcotics used for incisional pain are scheduled where you *can* take it PRN every 4 hours. However, since it is ordered every 4 hours PRN, please *do not* assume you will get it automatically when it can be given. Some nurses may ask you to call them when you want more pain medicine, and some may ask if you would like them to bring it to you when you can have it— *each and every time.* Then some nurses, like me, will offer to bring the medication when it can be given and on a routine basis to keep you as pain-free as possible. I highly recommend the latter as being best for most patients, and I will tell you why…

Reasons for recommended oral pain meds

After surgery, you will get up and move around rather quickly—usually within the first 6-12 hours. You will be sitting up to breastfeed/bottle feed the baby, taking care of the baby's needs, getting up to go to the bathroom, walking in the halls, showering, etc. So you can accomplish these tasks and stay comfortable, you will likely need to take pain meds regularly for incisional pain and muscle soreness/cramping. And as discussed previously, remember to move around in bed before you give your nurse your pain rating. Hence, you get the proper dose of meds you currently need. *(**As discussed in the beginning paragraphs of the "Pain Management" section.)*

All these tasks are important for your well-being and recovery, so take care and maintain control of your pain management. If you are as comfortable as we can make you, your recovery will be quicker and more controlled— and give you a more pleasurable experience. Remember that no one is completely pain-free after surgery, so don't expect you to be. I told my patients that if we kept their pain around 2-3, they are getting good pain relief.

It cannot be emphasized enough that pain management is a very important part of any patient's recovery. We, as healthcare workers, consider this "The Fifth Vital Sign." I know there are problems of opioid abuse out there, and it's directed at the healthcare industry for issuing vast amounts of prescriptions to patients. I believe, but it has not been or can be studied, that patient education is key to providing a remedy for this growing and continuous problem. If patients are handed a prescription for pain medication, they should also be educated on how to take it. They must be taught about their pain and how to best taper or "wean off" the narcotic as pain decreases. I'm fairly sure almost everyone prescribed narcotic medications by physicians was not properly given instructions or education. They were just handed the prescription and said to take it as prescribed. I know several in my family alone have not been educated like this. This can be remedied by simply *ed-u-ca-ting!* I firmly believe in pain management for patients. Still, education is the key to making it work for the best and shortest possible time. Remember, it is best to treat acute *(immediate)* pain effectively to avoid chronic pain in the future— which, if not done right, could lead to opioid addiction.

When you are getting ready to go home, you should have prescriptions given to you before you are discharged from the hospital. This should be for any or all of the pain medications you received during your hospital stay. Some hospital systems can e-file a prescription directly to your pharmacy if they have the information on file. Usually, you will receive about 10-14 days' worth of pain meds. As discussed earlier, you may not finish the whole prescription if you wean off the meds. Plus, *don't* forget to get your Colace® to go with the pain meds. This is an over-the-counter medication for which you will not receive a prescription. Your doctor may not remember telling you to keep taking it, so be sure to get this too. You will still need this while taking the narcotic pain meds and maybe for a short time after you stop taking them.

Women with a history of opioid use

This is a heads up for those with a history of opioid use/misuse during the pregnancy or without prenatal care or very little; you will be screened for narcotics in your system. This would be at admission and before administering any opioid substances, including the postpartum period. Non-opioid drug therapy and alternative pain therapies, such as heat or ice, meditation, etc., may be used to control and manage your pain.

Physicians would be concerned on behalf of the infant born to an opioid-addicted mother or who had prior opioid abuse in her history. In that case, opioids may then be prescribed to the mother to reduce the chance of the infant developing Neonatal Abstinence Syndrome *(**This is an immediate drug withdrawal from opioids after delivery.)* Additional medical support may be needed for these infants to help them recover from exposure to opioids during their mother's pregnancy. *(**Additional information about drug use is in more detail below in the section "To Mothers Using Illicit Drugs or Having Limited/No Prenatal Care.")*

Pain Management Conclusion

I know this was a long and drawn-out section regarding pain management. Still, I decided it was especially important to be very specific when teaching. It's one of the most critical areas which gets glossed over during patient care, whether the patient is in the hospital or not. You cannot have patient satisfaction if one of their issues, like pain, is uncontrolled. Pain is a significant factor that can affect many different aspects of recovery. I looked at pain management like I approached my patient care— I treated all my patients the way I would like to be treated if I were the patient. With that said, I will leave you with the last line of a favorite poem of mine, "Invictus."

> …I am the Master of my fate; I am the Captain of my soul.
> ~~ William Ernest Hensley

You are the "master" of your healthcare, so be diligent and stay in control of it! Fight for what you feel is best for you, and the rest will fall into place. I believe all patients should stay in charge of their care during their lifetime— I hope you will as well!!

Voiding (Urinating)

You may hear your nurse use the term "voiding" instead of urinating or peeing when they ask when you have gone to the bathroom. It's the term doctors, nurses, or other medical professionals use. Sometimes we forget you may not have ever heard it. *(**I know I've had a few people look at me strangely when using that term.)* Even so, your nurse will ask *if* you have urinated, *how* much, and *how* often? These three things are particularly important in your recovery after delivery.

The first question you will be asked is, *have* you urinated? If the answer is "no," we will want you to do so within 4-6 hours after a vaginal delivery or 6 hours after your catheter removal *(whether vaginal or cesarean)*. Your nurse may suggest you increase your water intake, making the urge or need to go come quicker. She may suggest that while attempting to void, have water running in the sink to make you think about urinating. She may also have you get in the shower if you are stable enough to and let the water run over you. She may even tell you to let loose in the shower if you can, that it's okay. Sometimes these tricks are effective enough to get the ball rolling. If you still cannot go, your nurse will check to see if your bladder is full or over-distended, and if it is, she must remove the urine. That means using a straight catheter to empty the bladder, but then they will remove it again. Patients asked me, "Why can't I pee? And I would tell them due to the initial trauma to the urethra *(tube releasing urine from the bladder)*, it may not start functioning again as it should. Then your bladder will fill up and become over-distended, causing your urine to back up into your kidneys. *Not* a good thing! Can anyone say— *pain and infection??*

The next question is, *how* much did you urinate? Was it just a little? It emptied some, but you still feel you could go more. Or do you feel as if you completely emptied your bladder out? Suppose it was a little or just some. In that case, we will continue monitoring you closely to ensure your bladder returns to functioning within the designated timeframe. Sometimes you may start and stop frequently when first going as well. This is a *normal* thing. You may have to sit on the toilet for a little while to finish. If it is completely emptying out, then that's a good thing. That's what we are looking for when we ask if you have urinated— complete bladder and urinary tract function.

Lastly, we will want to know *how often* you have gone. If you haven't been told by your nurse, you need to make sure and go at least every 2-3 hours to keep your bladder emptied, especially if you drink a lot of water or other liquids. (**Preferably water, of course!*) Suppose your bladder has a chance to over-fill. In that case, it will cause your uterus to become displaced, usually to the right but sometimes to the left. Then, if it's *really* overdistended, it will elevate your uterus up higher than it should be, which should be at your belly button or below. What happens then is the uterus, being out of place, cannot contract like it needs to do to close off the blood vessels where the placenta was attached earlier. Therefore, the uterus becomes soft or *boggy*, making you prone to blood clots, postpartum hemorrhage, or both. Not a good thing when you already had a significant amount of blood loss at delivery.

One of my biggest pet peeves when taking care of patients was that any or all visitors thought it was "okay" to use the patient's bathroom while they were visiting. *HEL-LO-O-O PEOPLE!!* This is *a HOSPITAL*, not a public place to share bathrooms! I strongly suggested to my patients not to allow visitors to use their bathrooms. As a patient, you are compromised and prone to contracting infections. You may have stitches, lacerations, and/or tears from a vaginal delivery. Or just the vaginal bleeding from a cesarean section. Either one makes you vulnerable to infection from bacteria or other diseases. And— you *never know* what someone might bring into your bathroom, which might infect you.

Now, with that said, I will leave this decision *up to you*. If you feel comfortable that your husband/significant other and/or your children aren't infected and will not pass something on to you, then it's your call. But— be aware even *they* might expose you if they have used any public facilities recently. *(**Especially at any outdoor events, such as Johnny-on-the-Spots. Yuck, yuck, and triple YUCK!!! Those are just NAAA—STY!!)* So, use your good judgment before you let anyone pass through your bathroom door, okay? The hospital's facilities are available close by, usually right on the unit, which is specially designated for visitors.

Bleeding/Clots/Hemorrhaging

This is quite a common issue that can happen to any patient during the delivery or within the next few hours, days, or weeks ahead. As a patient, you must report to your nurse anything unusual or "out of the norm" with your bleeding. If you aren't sure if it is a problem, ask anyway. It's always a better idea "to err on the side of caution" than to assume that the bleeding is okay or ignore it. This can put you at greater risk and your life in danger if it is not checked and addressed promptly.

It is very normal to begin bleeding again after giving birth. I know— you've had nine months of not having that blasted period, and now it *must* start again?! I don't know of any woman who wants to start that back up again, even if it must start— *and* it will— *and* it is supposed to happen even if we don't want it to. At first, the bleeding will usually be a little heavier than your normal period. For those of you who normally have heavy periods, they may be more like those or maybe a little heavier. Over the next few days, the bleeding will decrease and begin darkening, just like it does as you start to taper off from your period.

When the bleeding becomes concerning for your nurse is when you are filling your pad very quickly. If you are bleeding heavily, it will usually fill up a large portion of the pad within an hour and become much heavier in weight. When this happens, let your nurse know so she can check it and determine if additional actions need to be taken, or maybe watch and wait to see if it will resolve on its own. If she checks you and it's due to a soft or boggy uterus, expect a wonderful, *heavy-duty* massage again!! *IT'S CRUNCH TIME!!* You know, just like the ones that were not fun right after delivery? Well, this does the

Bleeding/Clots/Hemorrhaging

trick most of the time, and no other interventions are necessary, so it is a good thing. But— if you have returned home from the hospital and you are filling up a pad in an hour, *call your doctor immediately* so you can be evaluated.

Bleeding can be caused by any number of things. One of the most common is an over-distended bladder. When your bladder over-distends or fills up way too much, it can displace or push your uterus to one side or the other, preventing it from contracting. When the uterus cannot contract, it cannot close off those blood vessels where the placenta was attached. This causes additional bleeding from the uterus, which is relaxed and not contracted. In turn, it causes uterine bleeding to resume, pool in the uterus, and form blood clots. The best prevention for this problem is to get up and empty your bladder every 2-3 hours or *more frequently* if you are drinking a lot of water.

Another issue with heavy bleeding is that it may be brought on by too much activity shortly after delivery. This counts for when you go home— and over the next several weeks. Increased bleeding and clots are one of your body's natural ways of telling you that you are overdoing it. Too much activity, especially the first few weeks, can cause healing areas in your uterus or cervix to "break back open." This causes the additional bright red bleeding to start again. Your body needs to heal from your vaginal or cesarean birth, so you must take it easy over the next few weeks and not overdo it. When you take 6-8 weeks off from work during your maternity leave, it's for a very good reason— to heal!!

Blood clots form when the blood pools in one area or another in the uterus, cervix, or vagina and start to thicken up to the consistency of a piece of raw liver. It is *normal* to pass a few clots after delivery. They are usually very small pieces you may find on your pad or notice when you dry off after voiding— like what you may have during your monthly periods. They may be a little larger or stringy. You may also pass one or two golf ball-sized clots and then no others, which can be normal too. Anytime you are not sure if it *is* normal, be sure and ask your nurse.

Another reason for a moderate to large amount of blood loss can be caused by vaginal or cervical tears or lacerations not found after vaginal delivery. Or it could even be uterine tears or lacerations that cannot be seen further back in the body. Sometimes these "bleeders" may slowly trickle but fill up your peri-pads rather quickly, or they flow freely and quickly, causing rapid blood loss.

You may be given medications to stop the bleeding, which is better sooner than later. Suppose the issue is related to a blood vessel or vessels leaking and causing the hemorrhaging. In that case, the doctor will need to make the repairs. And suppose the cause cannot be quickly determined and corrected. In that case, your doctor may need to take you back into the operating room and perform surgery to find the source of the bleeding and correct it.

In most cases, this can be fixed quickly with a few stitches here or there. However, there are some rare instances in which the bleeding *cannot* be stopped and becomes life-threatening to the patient. In this unfortunate event, the doctor may perform a hysterectomy to save your life. I do not want to scare you into thinking this will happen to you. I only want to inform you of the possibility that it can happen, and quick decisions may need to be made to keep patients safe.

So, do not take your bleeding lightly— or, might I say, *heavily*. Because if it's heavy and produces lots of smaller clots that equal a big one, or you're passing several large ones, it can have very serious consequences. If you are not sure, ask your nurse. She will either check it and reassure you that it's *"okay"* or check it and watch it more closely if it's more clotting/bleeding than normal. If not, she will contact the doctor and report what is happening so that further care can be administered quickly. Or again— call your doctor if you are already back home. Do not second-guess yourself on this. You know what is normal and not normal with your bleeding. Anything out of the *normal* range for your bleeding needs to be addressed by your obstetrician.

Other Medications/Supplements

You may be given other medications or supplements during your hospital stay, which are used to either aid in your recovery or help give you a needed boost. We'll go over all the types of medications used for both.

Colace® (docusate sodium) or Peri-Colace® (w/added laxative)

Colace® *(docusate sodium)* is a stool softener that helps to make the stool— well— *softer.* So when you go for the first time after delivery, this reduces the chance of having a harder stool to pass. It helps your body to draw more water into the bowel, thus making the stool softer. Peri-Colace® *(docusate sodium w/sennosides)* contains a stool softener with added laxative to help increase the effectiveness of stool passage. Several things affect your ability to go to the bathroom easily after delivery:

- medications *(especially narcotics)*
- decreased intestinal motility *(moving the food down the GI tract)*
- dehydration
- not eating proper foods *(dietary "roughage," such as fruits and vegetables)*
- vaginal and/or rectal repairs
- hemorrhoids
- cesarean sections

You do not want to strain or cause increased pain in your nether region or abdominal incision when stooling. So you will generally be offered this medication to make it easier "to go" for the first time. It can be taken twice daily to help you along for that first stool you may be dreading. It's highly recommended you take this along with your narcotic pain medications since constipation is one of the side effects. If you are taking narcotics, be sure to pick up some Colace along with your prescriptions when you are discharged from the hospital. Take them the entire time you are taking the narcotics. Even if you are not taking narcotics, it is okay to take this medicine to make it less difficult to have that first stool, so take it if it is offered or ask for it if it is not. Also, increase your dietary fiber intake and continue your increased water intake. You will feel much better if you do.

MiraLAX®/Milk of Magnesia®/Ducolax®

These types of medications: MiraLAX® *(polyethylene glycol)*, Milk of Magnesia® *(magnesium hydroxide)*, and Ducolax® *(bisacodyl)* will help if you are having a tough time producing a bowel movement after you deliver. Sometimes, during your recovery period and beyond, you may have extreme difficulty having one or more bowel movements. You may need something stronger than Colace® to get everything moving through. These medications are laxatives, and they work on the small intestine to help push the waste through more quickly and easily by drawing in even more water. Still, they have side effects during that *"hastening"* period, especially the Dulcolax®. You may be bloated, gassy, crampy, and need to *run* to the bathroom more quickly with these medications because they work faster on your digestive system. These should only be used if you are prone to constipation, take narcotics, and not eating and drinking properly after delivery.

Also, Dulcolax® is for those who don't get up and ambulate after surgery as they should and become *extremely* uncomfortable due to gas and/or stool build-up. Take the Colace® whether you are taking narcotics or not, eat high-fiber foods, and drink plenty of water. You can avoid using these medications unless necessary.

MiraLAX® and Milk of Magnesia® are oral medications, but Ducolax® is offered in suppository form. This will make for quicker results. However, when asking for gas or bowel relief, most patients usually avoid taking Ducolax® since this medication goes up the *wazoo*. Warm prune juice, followed by hot tea or coffee, can quickly result in good intestinal relief from gas. But it may *not* necessarily have an immediate effect on a bowel movement. I tended to offer this alternative to my cesarean section patients. They generally had more issues with gas, bloating, cramping, and sharp pain versus bowel movement issues early on. (**See the section relating to "Cesarean Section Deliveries" under "What to Expect During Your Initial Recovery."*)

Today was not like many years ago when your mothers were told that having a bowel movement was a *must* before they were discharged. Physicians now know that your body will function properly within a few days, and having a bowel movement will come within a brief period without becoming a concern. But if you have difficulty before or after being discharged, these medications can be highly effective for you.

Tums®/Gas-X®/Phasyme®/Mylicon®/Mylanta®—and Others

These types of drugs: Tums® *(calcium carbonate)*, and others *(simethicone)*, are used for reducing gas and bloating. This can lead to heartburn, gas discomfort, and/or indigestion in your stomach and/or gut. These come in a chewable tablet for quicker digestion and relief. However, if you are having issues with gastric reflux, you may need something more to reduce acid production. Tagamet HB® *(cimetidine)*, Pepcid AC® *(famotidine)*, or Axid AR® *(nizatidine)* are tablets you swallow. They do not work as fast but provide more acid reduction and long-term relief than their faster-acting counterparts.

For some women, indigestion, gas, and bloating are big problems during pregnancy. This is due to the baby pushing all your intestinal organs up and out of their usual places. But sometimes, after your delivery, you may still have issues that have not gone away, so taking these medications may help you. Talk to your obstetrician if you have questions about what is best for your situation.

Prenatal Vitamins

During your pregnancy, your obstetrician or general practitioner would have ordered prenatal vitamins to give you additional vitamins and minerals you will need during the pregnancy. Also, some doctors recommend using prenatal vitamins even after delivery, especially if you are breastfeeding. They will aid your recovery and provide the necessary vitamins and minerals to replenish your body.

My personal OB/GYN and colleague told me that she recommends prenatal vitamins to be used as a supplement even if not breastfeeding or pregnant. She informed me that they are a good overall supplement to use for years to come. So, if you have taken prenatal vitamins during your pregnancy, I recommend taking them after delivery— and beyond. If you continue using them, be sure to let your husband or significant other know why you are taking them— so you don't freak them out if they see the bottle!! Let him know, even if you are not pregnant or don't plan to become pregnant again. I know my husband did when I started taking them again years after we quit having more babies. What an uproar that caused trying to convince him I *was not* pregnant. Lol!

Iron Tablets (ferrous sulfate)

If you are anemic, your doctor may have prescribed iron tablets or gel tabs be taken. This is because your body does not have enough iron to carry oxygen from your red blood cells *(hemoglobin)* into all the other parts of the body. You may have become anemic during pregnancy, which would hinder your body from providing much-needed oxygen, not only for yourself but for your baby as well. Severe untreated anemia can cause anemia in your baby, maternal death, and stillbirth or fetal death. So, it would be best to *not* take anemia and its treatment lightly.

Your doctor may prescribe iron tablets if you are:

- Anemic during pregnancy
- Become anemic due to larger-than-normal blood volume loss during delivery
- Become/remain anemic after delivery

Some women also have ongoing anemia even when not pregnant. There may be other blood-related issues you may personally deal with, which are uncommon. Still, your doctor should provide you with information and appropriate care if you do.

Lab work is ordered after every delivery to check all kinds of levels. Suppose you have a significant drop in your hemoglobin after delivery. Iron supplements are insufficient to boost your iron levels. In that case, your doctor may order a blood transfusion of a couple of units of red blood cells. This will help you bounce back much quicker from the severe drop in your hemoglobin than just taking oral tablets or gel pills. Then they may also order iron supplements to continue boosting red blood cell production after the blood infusion.

During my career, I had a Micronesian patient who did not seek prenatal care before delivery. Whether she didn't know prenatal care was available to her or didn't get care due to religious or cultural beliefs, she did not seek it. When she came into the hospital to deliver, no fetal heartbeat was found. Her labs drawn before delivery had come back showing she was severely anemic. She was close to full-term and came into the hospital in full labor. Unfortunately, the baby was stillborn. To me, this was a very sad and needless fetal death. This could have been prevented by having prenatal care *(even if it was just a few clinic visits)* to diagnose the anemia and take iron tablets. Iron infusions might have also prevented this from happening. This was a very, very sad situation to have happened.

Vaccinations

Children receive numerous vaccines as infants, up through middle school and junior high. Recently, additional vaccines have been offered to older high school and college students, such as for cervical cancer prevention or meningococcal meningitis. But some vaccines must be given again, as boosters, when the time frame has elapsed, and the previous vaccines are no longer effective. The Centers for Disease Control recommend updating these vaccines as soon as it is determined safe for each type.

Hepatitis B

This is a series of shots given over several months to protect you from contracting Hepatitis B and, in turn, passing it on to others—including your unborn baby. Once the series is given, no boosters are needed. If you have not received this vaccine and would like to, talk to your doctor when the best time to receive the vaccine. It is usually not offered in the hospital during your stay but may be at other hospitals. Just check to see if you can get the initial dose in the hospital or if you must wait until discharge.

MMR (Measles, Mumps, Rubella)

During prenatal visits to the obstetrician's office, your doctor will ask when you last had your vaccine. They will also evaluate tests on your blood to see if your previous measles, mumps, and rubella vaccine is still protecting you. Suppose it is not or is only giving you partial protection. In that case, your doctor will recommend you have a booster shot given in the hospital after delivery. Or you can get it any time after the baby is born and you have been discharged. This vaccine *cannot* be given to you during pregnancy, as this is a live virus and may be passed on through the placenta to your unborn baby. It will be offered to you after the birth before discharge. I recommend getting it in the hospital so you do not forget it. This will help prevent contracting any of the three diseases and passing them on to your newborn. It usually takes about two weeks to become effective, so there is that small window you won't be protected. Therefore, be careful who you come in contact with during those two weeks. "Two doses of MMR vaccine are about 97% effective at preventing measles; one dose is about 93% effective." (CDC)

- *Measles* - "…is one of the most contagious diseases there is. If one person has it, 9 out of 10 people coming close to that person and who aren't immune *(protected)* will also get measles. And it can be dangerous— serious cases of measles can lead to brain damage and even death," according to the US Department of Health and Human Services (DHHS).
- *Mumps* - according to DHHS, "…is a contagious disease— it spreads easily from person to person. And it can lead to serious complications, like hearing loss." They state, "…before the mumps vaccine, almost everyone in the United States got mumps during childhood. But thanks to the vaccine, the number of mumps cases in Americans has dropped by over 99%."
- *Rubella (German measles)* - "Rubella is a contagious disease caused by a virus. It can lead to serious complications, especially for unborn babies. If a pregnant woman gets rubella, she can lose her baby. Babies born to mothers who had rubella can have birth defects that last a lifetime." (DHHS)

Tdap (Tetanus, Diphtheria, and Pertussis)

This vaccine is only good for approximately 10 years, and it is recommended that everyone get booster doses after that time. If you do not know how current you are on this vaccine or if it has been more than 10 years since your last booster, it is recommended that you receive a new booster shot. For women, you may receive this during your pregnancy between the 26th and 36th week, preferably closer to the 26th week, as it can safely pass on immunities to your unborn child. *(**This is not a "live" virus. It contains an inactivated, noninfectious bacterial product.)* The longer your antibodies increase within your body before birth, the more antibodies are passed on to your baby. This protects them until they receive their vaccinations. Because of this, it is better to receive it before birth. If you do not, it should be offered during your hospital stay. You are highly recommended to receive it— I strongly suggest doing it if needed. If you've had other children but cannot remember if *you* have been given this vaccine, the CDC also recommends that you go ahead and get it. An additional booster will not cause any problems, so if you are unsure, go ahead and get it again.

- *Tetanus* - Better known as "lock-jaw," is uncommon but can be dangerous if contracted. According to DHHS, "…of every 10 people who get it, as many as 2 will die. Thanks in part to tetanus vaccines, deaths from tetanus in the United States have dropped by 99% since 1947." The dangerous complications for babies and children include pneumonia *(lung infection)*, convulsions *(uncontrolled shaking)*, and brain damage.

  Mostly this is contracted from a cut, puncture wound, or animal bite coming in contact with contaminated soil, dust, and manure infected with the *Clostridium tetani* bacteria.

Therefore, it is important for you and your family's safety to be vaccinated.

- *Diphtheria* - "In the 1920s, the United States used to see as many as 200,000 cases a year. Thanks to diphtheria vaccines, that number has dropped by 99.9%," according to the CDC. Although the disease is rare, cases have been found in the US. DHHS tells us, "Diphtheria can cause serious complications, like paralysis *(loss of the ability to move)*, pneumonia *(lung infection)*, and lung failure. It can also be deadly, especially for certain age groups — up to 1 in 5 young children and older adults who get the disease will die from it.

Be sure that anyone who comes in direct contact with your children regularly needs to get vaccinated:

- Babysitters
- Teachers
- Preschool or daycare workers
- Any family members caring for baby

Most daycare centers and schools require their employees to be vaccinated before coming in direct contact with children. Still, others who are not— grandparents, aunts, uncles, cousins, etc.,— might not have had a booster. If anyone comes in frequent contact with your children, insist they get the vaccine if they haven't. The Tdap vaccine is given to children over 7 years through adulthood.

- *Pertussis (whooping cough)* - Whooping cough is one of the diseases prevented by this vaccine that is the most needed for your protection and your baby's. Whooping cough can be extremely serious and potentially life-threatening to your newborn baby. If you have not been vaccinated in a long time or have never been vaccinated, you can pass this on to your baby if exposed to it. Getting the vaccine in the hospital is better than not receiving it at all. Still, having it by the 36th week of pregnancy is better. However, if you don't get it until you deliver, *be aware* that it takes about two weeks for the antibodies to produce enough quantities to be protected from the disease. During those two weeks, your baby *will not* be protected from others who might pass on the disease to them, even if breastfeeding. Your baby will be exposed for that timeframe and can still contract it. If you are breastfeeding, roughly two weeks later, when your body starts producing antibodies, you can pass those immunities to your baby. If bottle feeding, your baby will be exposed until they receive their DTaP shot at about 2 months of age.

I cannot imagine how devastating this can be for an infant to contract this horrendous disease. When my oldest daughter was in middle school, there was an outbreak of whooping cough within our school district. She did not contract it but "carried it" home to me— and I contracted it. I didn't put two-and-two together until several years later. I had been exposed to and contracted it. I had been immunized throughout my childhood but was unaware that a booster was needed for continued protection. It was a miserable two months of coughing so hard that I couldn't catch my breath or so hard it would cause me to choke and gag. Infants and small children are vulnerable and are frequently hospitalized due to its devastating effects. If you refuse some of the other shots because you have your reasons or just don't want them, please don't pass this one up!!!

Unfortunately, some "nay-sayers" believe *ANY* vaccine is responsible for autism. Even with all the evidence and studies conducted on this controversial subject— and proof there is *no* vaccine-autism connection— parents are still convinced to this day that there is a connection. All of the conclusions from the many health organizations worldwide are clear. There is *NO* connection. They would not be backing the committee's findings if there was evidence to the contrary. All health organizations worldwide want the best for every child and would not steer parents in the wrong direction. So you decide— are you for or against childhood vaccinations? Do you feel the risk of vaccinations far outweigh the risks of contracting one of these diseases and developing a serious or deadly complication?

Influenza Vaccine

These are also offered to moms-to-be and other hospital patients who have not been vaccinated during the flu season, usually between October 1 and March 30. They are safe to be given during pregnancy and during the flu season.

The CDC also highly recommends that pregnant women receive this vaccine to prevent them from contracting it. The influenza virus can be even more devastating to a pregnant woman due to her bodily changes during her pregnancy. Heart, lungs, and immune systems are greatly altered, putting them at higher risk during the flu season. Like the Tdap shot, it can be given during pregnancy if you are in the current flu season. It will allow your body to build up antibodies, which can be passed on to your baby prior to delivery, thus protecting them as well.

The misnomer with this vaccine is that a large population *"thinks"* of the influenza vaccine as preventing the stomach "flu" or virus. This is actually *incorrect!!!* The vaccine is made to prevent the influenza virus, which can cause:

- Respiratory congestion *(mucus-filled lungs)*
- Respiratory distress *(difficulty breathing)*
- Respiratory failure *(cannot breathe)*
- Heart failure
- And/or death

Each year the CDC provides a vaccine that will eliminate or lessen the severity of the four most prevalent strains predicted to occur during a particular flu season. Which means you can still get influenza after having the vaccine. You may contract another strain of influenza that the vaccine does not cover or another virus that presents symptoms similar to the flu that also spreads during flu season. You may also become exposed to the four prevalent influenza viruses just before receiving your shot or within the two-week window before the shot becomes effective. This would *not* prevent you from contracting it.

The stomach "flu" will generally not cause respiratory distress or heart failure. It's a short-term bug that causes fever, vomiting/diarrhea, muscle aches, and/or chills over the next few days. Once your body purges and rests, then it will heal. So, don't mix up the two when deciding to get the influenza shot or not, as so many others have done. Unfortunately, some people didn't understand how the shot worked, or they received the wrong information. This is again the issue of not educating patients *correctly* so that accurate and informed decisions can be made for themselves.

Pneumococcal Vaccine

This is generally offered to individuals at a higher risk of contracting pneumonia. Patients should be offered this vaccine if they:

- Currently smoke or have within the last year
- Have recurrent bronchitis or other respiratory issues
- Have or had asthma
- Currently using inhalers or other respiratory meds to combat the issue
- Have been diagnosed with emphysema or Chronic Obstructive Pulmonary Disease *(COPD).*

These respiratory issues put compromised patients at higher risk of contracting the pneumococcal virus. So, it is offered— like the influenza shot— to these patients during the pregnancy or after the delivery. So, if you are at risk because of respiratory issues, you will also want to be vaccinated against this.

Lab Work

During your prenatal visits with the doctor, you should have had initial lab work done in your physician's office or the local lab, usually during the first prenatal visit. These labs will be repeated upon admission to the hospital since the previous results will have changed since the initial baseline labs or the last time your blood was tested. This will give your doctor vital information, which helps them to decide what treatment will be administered to you.

Lab work will also be drawn the morning after delivery or sooner if there are complications during or just after delivery. Your doctor will want to see what changes have occurred, allowing them to give you the appropriate follow-up care.

CBC (Complete Blood Count)

This gives a baseline to see your:

- *White blood cell count* - shows if an infection is present
- *Hemoglobin & hematocrit* - shows the oxygen-carrying capacity of red blood cells
- *Platelets* - shows blood clotting ability
- *Glucose* - blood sugar levels
- *Blood type & screen* - check blood type and screen for antibodies
- *BMP or CMP* - chemical balance and metabolism. i.e., kidney or liver function, etc.
- *Various other labs* - HIV, STDs, etc.

Lab Work

These labs are important to your ongoing care until discharge and possibly beyond.

ABO & Rh Factor Incompatibilities

When checking your blood type & screen, the lab tests your blood type. So your obstetrician or other physicians taking care of you can get the appropriate blood needed should you have an emergent situation requiring a transfusion. The four blood types are A, B, AB, & O, but most are incompatible. Each blood type has antibodies against the other types *(Rh factor)*, except for O negative. O negative-type blood has no antibodies, nor does it have antibodies from the *(–)* Rh factor, so this blood can be used with *any* blood type, including Rh *(+)* or *(–)* patients. *(**This is why O neg blood is considered the universal donor.)* The screening determines your blood type and if you have the *(+)* or *(–)* Rh factor. The Rh factor is antibodies that can attack the opposite Rh factor. So, if you are Rh negative *(–)* and your baby is Rh positive *(+)*, this can affect any future babies if it is not taken care of. *(**If you know you are Rh (+), you may skip the next two paragraphs.)*

Generally, when a mom is pregnant and has the *(–)* Rh factor, she will get a shot around the 28th week called RhoGAM or Rhophylac. She will get another after birth if the baby's blood type has a *(+)* Rh factor. By getting the second shot, the mother's *(–)* Rh factor *will not* attack the *next* baby's red blood cells if it is *(+)* Rh. It can be a little confusing if your physician has not already explained this. Still, it's one of those easy fixes with RhoGAM or Rhophylac. If not corrected with one of these two blood products, it can have serious *(immune hydrops fetalis)* or even deadly consequences for the next baby.

Immune hydrops fetalis is a life-threatening anemia in newborns at delivery in which ABO blood group and Rh incompatibilities can occur. If a *(-)* Rh mom is not desensitized *(given the RhoGAM or Rhophylac)* soon after a *(+)* Rh baby is born or after a miscarriage, this can occur. This issue causes large numbers of red blood cells in the infant to be *destroyed,* which may cause:

- Severe anemia
- Skin bruising
- Respiratory issues
- Total body swelling
- Jaundice
- Heart failure

Treatment would include:

- Blood transfusions
- Needle aspiration of fluid from the abdomen and/or around the lungs
- Respiratory assistance with breathing
- Medications to help kidneys remove excess fluid
- Control heart failure

Being prepared for this eventuality may be necessary if the mother is *(-)* Rh and she has:

- Had no prenatal care and is not sure if she has ever had a miscarriage at any time.
- Unsure if she has ever had a miscarriage, and informed her physician or obstetrician.

- Had a miscarriage but never received RhoGAM after the fact and is pregnant again.

Suppose the mother is known to have *(-)* Rh, or there has not been any testing before coming in to deliver, and the mom is found to be *(-)* Rh. In that case, the obstetrician will order labs after delivery to determine how much RhoGAM or Rhophylac will be given. This medication will ensure immune hydrops fetalis does not occur. However, if there was a "chemical pregnancy," where miscarriage happens within the first five weeks, then RhoGAM or Rhophylac would not be needed.

Group B Beta Strep (+ or -)

This is another lab test you are checked for during prenatal visits, usually at about 36 weeks. It's an important test doctors need to know before a vaginal delivery. Group B Beta Strep can be part of any women's normal vaginal tract flora. If the mother is, what we call, GBS *(+)*, then she has the flora in her vaginal tract that can cause her unborn child to become infected when born. Suppose antibiotics are given in labor at least 4 hours before delivery. In that case, it can cross over the placental barrier and protect the infant from the GBS *(+)* colonization of bacteria. This prophylactic treatment of antibiotics greatly *decreases* the chance for the bacteria to infect the infant and cause various issues. This can lead to intensive care for the newborn in a Level II or Level III nursery— should they become infected. Sometimes delivery can occur before treatment or quickly after admission. If you cannot receive antibiotics in time to be effective, then your baby will be monitored during their hospitalization. Nurses will watch for signs and symptoms of infection and treat the baby accordingly. Treatment, however, is unnecessary if you deliver by cesarean section. This is due to the baby not passing through the vaginal tract, where the Group B Beta Strep is located.

Hepatitis B, Syphilis, Gonorrhea, HIV (or AIDS)

These are other diseases that can be potentially harmful to your unborn baby or be harmful during vaginal delivery. Generally, your physician will test for these along with your other labs during the beginning of prenatal care. However, these are tested upon admission if: 1) they weren't done during pregnancy, 2) you *did not* receive prenatal care, or 3) the hospital cannot access your medical records because you're delivering at a different hospital than planned.

To Mothers Using Illicit Drugs and/or Having Limited/No Prenatal Care

I also wanted to add this section to the book to cover this particular group of mothers who plan to deliver in a hospital setting when the time comes. This section *is not* added here to criticize *any* mother using illicit drugs during the pregnancy. Nor is it criticizing any mother deciding for personal reasons not to receive regular, if any, prenatal care. It is here to discuss the importance of fully disclosing this information to your nurses or doctors upon arrival.

Your doctors and nurses are professionals and must give the best care to every patient who comes into the hospital for treatment. This is regardless of the patient's personal choices or situations. To give the best care, they *need* to know *your complete history*. This includes telling them things that you feel might make them judgmental toward you. I cannot predict whether your nurse or doctor may not have something to say to you regarding what information you give them. Regrettably, some may give you a "dressing down" because of it. But they need all the information they can get to make sure you and your baby get the best care they can give. Just so you know— they will not withhold treatment from you on anything they deem necessary for a good outcome for you or your baby because of this.

This is *so* important to be totally honest with your nurse during your initial assessment and screening. They will get your medical, family, and current history information. This will help ensure that you get the appropriate care needed if there is anything in your history that might be an issue for the delivery or your baby afterward.

If you received a little prenatal care elsewhere, they would attempt to get records of what had been done during those visits, which will be important to them. If they cannot get records, your doctor will order everything necessary to check your current status. This is especially true if previously you had no prenatal care or they cannot get your records before you deliver.

Be sure to tell your nurse or doctor if you have used illicit drugs *(i.e., marijuana, cocaine, crack, meth, prescription painkillers, etc.)* during the pregnancy— and be *honest and specific. Especially* if you have used any in the last few days before arriving at the hospital. The doctor does not want to give you any medications you cannot have due to the drugs you have taken. If this did happen, it could cause serious complications for you or your baby. This is why giving them all the information about any drug use is so important when they ask.

The first thing collected for patients falling in all these groups will be your blood for testing. This will give an up-to-date look at your body system functions and give them a guideline on what specific actions will be necessary for your care. Suppose you have used illicit drugs in the past or have had no prenatal care. In that case, they will request a drug screen to test whether drugs are in your system. This will tell them what might be contraindicated *(not advised)* with other painkillers or medications you might receive. Your baby will be tested *as well* after delivery:

- *Urine* - to detect drugs passed on within the past few days
- *Meconium* - to detect what you would have taken at an earlier time during the pregnancy

This is also helpful for the baby's treatment, as the baby can have withdrawal symptoms if drugs are detected in either or both. If you

To Mothers Using Illicit Drugs and/or Having Limited/No Prenatal Care

have limited or no prenatal care, additional testing would be required to check for any diseases affecting your care and require additional precautions. This includes STDs *(sexually transmitted diseases)* or other contagious viruses that are easily transmittable.

With some STDs, there would be a need for a cesarean section because a vaginal birth might be dangerous for your baby. Vaginal herpes, chlamydia, gonorrhea, and syphilis are the main STDs for which cesarean births would be needed for a good outcome and to reduce or eliminate risks to your baby.

Testing for HIV and AIDs *(another group of STDs)* or any acquired virus through other means *(ie., shared needles or other equipment; contact with another's bodily fluids through broken skin, wounds, open sores, etc.)*, which the doctors and nurses caring for you and baby want to be aware of. Consent from you must be given to the hospital staff for this testing. However, it is preferred you get tested whether you know you have it or not— and it's ethical for you to provide this consent to protect the staff caring for you.

Although vaginal delivery occurs with these viruses successfully, testing is necessary to provide information for a primary care physician and/or pediatrician for follow-up care for you and your baby. The testing is also necessary to protect the hospital staff caring for you and your baby. Additional precautions need to be taken for patient isolation, and universal precautions for appropriate hand hygiene and use of non-porous medical articles of gloves, gowns, and masks for hospital staff. They want to stay safe to continue caring for other patients, now and in the future. So knowing if they are at risk for contracting one of these diseases is very important for the safety of all involved.

Ultrasonography *(getting an ultrasound)* will also be ordered, if time allows, before delivery. This gives information to the obstetrician and nurses concerning:

- The possible age of the baby *(in weeks)*
- How big is the baby
- Which position the baby is lying in
- If there is anything visibly wrong with the baby, cord, or placenta
- Where the placenta is positioned
- How much amniotic fluid is present around your baby

This also helps determine whether it would be safe to deliver vaginally— or if a cesarean section would be necessary.

Per the obstetrician's orders, you should also expect a social services visit during your hospital stay. This is necessary for helping to:

- Determine your current living conditions and if it is a safe environment for your baby.
- Determine if additional services might be necessary to help you and the baby once you leave the hospital.
- Provide information for financial assistance programs.
- Get signed up for WIC benefits or Medicaid *(if you're qualified)*.
- Provide aid or information for homelessness, abuse, or baby needs.
- Offer drug rehabilitation programs.

Our goal is to provide optimal care for you and your baby and acquire useful information that will allow us to provide all the care safely and securely. All information remains confidential and is only available to the nurses and doctors providing that care. Our *ultimate goal* is the best outcome— for you and your baby! So, trust your medical staff to do just that.

Q&A on Other Post-Delivery Concerns

This is the section we will be covering numerous questions or concerns that might pop up during your hospital stay or even for a time after you return home.

Q *Why am I running a low-grade temperature? Should I worry about infection?*

A You may run a low-grade temperature for a couple of reasons. Spinal or epidural anesthesia may cause you to run a low-grade temperature briefly during or after delivery. This is nothing to worry about unless you have other complications after having anesthesia, which your nurse will monitor you for during your stay.

The other will be if your milk has come in. Some moms have what is called a *"milk fever,"* which isn't a fever at all. It occurs at the onset of lactation, or milk production, and lasts only a few hours.

If you were to have any infection going on, your temperature would be at least 100.4 degrees or higher, and for a longer period. Again, your nurse will monitor your vital signs for any indication of infection during your stay. If you have been discharged from the hospital and have a fever of at least 100.4, you should contact your doctor.

Q *Do you have any pills to dry up my milk since I am not breastfeeding??*

A Unfortunately, this is very outdated. You probably have your mom, grandmother, or older family member/acquaintance giving you that advice to ask about it. Simply put, medication for this has not been given for many years due to serious side effects. There are several other ways to help suppress your milk production during the beginning of your lactation.

- Wear a well-fitted support bra.
- Use cabbage leaves placed on the breasts inside your bra, then exchange the wilted leaf with a new one when needed.
- Pump or hand express breasts *only* enough to reduce discomfort, and *only* if necessary during engorgement, but not enough to empty them.
- When you take warm showers, *do not* expose your breast to the direct spray of water; shower with the spray on your back or any other body part, just not the breasts.
- Use ice packs to help reduce the pain and tissue swelling.
- Take ibuprofen or acetaminophen *(Motrin or Tylenol)* for pain relief. *(** Do Not take additional Tylenol if you are taking narcotic pain relievers at the same time, as they already may contain acetaminophen.)*

This process may take a week or two, but remember, every woman is different, and it depends on your body's amount of milk production. And also, remember, even if you are formula feeding, any milk you have already pumped or hand-expressed can be fed to the baby. Even a little bit is good for them.

Q&A on Other Post-Delivery Concerns

Q *I weighed myself on the scale in the hall, but I only lost a few pounds. How come? Shouldn't I lose more?*

A You would think just by having had your baby, you would have lost more than a few pounds after delivery. I mean, there is the weight of the baby, so you should have at least lost that much, right? The answer is "not necessarily so." The reasoning for this is the enlarged uterus, additional blood volume from pregnancy, swelling of the breasts in preparation for lactation, and the extra fluid pumped into you during your labor or cesarean section. This accounts for very little weight loss after delivery, even though we would like it to be much more.

Q *Why am I swollen? (or swelling more?)*

A During the pregnancy, women will sometimes retain some of the fluid in their legs, feet, hands, and face, which the physician will monitor throughout their recovery for any underlying complications. Any fluid you might have retained during pregnancy and all the fluids given to you before, during, and after your delivery can cause you to swell— or swell even more than you already have. The added IV fluid infusion during labor and/or delivery can *"get worse before it gets better."* You may wake up anytime and realize your fingers and toes feel like "sausages," or your feet feel like "you are walking on soggy or squishy sponges."

After delivery, your body reverts to its pre-pregnant status now that you are no longer pregnant. Due to all the hormonal and physical changes, you may swell *more* within the next couple of days or *start* swelling even if you had none before delivery. This is what is called *Third Spacing*. Fluid is finding its way outside the body's cells and floating in the spaces around the cells. This normal physiological issue usually takes a few days or so to remedy. One way to help remedy this is to drink lots of water. It really sounds funny your nurse would instruct you to do this when you already have lots of *"water swelling."* But the fluid in your hands, feet, legs, and face is actually not in your cells— it's now *third spacing* or going outside the cells into the tissue and floating around. By drinking water, you are causing an osmotic process that helps to *"draw"* the water back into the cells so your body can flush the excess fluid out. You will definitely know this is working because you will start going to the bathroom frequently and urinating quite a lot each time.

The second would be getting up and walking around, *not* sitting for extended periods. By getting up and moving, you are helping to get the circulation going, especially in your lower extremities, to help move the fluid out.

When sitting or lying down, the third way is to elevate your feet to help shift the fluid in the lower extremities away from your feet. If the swelling or edema gets extremely bad, it can put additional pressure on your blood vessels. This might cause your blood pressure to increase. The swelling can also cause constriction of the nerves, which may cause pain, tingling, or weakness in your arms, hands, legs, or feet. Once the fluid begins to shift, and your body starts the fluid removal process, you will notice relief from the pain or swelling.

Q&A on Other Post-Delivery Concerns

Q *Why am I crying or emotional? Hot? Sweaty?*

A There are several of the strangest things you might notice after you have delivered your baby. Why am I burning up? Feeling like I have been in a sauna? Why am I getting drenched in sweat? Crying at the "drop of a hat?" You've been in good control or feel you have since you delivered, but these things which are happening seem strange. Why are they happening? Is anything wrong? The answer is a big resounding…. *"NO!"* All of this funky stuff happening is all due to— hormones. Hormonal and physiological changes.

Now that you are no longer pregnant, all the hormones that shifted around when you first became pregnant are *shifting back* to your pre-pregnant state. Also, physiological systems which changed to accommodate the pregnancy are shifting back too. These hormonal and physiological changes can last a few days to weeks. It's normal if you are throwing off the blankets, trying to strip down to the bare minimum of clothes, asking for a portable fan, feeling like everything is falling apart, and you want to cry over what you think is the silliest thing. Just remember— *it will get better* with time when the hormones readjust to their normal state.

****Postpartum Depression*— I had to put this one right behind the hormonal fluctuations, as this follows the same guidelines. But this is usually just slightly different— it can be more severe.

Postpartum depression is a condition that generally does not start affecting you right away. This comes with time, approximately 3-12 months after delivery, and may be minor or major in severity. Or, this can hit sooner if any risk factors are affecting you, along with anything happening after you have returned home from the hospital. *(i.e., lack of sleep, pain, isolation, no help once going home, etc.)* This can affect 1 out of 7 women in the postpartum period, and in which a family history of mood disorders can predispose you to this condition even more. Other risk factors can include:

- Depression or anxiety during the pregnancy
- Stressful life events during the pregnancy or postpartum period
- Infant NICU admission or preterm delivery
- Low-income family
- Poor social support
- History of depression
- Problems with breastfeeding

Any one or more of these risk factors can make things difficult for you and your family, and even more so if you do not have a support system to help you through some or a lot of these issues.

Unfortunately, as the patient, you may not notice this creeping upon you and taking hold. You also may not realize the "signs to look for" have started occurring when watching for postpartum depression *(PPD)*. This is where your husband, significant other, family, and/or friends can help you. They will be able to see the signs when you may not. And if you do not have a support system, try to be mindful of these signs so, hopefully, you can recognize them.

Q&A on Other Post-Delivery Concerns

Some of these signs might be:

- Loss of weight and/or appetite
- Depressed mood
- Inconsolable crying
- Not wanting to take care of yourself or the baby
- Feelings of helplessness or hopelessness
- Wanting to withdraw from everyone

The others will more likely be able to see these changes coming about when you may not. Your friend or loved one may let you know you might be showing signs of PPD. If they do, don't hesitate to contact your OB doctor *(if still under their care)* or your Primary Care Physician. They may be able to prescribe medications to take for short-term mental health therapy and then wean you off once the crisis is resolved.

Q *Why do I have trouble sleeping?*

A That first night, or day, depending on when you deliver, you may be physically exhausted and want to sleep— but are having trouble getting there. For most women, shortly after delivery, they find sleep somehow eludes them and don't know why. There is a simple explanation for this problem— *Adrenaline Rush!!*

I tell patients this adrenaline rush is caused by the birth of their baby. The excitement of the birth, the inundation of visitors, numerous recalls of events during the delivery, and the fact that you "can't shut your brain down." It's no wonder you are having trouble sleeping. It also makes it difficult to get sleep when your baby is right in the room with you, and any little squeak or squawk brings you to immediate attention.

You hold your baby, cuddle, and kiss, and are in total awe of this new life before you. You don't want to put your baby down or send your baby to the nursery for fear you might miss out on even one precious moment of your baby's new life. And thus, we move on to…

Q *Why am I so exhausted?*

A Think back to just before you entered the hospital and what happened until then. Have you gotten any sleep during the last week or so before coming into the hospital? How long were you in labor before you delivered? Were you anxious and not sleeping because you had a scheduled delivery date the next day? Any one, or a combination of these, could be playing a role in this sleep deprivation. Then after having the baby and being *adrenaline rushed,* you now have compounded this problem. Nothing like starting off "behind the eight ball" when it comes to sleep. Next, there are the new demands of feeding the baby every 2-3 hours, changing diapers, soothing or comforting a crying baby, and having visitors outstay their welcome— and it snowballs!!

Once you are able to sleep, try and get as much rest as you can between your baby's feedings. Sleeping for a couple hours at a stretch every few hours will help you overcome this deprivation. You'd be surprised at how a couple of hours of solid sleep between feedings will help to rejuvenate you, and two or three more of these "power sleeps" will help even

Q&A on Other Post-Delivery Concerns

more. But remember, this will go on for months, with a few curveballs thrown in *(i.e., colicky baby, sick baby, overstimulated and cranky baby, etc.)*. Do your best to rest *when* you can because there is a light at the end of the tunnel— I promise!

Q *Why am I lightheaded? Dizzy? Loopy?*

A There may be several causes for you to be lightheaded or dizzy during your recovery period. First and foremost would be blood loss. During the delivery process, blood loss for a vaginal delivery is generally less than 500 ml, and for cesarean delivery is less than 1000 ml. Having blood loss decreases the amount of blood flowing in your system and the number of red blood cells, which help provide oxygen to all your body systems. This can cause you to be lightheaded or dizzy easily. This is one of the reasons we discussed earlier about getting out of bed slowly— and with your nurse present at least the first time.

Another probable reason could be a lack of sleep combined with your pain medications. Sleep is key to recovery when your body is trying to heal. If you have not had sufficient amounts of sleep and you put pain medication on top of that, it may make you feel loopy, dizzy, and in a "fog." The pain medication helps give you pain relief and, in turn, helps to relax you. If you are already exhausted, the pain medication can amplify the effect, causing you to feel "out of it." *Listen. To. Your. Body!!* If you are sleep-deprived, with your body trying to heal from the delivery, you are just compounding the problem for yourself.

Be sure you get in and out of bed slowly during the first day or so, and not moving too quickly— take your time! Also, when you get into the shower, *do not* take a hot one! Hot water will zap what little energy you may have and increase your chances of becoming dizzy. Hopefully, your hospital has a shower bench available, so be sure to use it at least the first time.

Q *Why does my tailbone really hurt when I sit?? I can hardly put any pressure on it!*

A The cause of tailbone pain *(coccydynia)* is due to the vaginal delivery of the baby. The delivery may be difficult due to a large baby or fast delivery, small or abnormally shaped pelvis, or abnormal positioning of the baby as they are delivered. The joints between the individual coccyx bones can break open, causing pain, or a coccyx bone can become fractured. As the baby is born, it may force the coccyx back, damaging the joint. Unfortunately, there is no cure for this. With time, approximately 4 weeks for a joint break and 8-12 weeks for an actual bone fracture, the tailbone will heal.

Here's a list of helpful things to aid in healing:

- Rest and stop any physical activity which causes you pain. This will help in the healing process.
- Apply ice to your tailbone for 20 mins every hour for 48 hours while awake— *DO NOT* apply ice directly to the skin *(wrap in a damp washcloth or hand towel)*.
- Avoid sitting up as much as possible.

- Lay on your stomach to take pressure off the tailbone while sleeping.

- When sitting, alternate between sitting on one cheek or the other.

- You can breastfeed side-lying to avoid sitting up during this time. If you must sit up, sit on a cushion or inflatable donut to take the pressure off your tailbone.

- Take prescribed pain meds for your pain. Your doctor should suggest certain meds for pain relief.

- Take a stool softener throughout this healing time to avoid constipation. Straining will put extra pressure on your tailbone, causing additional pain.

- Drink plenty of water and eat fibrous foods *(i.e., fruits, vegetables, legumes, nuts, beans, etc.)*

Follow up with your doctor on your progress. If it is not healing well, they will help find other treatments to aid your recovery.

Q *Why is my lower back so sore?*

A Two common issues can cause lower back pain after delivery. First off would be having an epidural or spinal during your delivery. During the procedure, the anesthesiologist will numb the area around the tube placement site. This will cause tissue bruising in that location, leading to soreness. Then the anesthesiologist pushes the spinal needle into the epidural space of your spine, which takes a little added pressure to achieve. The combination of these will cause some of your back pain after delivery.

The second cause of lower back pain would be the weight redistribution after the baby is delivered. During pregnancy, your posture slowly changed to redistribute your growing weight. This gradual change did not cause back pains until the weight became heavier out front later in the pregnancy. Now that the baby has been delivered, the weight distribution shifted suddenly, so this quick change has strained your lower back muscles.

Q *Why do I feel sore all over??*

A This is a fairly easy question— you have just been through labor and/or delivery!! For vaginal deliveries— you use a lot of muscles you don't normally use, and they have had a workout!! About Day 2, you'll feel like you have been hit by a *Mack truck*, with sore muscles all over your body. For cesarean sections— most of the muscles and organs in your abdomen have been pushed and shoved around during the procedure, which will make you sore. Ibuprofen *(Motrin)* is recommended to relieve your overall muscle soreness.

Q *Why do I have difficulty going to pee?*

A Whether vaginal with an epidural or cesarean section with an epidural or spinal, a Foley catheter was inserted to empty your bladder when you could not get up to do so on your own. When a catheter is in place, the urethra *(tube emptying your bladder)* and the bladder become inactive. Having the catheter inserted and left in, even briefly, can block the nerve

Q&A on Other Post-Delivery Concerns

signals to your bladder when you attempt to urinate after its removal. This is called a neurogenic bladder.

Trauma from delivery, foley catheters, general anesthesia, pain medications, and IV fluids can cause a neurogenic bladder. Most of the time, this issue will resolve on its own without intervention. It may take some time for those nerve signals to fire again, so the urethra can resume emptying the bladder. You will be given a few hours for this to start functioning independently. It may be slow going with the flow until it starts working again, so be patient. You may start and stop several times before you feel you have emptied your bladder. But if it doesn't start working in a timely manner and your bladder starts to fill, it will be emptied by your nurse.

Q *I feel like I have to pee, so why is my catheter not working?*

A One of the problems I have found with cesarean section patients is having a Foley catheter that does not empty as it should. The catheter has two oblong holes on each side of the tip, but one side can be covered by the balloon that keeps it in the bladder. That leaves only one hole to allow for drainage. With continuous movement and the position changes you make in bed, the catheter can "butt up" against the side wall of the bladder. Now *both* holes are blocked, so the bladder fills up, and you feel the need to urinate. Let your nurse know when this happens so she can help drain the catheter and keep the bladder empty until its removal.

Q *Why does it burn when I pee?*

A Episiotomies and lacerations to your hoo-hah after a vaginal delivery can make urinating painful. The more concentrated your urine is, the more it will burn. Try using your peri-bottle, Hygenique® sprayer, or sitz bath while you are going. The water will help to dilute the urine and lessen the burning sensation on your cuts and lacerations. Continue to do this until they start to heal and it no longer burns.

If the burning sensation feels like it's coming from *inside* you, let your nurse know, as you may be developing a urinary tract or bladder infection.

Q *My stitches feel like they are pulling out when I sit down. What can I do??*

A The suggestion I made earlier in the book seems to work well for my vaginal-delivered patients when they sit down. During the pregnancy, your doctor or nurse may have instructed you to perform Kegel exercises to help strengthen your pelvic floor muscles in preparation for delivery. As you get ready to sit down, do a Kegel, hold it, then sit down and relax. This will help draw in your muscles and vaginal skin so it won't pull as much when you sit and relax. Do this anywhere you sit— bed, chair, toilet, car seat, etc.— until you no longer feel the pulling and tugging.

Q *I feel like I've got more pressure on my bottom (from vaginal delivery).* OR *My knees are pressing against my incision, which hurts (from cesarean section). Why is that happening??*

A One of the things I found with some hospital beds is that when you raise or lower the head of the bed, the knees of the bed start to slowly rise on their own. This is such a subtle change over time, and you do not even realize it's happening.

Q&A on Other Post-Delivery Concerns

Because of this phenomenon, patients had more vaginal area pain or pressure than before, or cesarean section patients had added pain with their thighs pushing up against their incision. Once the knees of the bed were moved back down, this produced instant relief from either vaginal or incisional pain, respectively, and reduced the rating given for their pain.

When you go to get out of bed, be sure to check that the knees of the bed are completely down before you attempt to crawl out. This way, you will not try " crawling out of a hole" in your bed. I find it bizarre that something so simple can cause pain in either patient just by "having a ghost in the machine…" but it's an easy fix with a remarkable outcome.

Try this solution if you find yourself in this situation. You will be glad you did!

Q *I cannot hold the baby. So, why are my hands tingling and/or numb?*

A Usually, you already had some swelling during pregnancy and had additional swelling after the baby was born. The added swelling in your hands, arms, etc., puts pressure on your nerves— making your hands feel like they are "going to sleep." This is known as *Carpel Tunnel Syndrome*. The tingling and numbness will subside as the fluid leaves your body, and the swelling goes down in your hands and arms.

If you had swelling and carpel tunnel syndrome before delivery, it could get worse before it gets better. This is just like post-delivery swelling all over your body. Again, walking the halls will help with the circulation of this fluid, and drinking lots of water will help to draw the fluid back into your cells to be flushed out.

Q *I'm having terrible shoulder pain... What is causing this?*

A Patients who have had a cesarean section may find this a problem. This is known as *"referred shoulder pain."* There are two schools of thought regarding referred shoulder pain after surgery. One thought, this is caused by the trauma of the abdominal surgery and manipulation of the abdominal muscles. The other is it is a sign of gas build-up in the intestines, causing carbon dioxide-induced irritation to the phrenic nerve, which causes pain in the C4 area of your neck.

Usually, this pain is located on the right shoulder versus the left. I have found the right shoulder seems to be more accurate, but I have had patients with both at the same time. As the patient ambulates or rocks in a chair and starts passing gas, the pain in the shoulder starts to work its way out.

Q *Why am I shivering uncontrollably right after delivery?*

A Again, there are several schools of thought concerning postpartum shivering. Sudden thermal imbalance from the separation of the placenta, postpartum hemorrhage, sudden decrease in body temperature following delivery, hormonal changes immediately after delivery, and anesthesia-related effects can contribute to this. Thermal support, such as warm blankets, will help, along with administering meperidine *(Demerol)*, if an epidural or spinal has previously been administered. This resolves within the first couple hours after delivery, usually during recovery.

Q&A on Other Post-Delivery Concerns

Q *I have an excruciating headache that will not go away unless I lie down... What is causing this?*

A If you have received an epidural or spinal before delivery, sometimes this is a side effect after removing the catheter. If your body does not "clot off" the puncture site on the spine, cerebral spinal fluid can leak out, which in turn can cause this headache. This might resolve on its own by lying down for an extended period, taking pain meds, and consuming caffeine. If severe enough to cause incapacitation, the option for a blood patch to be placed over the puncture site might be in order. This blood patch will cover the site and stop spinal fluid leakage, reducing and resolving your headache. The anesthesiologist will complete this task.

Suppose your headache is accompanied by epigastric pain, increased blood pressure, visual disturbances, shortness of breath or painful breathing, or altered mental status. In that case, they *may be* symptoms of pre-eclampsia/eclampsia in the post-delivery phase. Usually, this is found in patients who show signs or symptoms before delivery. Still, it can begin after delivery in some patients, even without having prior preeclampsia. Let your nurse know immediately with either of these findings, so proper assessment and treatment can be started as soon as possible.

Post-Hospital Complications / Emergencies

There can be complications after delivery, such as hemorrhaging, quickly becoming a genuinely concerning issue with your nurses or the doctor. Some post-delivery complications occur during your hospital stay and can be addressed and managed quickly. But, over half of all postpartum complications can occur in the days, weeks, and months after delivery. Don't think you are "in the clear" after delivering and recovering some in the hospital. You may find some of these issues occurring with you after discharge.

After you have returned home, you may find that your vaginal bleeding has picked up and become heavier than it had been. Sometimes this is due to increased activity on *your* part. Let others do what needs doing and concentrate only on caring for yourself and your baby. *(**I know some of you out there may feel the need to keep busy all the time, but this time IS NOT one of those times.)*

When you go home, it is important that you take it easy for a few weeks before you increase your activity. This gives your body time to heal, *even* after a vaginal delivery. Delivery is a very traumatic event for your body, and it needs time to heal, so don't try and overdo it too soon. Suppose you suddenly start doing more around the house, such as laundry, dishes, cleaning, and caring for your baby. In that case, you might find your bleeding picking up and becoming more reddish in color again. Areas in your uterus that previously had clotted off may have "broken back open," increasing the reddish bleeding. This is a good indication you are doing too much and need to *slow way down—* let your body *heal.*

There are other signs of complications you need to look for after going home. More and more hospitals today give a hand-out

Post-Hospital Complications / Emergencies

regarding complications to mothers before they discharge from the hospital. This handout is written by AWHONN *(Association of Women's Health, Obstetric, and Neonatal Nurses)*. It provides information on signs and symptoms you must watch for, and some can become *medical emergencies! (**If you do not read anything else the hospital hands out at discharge, be sure to read THIS one.)* If you didn't receive this hand-out upon discharge, here are the contents of the warning signs given in the acronym: **P.O.S.T. B.I.R.T.H.**

- **P**ain in the chest *and/or*
- **O**bstructed breathing or shortness of breath; either of these two can mean a clot in your lungs or a heart problem.
- **S**eizures, which can indicate the condition of eclampsia.
- **T**houghts or feelings of hurting yourself or your baby may mean you have postpartum depression/postpartum psychosis.

All four are life-threatening emergencies; you must seek help immediately by *calling 911.*

The following symptoms are indications you need to call your healthcare provider. Generally, this is your obstetrician as you are still under their care for at least 6 weeks post-delivery:

- **B**leeding, soaking through a pad in an hour, and/or blood clots the size of an egg or bigger may mean you are having or starting to have a postpartum hemorrhage.
- **I**ncision that is not healing, or increased redness or pus at the site of an episiotomy or cesarean incision may indicate an infection.
- **R**edness, swelling, warmth, or pain in the calf that is painful to the touch may indicate a blood clot.

- **T**emperature of 100.4° F or higher, bad-smelling blood or discharge may indicate infection.

- **H**eadache *(excruciatingly painful)*, vision changes, and pain in the upper right area of your belly can all indicate high blood pressure or the condition of post-birth preeclampsia.

Your obstetrician will determine if you can come into the office to have this checked out or if you need to go to the emergency room for treatment.

Trust your instincts whenever you have anything that just doesn't feel, look, or smell right. You should always seek medical advice or care if you are not sure. It is *always* better to err on the side of caution and make that phone call. Doesn't matter if it is day or night. If it's at night, an answering service should connect you to the on-call obstetrician.

Baby's Care

This is the section you will most likely refer to often, given that your new baby is here. As parents, we tend to be more concerned with our children than ourselves, but we must not overlook our own care to focus on just the baby's care. Remember, *you must take care of yourself in order to take care of your baby.*

Many events and situations during the infant's time in the hospital and shortly after returning home are normal and become routine. Some things might appear abnormal but are expected during the baby's first few days after delivery. The focus will begin with regular assessments, activities, changes, and education, then move on to some more issues which creep up unexpectedly but are still normal in this timeframe.

Every post-delivery situation is unique to the recovery of each baby. Still, sometimes little "curve balls" can be thrown into the mix. They may cause you some anxiety and concern when they happen. So, we will address all the possible "routine" stuff and then come back and talk about the "other" stuff. Be reassured that even if something is "out of the ordinary" in your mind does not mean it is. Sometimes it just happens and usually resolves itself in its own time. This is one of the reasons for providing this information to you; to help educate you ahead of time or be a reference during this time to help put your mind at ease.

Beginning with Recovery

Congratulations!!! Your baby is born— and now begins the recovery process for him or her— *or* them. The mouth and nose are suctioned out by your doctor, the cord is clamped, then cut, and the baby is placed on your chest within the first minute or two. Your nursery nurse will then take over from there, drying the baby off with a towel and removing wetness and some vernix from the baby's skin and head. This is all while stimulating the baby and placing a cap on the baby's head. By rubbing the baby's skin, the nurse removes lots of moisture *(ie., blood, amniotic fluid, urine, meconium)* covering the baby's exposed skin— which can quickly decrease the baby's temperature. During this time, the baby gets body heat from you by laying on your chest, thus helping maintain a more stable body temperature. Rubbing or stimulating the skin also helps to elicit the baby's first cries, which help to "open up" the airway and expand the lungs. This helps to provide oxygen to the baby and helps the lungs absorb the amniotic fluid remaining there.

When your baby is crying good and loud, the bluish skin color begins turning pinker and pinker with each cry. It's a good thing to allow your baby this time to cry excessively for a while after birth. This gives the lungs ample time to absorb all the fluid inside and provide much-needed oxygen to all the body's cells. Once the cord has been cut, this is an especially important step for your new baby. You are no longer providing that oxygen for them, and they must be able to provide it for themselves now… "♪ *So let her cry!!* ♫"

During your baby's "crying time," your nursery nurse will quickly check their vital signs and do a visual assessment to determine their well-being. Soon after, if you are breastfeeding, the nurse will assist you and the baby with latching on to the breast for the first time. If needed, your doctor will begin to make repairs from the vaginal delivery or finish with your cesarean section surgery. Your delivery nurse will continue to monitor and assess you simultaneously and provide care until recovery is completed.

*[**Some hospitals are now changing their procedures to allow cesarean section deliveries to experience much of this immediate delivery occurrence, where they were not allowed before. Our facility calls this the "gentle c-section."]*

The recovery period for the baby generally lasts two hours, just like yours, so you will see the nursery nurse or postpartum nurse recheck vitals and reassess often. Generally, this occurs every 30 mins for the first two hours. Depending on your hospital's policies and procedures, this time is also for bonding between the parents and baby. Other procedures, such as weights and measurements, medication administration, and baby's first bath, will be delayed to give you this time to bond as a family unit.

Many hospitals nationwide use this recovery method for the family to enhance the bonding experience. Whether this is your first delivery or your 6th— enjoy this time *alone* without visitors swooping down on you and invading. Nothing is worse than not having gotten mom out of stirrups and the room a mess from the delivery, only to have your room— and *your privacy* invaded by impatient family members. *(Or— barge into your room as soon as you return from surgery.)* They have waited just as long as you have to see your new baby, but this is *your right* as a family to have this time alone together. And this will be the only *"first time"* you'll get, so take advantage and enjoy!! Better yet, tell anyone planning to be at the hospital at delivery— this *will* be happening with your new family. *(Even if the hospital doesn't routinely do this.)* Put your foot down and declare, *"No Negotiations... at All!"* regardless of how you deliver. If they know this in advance, they will expect it and should have no hard feelings about it.

When the recovery and bonding period is completed, you can enjoy spending time with family and friends. Now your anxious visitors are let in to greet the newest addition to your circle. But just remember, you've just been through delivery and are likely exhausted from your experience. Don't let them overwhelm you for hours on end. You and baby— *and* Daddy *(or significant other)* need rest, feeding time, bonding time, etc.,— and the adventure has only begun. *(**See the section on "Other Topics" under "Visitors, Visitors Visitors".)*

Detailed Recovery for the Baby

This section will discuss the baby's recovery period in more detail. This way, you will know what to expect as each event unfolds—and why they occur. Hopefully, this will put you at ease knowing everything that can happen beforehand.

Suctioning Out the Baby

Right after the baby's head is born, your OB doctor will take a bulb syringe and remove any excess fluid still in the baby's nose and mouth. This will help to unblock their airway so that the first breath can occur. If your baby had his first stool inside before he was born, which is very thick, the doctor might use a suction catheter to remove it from the mouth. *(**Sometimes those darn babies will try and cry just with the head delivered— it happens!)*

As of 2005, if any babies passed their first stool before delivery, only a bulb syringe can be used. Deep airway suctioning is not recommended with suction catheters *(ie., back of the throat and down the airway)* and should not be performed unless absolutely necessary. Doctors should only use the bulb syringe to remove the fluid in the mouth and back of the throat. Still, the baby will be monitored closely for any signs or symptoms of meconium aspiration. It *can* make the baby sick, but they usually tolerate it without any additional concerns. If the baby has difficulty recovering from it, appropriate neonatal support therapy will be initiated.

Vital Signs

Right after the baby is born, the nursery nurse will check the baby's heart rate, respirations, and temperature. These vital signs give nurses a baseline on how the baby transitions from delivery through recovery to the outside world. One vital sign, or all, can be outside the normal range, telling us the baby may need additional medical care above and beyond that of a well-transitioning baby. Whether sick- or well-baby, these vitals are monitored throughout their hospital stay until discharge. They can change at any time during their stay.

- *Temperature* - Immediate post-delivery temperatures range from 96.8 to 100.3. The normal range after recovery is generally between 97.6 and 99.0. Anything above or below these could indicate issues that may need medical interventions to correct if it is outside this range. At this early age, infections are not just registering in the high ranges for newborn babies; they can also be too low.

Skin-to-skin contact with the mother can help keep temperatures up, along with warmed baby blankets. But if the baby is not warming up either way, then placement under a radiant warmer will help with this. Warmers are generally used briefly and only as needed because long-term usage of warmers can cause dehydration.

- *Respirations* - How fast or slow the baby is breathing and if they are making sounds can help determine if there is respiratory distress, possible infection, or both.

Sometimes right after birth, a baby may struggle with breathing because of airway blockage from substantial

Detailed Recovery for the Baby

amounts of fluid in the nose and mouth that had not been completely removed at delivery. Additional suctioning with a bulb syringe and some supplemental oxygen may be needed.

If the baby does not spontaneously breathe on their own, CPAP *(Continuous Positive Airway Pressure)* may be administered with a mask and oxygen source to help push air into the lungs and start spontaneous breathing. This is usually a short-term solution that quickly improves the baby's airway within minutes, requiring no other assistance.

- *Heart rate* - If this is too high, along with fast respirations, this can indicate the beginning of respiratory distress or infection. If too low, the baby may already be in respiratory distress, and the heart may have difficulty pumping due to lack of oxygen.

   Generally, if the heart rate is too low, it is due to a respiratory issue where the baby is not breathing well on his own. Respiratory assistance would be necessary, along with possible medications to help with resuscitation. Your nurses and doctor will assist your baby in overcoming this rather quickly. So unless your baby has other contributing issues, they should do just fine. Additional monitoring would be needed in the Level II nursery to ensure your baby recovers well and can return to normal newborn care.

Combinations of any or all of these can indicate other potential issues such as— low blood sugars, temperature instabilities, apnea *(periodically stop breathing)*, etc., which is why they are monitored. So, if the vital signs are in the ranges where they should be, the baby is transitioning well on this part of recovery.

Baby's Other Recovery Needs

Here is a list of all the rest of the baby's recovery needs beyond the vital signs. Although vital signs are *the* most important part of recovery, others need completion, too. These other things help to round out what occurs during the recovery period— and how we care for the baby from recovery moving forward.

Apgar scores

This tool is used within the first few minutes of life, which also helps determine how well the baby is transitioning, but much quicker. These are done at 1- and 5-minute increments after birth. They are scored based on these five observations rated 0-2 for a maximum score of 10:

- *Heart rate:* 0= None, 1= <100 BPM, 2= >100 BPM
- *Respirations:* 0= No cry, 1= Weak cry, 2= Vigorous cry
- *Muscle tone:* 0= Limp 1= Some flexion, 2= Active
- *Reflex:* 0= No response to airway stimulation, 1= Grimace with stimulation, 2= Grimace and cough or sneeze during stimulation
- *Color:* 0= Entire body blue or pale, 1= Good color, but blue hands and/or feet, 2= Completely pink or good color

These can quickly indicate the need for help with their airway or breathing. Still, most normal births score in the 8-9 range at 1 and 5 minutes, usually taken 1 off for color and/or 1 off for tone. Just know that when your baby has been given a low Apgar score(s) at some point during the first few minutes of life does not mean the baby will have issues later because of this. This is just a quick indicator for us if the baby might need some assistance to help with breathing.

Baby's measurements

After the first couple hours, when the recovery is over, or you're anxious to know sooner *(who won the baby pool???)*, the baby's measurements will be completed. The baby will be weighed and then measured for length, head circumference, and chest circumference. These measurements are not just information about your baby for you to have and for everyone to rave and boast about. They are useful diagnostic tools in determining your baby's plan of care during hospitalization.

With the weight, we are looking at the birth weight as a baseline and will have daily weights until discharge. This helps us to determine if the baby is losing an appropriate amount of weight or too much. Losing too much weight can show baby is not getting enough nutrition and may need additional supplementation, whether breast milk or formula. Pre-term or lower birth weight babies need specialized care to help with weight gain and other issues. There can be other reasons for weight loss, but these are just a few more common ones.

Head circumference measurements help determine if the baby's head is in the normal range for its size *or* too big/too small. An enlarged head might indicate something as simple as macrocephaly *(larger than normal head w/o any other sign or symptoms)*. This can be simply a "big head" which runs in the family to something more serious, such as macrocephaly, including more serious signs and symptoms. Most of the time, macrocephaly is benign and has no cause for concern. Then there can be macrocephaly due to hydrocephalus *(build-up of fluid on the brain)*. This can also be nothing to be concerned about, but at times it can be dangerous, and more medical treatments may be needed.

Microcephaly *(too small of a head)* is a rare condition generally related to problems with brain development in the womb. Still, it can also be related to infections, genetic changes, cerebral anoxia *(decreased oxygen to the brain)*, exposure to drugs, alcohol, certain toxic chemicals in the womb, or severe malnutrition *(not getting enough nutrients)*. But don't worry needlessly if your baby's head is smaller or larger. If the pediatrician has reason to be concerned, they will certainly let you know. But most of the head circumference may be just outside the normal range, and the baby is fine.

Length measurements average out to about 20" *(or 51 cm)*, and the range is usually 18" *(46 cm)* to 22" *(56 cm)*. If the baby's length falls outside the range, other health complications could contribute to this or issues during growth in the womb. Health factors of the mom, such as gestational diabetes, maternal anemia, high blood pressure, or obesity, can affect the baby's length issues. Genetics and/or genetic conditions, hormonal imbalances, medications, etc., can also contribute to this. Again, most babies fall into the acceptable range, so don't be concerned about your baby's length if it falls outside. Your pediatrician will let you know if there is cause for concern.

Ballard scoring

This assessment tool is used to help determine the baby's gestational age by the physical and neurological characteristics found at birth. Usually, this is accurate within a week or two of the number of weeks you were pregnant. Your baby's assessment may also determine if your dates were inaccurate. This is also a practical assessment for healthcare workers to determine the baby's age if the mother has no idea how many weeks she might have been pregnant.

Ballard scoring determines the care given by matching the baby's needs to their assigned gestational age. If this is close to the gestational age based on your dates, and you are 37 weeks or more, then regular routine baby care will usually be provided. If the dates are less than 37 weeks or greater than 42 weeks, then the healthcare given will be based on this assessment and any other findings indicating additional individual care. Your nurse or physician should discuss this with you if additional care is needed. They should inform you about what happens and why it is necessary. You can always ask if you do not get much of an explanation.

The scoring results, weight, and length are then charted on a grid. This helps to categorize the baby as Small for Gestational Age *(SGA)*, Large for Gestational Age *(LGA)*, or Average for Gestational Age *(AGA)*. It also helps to determine additional procedures required if the baby falls out of the AGA range. This is based on the three elements of measurements discussed above— weight, length, and head circumference. It also includes neurological and physical scoring.

Erythromycin eye ointment

This prophylactic antibiotic is placed in the baby's eyes to prevent ophthalmic neonatorum. This disorder can cause corneal scarring, ocular *(eye)* perforation, or blindness if the baby is exposed to bacteria from Gonorrhea or Chlamydia in the mother's vaginal tract during vaginal birth. Unfortunately, this can happen if not treated. However, a child delivered by cesarean section would not be exposed to these sexually transmitted diseases, but there could be other types. Exposure to infections such as Herpes simplex or Staphylococcus Aureus may also cause eye damage. So, the CDC *and* US Preventative Services Taskforce recommend that *all* infants receive this antibiotic at birth.

After its application, the baby may have redness and swelling around the eyelids, an occlusion or blockage of the lacrimal ducts *(tear ducts)*, and some yellowish discharge for a brief time. If the discharge concerns the pediatrician, additional eye medication may be ordered.

Vitamin K

Vitamin K is a shot given to all newborns within the first 24 hours of life. Babies are born *with limited* ability for their blood to clot, which increases the chance of bleeding issues. This is called vitamin K deficiency bleeding and can be very serious to the newborn.

Your baby has a small blood volume and cannot afford to lose much if they were to start bleeding. This shot helps boost blood clotting and prevent complications, which have been given routinely in hospitals since 1961. If you do not want your baby to receive shots in the hospital, don't refuse this one, as this is not a vaccine but a vitamin your baby needs to help with blood clotting. Since your baby is born with this limited ability for blood clotting, this puts the baby *at risk* for uncontrolled bleeding in the first 6 months of life. So this one shot is greatly needed.

Hepatitis B vaccine

This vaccine is recommended to all persons to prevent contracting this virus, which attacks the liver. It is offered to the parents for the baby's first vaccination shot in the hospital. The liver is a vital organ that filters out toxins and broken-down red blood cells *(bilirubin)*. It also processes nutrients for your body, regulates the composition of the blood, and makes certain proteins— Vitamin A, cholesterol, and clotting substances.

The Hepatitis B virus can damage the liver's ability to function by causing lifelong infection, liver cirrhosis, liver cancer, liver failure, and death. With the Hepatitis B vaccine, this virus can be prevented by vaccinating the baby with the first dose in the hospital at birth. The two remaining doses in the series will be given in the pediatrician's office before the baby's 18th month.

You do not have to decide during the hospital stay to administer the first dose of the vaccine. There is time to make this decision, and the shot can be postponed until the baby's first series of vaccinations. Some parents decide to wait until it could be given in the pediatrician's office so the records of the vaccines would all be together. However, some parents decided to get the first dose in the hospital when it was ordered so the baby would have one less shot during the baby's office visit. The hospital will provide a vaccination card, and the first dose can be documented on it. Then the card can be updated with any other vaccinations your baby receives in the pediatrician's or primary care physician's office. It's up to you which way you want to go with it.

Blood sugars (blood glucose)

Before the delivery, or at some time after, it may be determined your baby needs to have her blood sugar checked. The first glucose check is right after birth. It provides a baseline reading and alerts the nurse to provide any needed assistance to bring the sugar up if indicated by a low reading. *[**This is measured from an algorithm (chart) for a low reading based on the baby's age and the timing of reading. It also indicates the course of treatment to be given.]* Several factors would indicate the need for testing the baby's glucose levels and possibly for several intervals. Babies born *before* 37 weeks or SGA *(small for gestational age)* will have a series of glucose checks. These will start 30 minutes after the first feeding and each time right before the baby feeds over the first 24 hours. This is regardless of the initial glucose check after birth. Babies born LGA *(large for gestational age)* will also have a series of glucose checks. Usually, they are born to mothers who are either insulin-dependent diabetics or have gestational diabetes *(during pregnancy)*. Glucose checks occur 30 minutes after the first feeding and before feedings during the first 24 hours of life. This is also regardless of the initial check.

Suppose the mother is not gestational or insulin-dependent, and the baby is large for their age. In that case, the glucose checks occur 30 mins after the first feeding and before the remaining feedings within the first 12 hours. Any additional treatment will be based on the algorithm chart and the glucose reading.

When babies are born and fall under these two categories, they are at higher risk for their blood glucose levels to drop *(neonatal hypoglycemia)*. Therefore, monitoring is necessary to ensure the glucose level does not drop too low and requires intervention to bring those numbers up to the required levels. Recently, the use of a glucose gel within the first four hours after delivery has been very effective in rapidly raising the baby's blood sugars to appropriate levels. It also has decreased the need for IV glucose therapy and separation from mothers. *(**IV Glucose administration requires monitoring and treatment in the Level II or III nursery.)* This has helped keep the mother and baby together, which has helped with continued breastfeeding before and after discharge.

AGA babies, who fall out of these categories for monitoring, may also require blood glucose testing if they become symptomatic of Neonatal Hypoglycemia. They may become too cold, so the baby must expend more energy and use more calories to self-regulate their temperatures. This can cause glucose levels to drop. Other symptoms of Neonatal Hypoglycemia we watch for are:

- Poor feedings
- Floppiness or lethargy
- Jitteriness
- Apneic episodes *(stop breathing for greater than 20 seconds)*
- Losing their pink skin tone
- Seizures
- Weak or high-pitched cry
- Eye-rolling, and
- Tachypnea *(more than 60 breaths per minute)*.

Baby's 1st bath

To bathe or not to bathe… that is the question. Do you want your baby cleaned and "baby fresh" smelling? Or— do you want the vernix *(greasy, whitish covering on the surface of the baby's skin)* to remain for at least 24 hours or more to gain the benefits before the vernix is shed?

Some "old school" nurses still bathe the baby within the first couple hours after birth and get all the "yucky gunk" off the skin and out of the hair. But research results from several years ago stated that waiting to bathe the baby or not bathing during the hospital stay is very beneficial.

It's been found that the vernix has antimicrobial properties to protect from infection exposure during delivery and natural skin emollients to keep the skin softened. It also becomes a skin barrier while the baby is in the uterus, protecting him from amniotic fluid maceration *(shrinking or dehydration of skin)*. It also helps maintain electrolyte and fluid balance by greatly decreasing the transdermal *(skin)* release of those electrolytes and fluids.

Based on the evidence from several studies, more hospitals and birthing centers are migrating toward this practice. It's up to you, as parents, if you want to follow this newer practice of not bathing the baby. It won't hurt your baby if you decide you want your baby bathed, but it might be very beneficial for him not to be. Just remember, it's ultimately your choice.

If, or when, you bathe the baby for the first time, you will more than likely be giving the baby a "sponge" bath— meaning no tub bath for the immediate future. Until the umbilical cord stump falls off and the site heals, and— for male babies who have been circumcised and the penis heals, you should *not* place the baby directly into a bath. Both sites are portals *(entrances)* for infection, especially the umbilical cord site, which goes directly into the baby's circulatory system.

When giving "sponge" baths, you use really, *really* warm water, as the washcloth will begin to cool down when you go from the tub of water or sink to the baby's skin. You will start at the baby's face, work your way down and around to the back, and leave the hair for last. By bathing the baby in this order, you decrease the heat loss by saving the head for last, which is a large surface to be exposed for the baby.

The easiest way is to use two washcloths for bathing the baby— one to wash and one to rinse, and a dry towel to dry each section as you go. Wash the face *(without soap the first few times)* and dry it off, then move to the neck and gently lift the baby's jaw with your fingers, allowing access to the neck area. Wash this and the arms, fingers, underarms,

Detailed Recovery for the Baby

and chest. When washing the baby's underarm area, grasp the baby's hand and gently pull the baby's arm up straight. This makes it easier to access. And— don't be afraid to do this! Use firm but gentle, steady pressure to pull the baby's arm up, and it will straighten out easily. *(**Dads—you don't need to be afraid you'll hurt your baby doing this.)* Once done from the neck to the waist, then rinse and dry off. Next, open the diaper and leave it underneath him unless visibly soiled with stool. Remove any excess stool using the diaper to swipe down from front to back. *(**See "Diapering Your Baby" for additional tips.)* Move below the waist, clean the legs, feet, toes, and groin area, then rinse and dry off. Turn the baby over onto his tummy, turn his head to the side, wash his back and bottom, then rinse and dry off. Turn the baby back over gently. When finished, place a new diaper on the baby and wrap him in the towel you dried him with his arms contained, leaving only his head exposed.

Before washing his hair, turn the temperature of the water down to warm. You may have been given a soft-bristled scrub brush and a baby comb during your stay, so use these during this and future hair washing. Holding the baby tucked under your arm, like a football, supporting the baby's neck with your hand wrapped behind. Run the top of the baby's head under the running water to wet it, then place a dollop of baby shampoo *(or head-to-toe body wash)* on top of the baby's head. Use the scrub brush to gently clean the head all over. If you still find some stiff or sticky gunk, use the comb to gently comb through the hair and remove the debris. Once thoroughly cleaned, rinse and dry the head with the baby's towel.

Once you start bathing your baby, it should only be about every 2-3 days for the time being, as your baby's skin is sensitive, and daily bathing will dry it out. Daily face, neck, and groin cleaning are sufficient for the days between a full bath. But, if you bathe the baby daily, use lotion immediately to help trap moisture and keep the skin hydrated. This soft, sensitive skin can dry out quickly, so take good care of it. As your baby gets older, baths can be given on a daily basis if you wish.

Diapering Your Baby

Some parents can be "old hats" at changing diapers. Still, with others, they either have never been around newborn babies or have never changed diapers, especially newborns. Whether you know what you are doing or don't, rest assured that your nurse will assist you in tackling this feat.

For the "pros" out there who's "been there, done that," you may still need reminders on "starting off at square one" again. You may have gone from the previous baby's sex to the opposite one with the new baby. Now you have no idea how to clean this baby's diaper area. Don't be afraid to ask your nurse to show you how to do it again— that's what they are there for, so ask away!! And— don't let your nurse make you feel stupid if you *do* ask! You may have forgotten some of the "little details" in changing a newborn's diaper, and I would be surprised if you didn't. Remember, you only retained about 25% of the info from last time *(if that)*, so little reminders of how it's done *or* how it's done with the opposite-sex baby is totally okay!!

As with all babies, you want to make sure you have your new diaper out and ready before you begin changing the diaper. That means unfolding it completely and setting it aside until you are ready to use it. These little kiddos *really* like to go some more when you just remove the old diaper and expose them to the air. So if you have it out and ready, you can switch out diapers quickly after thoroughly cleaning your baby's nether region. Another trick would be to place the new diaper under the old one until you have cleaned them up. That way, you can remove the old diaper and already have the new diaper underneath just in case the baby goes pee or poop at that moment.

With little boys, you may want to place your hand, diaper wipe, or washcloth over his penis to keep him from spraying everything in sight— especially since you're right in the path of his aim. He may or may not do this every time you change him, but do you really want to find out the hard way?? *(**Just a little tip to help you avoid this: I learned very quickly with my son— the hard way! He was notorious for doing this every diaper change.)* Then pull out one wipe *(for just pee)* and two *(for poop or both)* from the wipe package or container. Before you get ready to clean your baby up, place the wipe between both hands and hold it there for a ½ to a full minute. By doing this, you are warming up the wipe so it is not so cold before you clean them up. If the wipe is cold, your baby may "let you know" very quickly they are not too happy with having a cold wipe touching their skin.

(…And there is no need to have electric "diaper warmers" now that you know this trick. When you use an electric warmer, by the time you get to the bottom of the package, they're starting to dry up or have dried up.)

Next, you need to see what you have that needs to be cleaned. If it is just urine, then wipe the entire diaper area clean. *Do not* skip this step!! For the sake of using fewer diaper wipes or just downright laziness, some parents do not always wipe the urine off the skin. Even though disposable diapers are rather absorbent, that doesn't mean there isn't any urine residue *still* on the skin surface. If it is repeatedly not wiped away, the urine can cause skin breakdown in the form of diaper rash. Moms, you wouldn't *NOT* wipe your nether region when you pee, would you?? *(**Dads, I don't know about you. You might be a different story. Lol!)* So why would you skip this step with your baby?

If there is stool *(ie., poop, feces, doo-doo, doody, caca, or whatever you call it)*, first use your dirty diaper to remove all the excess from the baby. You do not need to be overly gentle to do this. Place the diaper firmly against the top of the baby's crotch where the stool starts, and wipe downward firmly *(not hard)*. When you get lower on the crotch, lift the baby's bottom off the bed by the legs/feet to wipe further back. Usually, one swipe will remove the majority of stool there, so you have a much cleaner surface to use your diaper wipes on for the remainder. This technique will change the need for diaper wipes from— say, 10 to only 1-2 wipes.

With little girls, only wipe her off from front to back when stool is present. You *do not* want to wipe from back to front, as this may cause some stool to be pushed into the vagina and urethra, possibly causing infection. With little boys, it is okay to wipe in any ol' direction. Doesn't matter. It is also okay to place a finger or thumb on the scrotum and lightly stretch out the skin to make it an easier, smoother, and more stable surface to wipe on. You may need to do this all around the scrotum to clean it thoroughly. Make sure to check in the creases of their hips and legs and ensure those creases and the ones at the top of the bottom's crack are thoroughly cleaned.

If you don't already have a new diaper under the old one *(**like the trick I mentioned at this section's beginning)*, proceed with the next step. Once cleaned, place the new diaper under the baby, bringing the front part up between their legs and releasing one tape from the side. Apply the tab to the *middle* of the diaper along the diaper strip. Release the other tape with one hand, grasp the front top of the diaper in the other, and bring the tape again to the middle of the diaper. *(**Or crossing over the middle, depending on how big or little the baby is.)* Then, fold the diaper's upper "flap" over the top side of diaper covering the diaper strip. This will help to cover the tape tabs, which can be scratchy for the baby's belly if not covered. Some nurses fold this flap the other way, tucking it inside before taping the diaper down. Still, if you want to ensure the little tape tab doesn't come in contact with your baby's belly and be irritating, this would make for a better method. Make sure the diaper is around the waist snuggly, because if it is too loose, the diaper may fall off the bum, and you may have quite a mess to clean up later— and I mean *A MESS!! (ie., squirting out of the leg holes and waistband, getting all over the baby's clothes— and maybe the blanket— and the bed— etc. You get my drift. . . ?)*

There— you have now changed your first of many diapers, and soon you will become an expert— changing diapers while talking on the phone, folding laundry, making dinner, etc.— all at the same time!! LOL

Some "Oddities" Found When Changing Diapers

This section will address "odd" things you might find while changing the baby's diaper— and specific things you would find with girls and boys, respectively. First, I'll address the features found with either sex, then approach the details you might find with each sex individually. This way, you will know what to expect if you see these when changing diapers and feel comfortable that they are "normal" features that may present themselves with your baby.

Small Number of Diapers

Your baby is starting his brand-new life outside your womb and is beginning to have wet and dirty diapers. We expect to see at least one wet and one poopy diaper in the first 24 hours of life, then two of each the next day, then three on the third, and so on. This is normal for breastfed babies because the colostrum volume is generally in smaller quantities when first starting out. When your baby starts to have 6-8 wet and 2-3 poopy diapers, they are starting to get more volume of fluids, either from breast milk when it comes in *or* from the formula, if formula-fed. Any additional diapers over and above what is expected for the first few days of life are just a bonus. So, if your baby is not producing enough wet and dirty diapers expected of their age, your nurse will address this and provide solutions to help remedy it.

Your nurse may provide you with a chart to help keep track of your baby's feedings and diaper changes. Watching the number of diapers is important as this is one tool to determine if the baby is getting the needed fluids to prevent dehydration. The doctor may order supplementation of formula or donor breast milk (if available) for the baby if they're not getting enough fluids from their breast feedings. For formula-fed babies, they will want the baby to increase the amount of formula from what they are currently taking. *(**I will discuss supplementation later in the guide when I address the baby's feedings.)*

Pink-Tinged Spots on the Diaper

You may notice when you change the baby's wet diaper that on the surface, there is a little spot or a few spots that look pinkish in color, almost a salmon color. What this is— is uric crystals. If the baby is not getting a large volume to eat, the urine might be very concentrated, and you might see this pink-tinged stuff on the diaper when the baby pees. This is normal for breastfed babies who get small to minute quantities of colostrum. The urine will be very dark, and these uric crystals may be present. As the volume of fluid increases, the crystals will go away.

When we use the toilet and our urine is concentrated, we see darker-colored urine in the water. This may be because we haven't had enough fluids or urinated in a long time. The uric crystals would be there, but you would not see them as the water would dilute the urine somewhat. In the baby's diapers, the urine is *not diluted* by water. Thus you will see these uric crystals when the urine is concentrated.

Sacral Dimples

You may see a sacral dimple if you change a diaper or have the baby on their tummy with the diaper off. These will be deep pits in the skin right where the tailbone *(coccyx)* is located at the base of the spine. *(ie., at the start of "butt" crack).* Generally, these are considered common and do not affect the baby or cause any problems. But— the pediatrician will want to know if a tuft of hair is present, a skin tag, birthmark, skin discoloration, or if it's very deep. *(**The pediatrician should see this during the first assessment.)* There may be testing done to determine if there is a need for further evaluation and treatment of any possible spinal cord abnormalities.

If the baby is moving the legs around normally and the dimple is small or shallow, then the dimple is more than likely not a concern for the doctor.

Lots of Large Stools at the Beginning— and Then None

Your baby may have a lot of stools during the first day or day and a half. They may have very large stools that would equal several diapers' worth. Then they might suddenly stop having stools, *especially* if they are breastfed. This is because babies are born with meconium throughout their intestinal tract and have completely pooped out all the meconium.

If the baby is not getting much colostrum, their system must wait and digest what little amounts they have received. It might take a day or two before they resume stooling again. This is normal and will correct itself once the baby gets more breast milk volume. This can also occur with bottle-fed babies if they are not taking in much formula. It can be because they refuse to eat or do not retain what has been eaten or because they are throwing up the formula given. This, too, will resolve as higher quantities are eaten and digested.

Swollen Genitals

When changing your baby's diaper, you may notice that their genitals are swollen and maybe even reddened. This is also a normal finding for either sex, as this comes from the hormones the mother passes on to the baby prior to birth. Also, the additional fluids the baby is born with may contribute to genital swelling. The swelling will also decrease as the fluids and the mother's hormones decrease.

Findings with Little Girl's "Parts"

Here, you will see other findings with girls, following the swollen genitals and additional hormones.

Vaginal discharge

The hormones passed from mother to baby may cause a thick, whitish discharge. *Or* it may be pink or reddish bloody discharge, like a small "pseudo-period." This is called physiologic leukorrhea. This, too, will go away once the hormones have left her body.

Smaller outer labia

A small outer labia is common with baby girls born 37 weeks or less and may be noted by parents when changing their diapers. Lack of fatty tissue in preterm or premature baby girls is a normal finding. Therefore, the outer labia *(labia majora)* will be smaller and less prominent than the inner labia *(labia minora)* and clitoris. This will correct itself over time as the body grows and more baby fat is added.

Labial skin tags

These skin tags *(hymenal tags)* are skin protrusions from the inner vagina and are visible when changing the diaper. The skin tags are not an issue and will resolve themselves over time. Only 3-13% of infant girls are born with these tags.

Findings with Little Boy's "Parts"

Besides possibly having swollen scrotums *(testicles or "ball" sac)* after delivery, boys can have other genital issues. They may not happen frequently, but they would be an entirely common finding.

Undescended testicles

At birth, one of the checks a nurse completes with male babies is checking if the testicles are descended into the scrotum. Undescended testicles are a more common finding in preterm or premature boys *(~ 21%)*. Still, it can occur even with full-term infants *(1-2%)*.

It is not unusual for one or both testes to be undescended. If it occurs, they will have regular assessments to check if one, none, or both have descended during the baby's hospital stay. If they continue to be undescended, the pediatrician will continue to monitor the issue during follow-up office visits. Surgical intervention may be necessary if they remain undescended and have not corrected themselves by 3 months of age. But in approximately 99% of the cases, the testes will descend independently, and no other evaluations are required.

Penile torsion

When changing the baby boy's diaper, you may see that his penis looks twisted or rotated, generally in a counterclockwise direction *(to the left)*. This can be mild to severe; in most cases, surgery does not have to be done if it is 90 degrees or less.

Approximately 1 in 80 boys are born with penile torsion. It is not known to cause issues with urination or sexual intercourse unless accompanied by either hypospadias or congenital chordee *(see below)*. Some parents may opt for surgery to correct this defect for cosmetic reasons. They feel this might have psychological effects later in life from being tormented by other males who see it.

Hypospadias

Hypospadias happens in about 5% of male infants, making it the most common "congenital condition" in baby boys. This defect is noted as a urethral opening on the lower segment of the penile shaft. This can be anywhere from the head of the penis to the site where the shaft and scrotum meet. Hypospadias can cause the penis to curve downward, making urinating standing up in the future difficult and/or sexual intercourse difficult. Depending on the type or location of the hypospadias will depend on the type of corrective surgery needed. A few hypospadias are very minor and do not require intervention.

In most cases, this will need correcting by a urologist between 3-18 months of age, and these boys will not be circumcised due to this defect. The reasoning is the foreskin may be needed for any repair being made to correct the location of the urethral opening. The surgery may be completed all at once or in stages, depending on the severity of the hypospadias.

Congenital chordee

This is where the penis curves downward and would be especially noticeable during an erection. The cause is due to the more elastic tissue on the top side of the penis than the bottom. This may not be noted at birth but years later when an erection occurs. Again, only surgical intervention can correct this defect.

Natural circumcision

A natural circumcision is where the prepuce *(foreskin)* does not completely cover the head of the penis— only partially *or* not at all. Pediatricians do not generally circumcise these boys when this is a natural occurrence. It would not be necessary.

Changing Baby's Clothes

This, of course, goes hand in hand with diapering your baby. We both know that's what comes next— unless you're taking this time to have some skin-to-skin bonding. Putting on or removing clothing on your baby can be a little intimidating, but in many ways, it's like when you give your baby a sponge bath. Depending on what kind of clothing you have— sleeper sack *(long sleep "dress")*, t-shirt/shirt and pants, dress, onesie *(one-piece pajamas)*, etc., depends on how you approach putting the clothing items on. So—we'll go over each type so you feel more comfortable with what you're putting on or taking off.

We'll start with a sleep sack, which is the easiest to use. This is like a long gown with long sleeves. It may or may not have little fold-over hand covers to keep your baby from scratching her face. *(** A lot of long-sleeved articles of clothing are made like this today, which comes in very handy.)*

The easiest and less stressful way of putting the sleep sack on would be to put it on like you would a pair of pants. You might think, "Why would I put it on this way? Wouldn't you put it on over the head first?" Well, you can certainly put the sleeper sack on this way, but my way seemed to be a little less stressful because you don't have to worry about juggling their little body with the big floppy head and neck. What you will do next is to gather the long sack up just like you would with a sock. Then you slip it over both legs and under their bottom. Then grasp ahold of one leg and gently lift the baby up and roll to one side so you can work the dress up the back. Once you have done that side, you grasp ahold of the other leg and do the same thing, which you should now have the sack worked up to their shoulders or above. Then you reach inside for one sleeve and gather that up like a sock. Once you have done that, gently take the baby by the hand and place it inside the gathered sleeve. Once the hand can be grasped on the other side of the sleeve hole, gently pull the arm upward with one hand while you work the sleeve up the arm to the shoulder. Repeat with the second side. Once you have the sack on, snap it up at the top.

You can do just about the same method with the full-body onesies too. However, this time you gather a leg of the onesie and slip over the foot. Gently grasp the covered foot and lift the leg, turning the baby to the side, and work the outfit up the back. Do the same to the other side and work the outfit over the shoulders, then over both arms. Now comes the fun part of figuring out how to snap up the onesie. Not all onesies are made alike. Some snap up on both legs, then up the middle or one side. Some have a lot of snaps, and some don't. Some are harder to align than others. You just have to be patient and figure it out. *(**Trust me, you will snap up onesies more times wrong than right when first starting out, but it will get better and easier with time.)*

These methods described above make putting on sleeper sacks and onesies a little easier— and less awkward. When the baby is newly born, you won't have to try juggling with the sack going over the baby's head first. As your baby gets a little older and you get a little better and more confident at changing clothes, you can put on over the head first if you like. Whatever way works easiest for you— go ahead and do it.

When it comes to a t-shirt onesie, and you have to put it on over the head, at least the hole for where the head goes is usually pretty stretchy. Sometimes it is not, making it a little harder to put on, but most are fairly easy. First, gather the onesie until all the material is gathered at the neck hole. Once it's gathered, slip it gently over the top of the head while the head's still on the crib mattress. Use your fingers to gently lift the head slightly while slipping the onesie further over the head. Then, gather the sleeves like noted above and "work" one hand in, grasp the hand through the other hole, and work the sleeve up the arm, then repeat on the other side. Once the upper section is done, gently lift the baby upward by grasping one of the legs. This way, you can work the remainder of the onesie down the body and repeat on the other side. At least when you finish putting this one on, it is usually just two or three snaps at the crotch to secure it. *Yay!*

Putting pants or shorts on the baby will be like putting on a full-body onesie. Gather the leg, slip it on, gather the other, slip it on, then roll the baby gently to each side to work the pants over the bottom. Putting a dress on would be like putting on a t-shirt onesie to slip on over the head. Then when you go to take off the clothing, just do everything in reverse of how you put it on. Now that we have covered the clothing aspect let's move on to the next step.

Wrapping Baby in a Blanket

After diapering the baby and putting clothes on, the next step is wrapping your baby in a blanket. Parents always wondered how the babies wrapped by the nurses didn't seem to come loose like the ones they might have done. The difference is that nurses wrap them a little tighter— but not too tight, which might make breathing difficult. This way, the baby feels more confined, like inside the womb, making them feel more secure. When a baby is newly born, having nothing to keep them wrapped like a cocoon can be *pretty* scary. Arms flail around, which tends to frighten the baby because they don't realize those arms are attached to them. Securing those arms down for now, until the baby gets a little more acclimated to being outside the womb, makes them stay more relaxed and comfortable. If your nurse doesn't demonstrate how to wrap the baby, at least it will be covered below.

The first step is to lay the baby's blanket on the bed with the corners at the top, bottom, and sides. Then take the top corner and fold it down about 12 inches. Next, place the baby on the blanket with the baby's neck in line with the top fold. Grasp the side of the fold and the baby's arm and tuck the hand upward under the fold by their neck and cheek. Hold on to the baby's tucked-in arm and gently roll the baby onto that same side. Take the side corner and wrap it around the baby, tucking it in behind the back. Then, take the bottom corner pulling it up along the same side as the first tuck. Either lay it to the side or tuck it slightly behind the back. Repeat with the second arm, tucking it into the side fold. When you go to wrap the flap around the baby on the other side, pull it a little tighter or snugger around the baby. *(**Roll the baby toward one side while you pull the flap toward the other.)* Congratulations, you have just now wrapped your little "baby burrito."

Other Newborn Observations

In this section, we'll go from head to toe, discussing other occurrences found on a routine basis with newborns. Some will normally occur frequently, and some will not. Still, we will discuss each one and if anything needs to be done to correct the issue or whether it will resolve on its own. Some of this is in shorter sections with very little needed information or care on your part. Some have lots more detail, but they still could cause some anxiety if you do not know what it is or if it's a problem. So, it's better to cover each of these things than not.

Findings on the Head

Some things you see or feel on the baby's head can be very concerning for parents if they don't know what to expect. Below are several issues that can happen because of the delivery or what is normally found on a newborn's head.

Conehead (elongated head)

When a baby has been engaged deep in the pelvis for a long time, the skull segments overlap and mold themselves to their extremely snug surroundings. This causes a "cone-shaped" head when the baby is delivered. Over time the head will re-mold and become rounder in shape as it should be. But this molding can affect the scalp and tissues beneath the scalp, causing caput succedaneum. *(**See below)*

Caput succedaneum (swollen head)

When the baby has been engaged deeply in the pelvis for a long time during labor prior to delivery, the mother has been pushing for an extended period, or the doctor needs the use of forceps or a vacuum extractor to get the baby delivered quicker, fluid and/or blood can gather between the layers of the scalp due to pressure on the head during delivery. This causes swelling and possibly bruising. It is a common occurrence that will resolve in the next few days as the body reabsorbs this additional fluid.

You may notice that the fluid will shift under the scalp when your baby lies with her head to one side or the other. This is called "dependent drainage," where the fluid falls by gravity to the lower portion of the scalp. You might notice it on the side the baby is lying on.

You may want to avoid touching or holding on to the head where this fluid is located. The baby likely has bruising, soreness, and/or a "little bit of a headache" from this trauma. They will probably cry whenever you place your hand or arm against it or even when the baby is lying in the crib face up. So, to support the head until the swelling resolves, place your arm or hand against the neck only—and no fingers should be placed anywhere on the caput or head. If the swelling is substantial, the baby may cry whenever you lay them down in the crib. The nurse might place a small roll under the neck to slightly elevate the head to relieve some pressure. *(**This would only be a temporary solution until the swelling goes down and is NOT meant to become customary practice when you go home.)*

Cephalohematoma (blood-filled, swollen head)

This differs from the caput succedaneum. This is blood collection from broken capillaries between the periosteum and the bone but does not cross the central suture line on top of the head. This is commonly caused by the same issues during delivery as the caput succedaneum. It is just that the fluid/blood is in a different location and will possibly take a month or so to totally resolve.

(**To eliminate repeating the same information, if you are holding or feeding the baby, use the techniques suggested above in the "Caput succedaneum" section.)

The cephalohematoma will usually resolve on its own without any further health concerns. But an increased risk for jaundice might occur with this issue during your hospital stay. When the body breaks down excess red blood cells, this makes bilirubin— and when there is bruising or trauma such as this, the body must break down this collection of blood. This creates an excess of bilirubin. If the baby's body does not successfully break down and eliminate the excess bilirubin, the bilirubin "backs up" in the liver, causing jaundice. *(**Information on jaundice, bilirubin, and treatment in more detail down further under "Skin Color and Conditions.")*

Sutures on the skull (ridges)

When you feel along the baby's head, you will notice several ridges— around the front, the sides and top, and the back of the skull. Some parents wonder or worry about these ridges they feel, thinking there may be something wrong with their baby's head. I can assure you this is not the case.

The baby's skull is divided into sections— *six* separate skull bones, to be exact:

- *Frontal bone* - where the forehead is
- *Temporal bones* - on each side of the head by the temple

- *Parietal bones* – slightly above and behind the Temporals
- *Occipital bone* - on the back of the head

So the baby's head can pass through the birth canal, its head needs to "mold" itself to the pelvis and cervix, enabling it to come through the birth canal. If the bones were completely fused, this would make birthing babies exceedingly difficult this way. Since the bones are *not* fused, it allows the skull bones to overlap and mold themselves to deliver more easily.

After the baby is born, you may periodically notice some of the skull bone edges protruding a little more or less. This depends on the baby's head's position on the crib mattress. Those bones will keep moving around a little and may sometimes be more noticeable or prominent. As the baby ages, the suture lines between the bones begin to fuse. Eventually, the ridges will no longer be noticeable.

During the assessment, the nurse lightly runs her fingers all over the baby's head, feeling for changes. This is how she is locating the suture lines. She will determine at that moment if the suture lines overlap, spread apart *(a little or separated)*, or fit together like a puzzle *(approximated)*. Each time the assessment of the head might change, the nurse notes that, so the pediatrician can address any big changes during rounds.

Fontanels ("the soft spot")

Your baby will have several of these "spots" on the skull, but two main ones are used for observation. One on the top front of the skull and one on the crown of the head. These two fontanels are observed during the baby's assessment. The posterior one, at the crown, is small and should close up at about 1-2 months of age. Sometimes this one is difficult to feel on some babies because they are much smaller. The anterior *(front)* fontanel is much larger and more noticeable and will close completely between 7-18 months.

The fontanels have a tough membrane that helps to protect the brain during the baby's 1st year, allowing room for brain and skull enlargement. It is not dangerous to touch this area of the head because the membrane is durable and will withstand normal pressure from touch. In fact, your nurse will be assessing the anterior fontanel regularly for signs of dehydration or swelling.

Dehydration in babies can be detected by a sunken-in fontanel, along with other signs, such as decreased or no urine output and dry membranes in the mouth. This finding can help the nurse know that intervention is needed by increasing the baby's breast milk or formula intake to correct dehydration.

A raised or bulging fontanel *can* be a serious finding and only should be assessed when the baby is quiet and the head is raised. This finding could indicate brain or fluid swelling inside the skull or a possible sign of infection. Immediate testing is needed if this is a "true" finding observed from the assessment. The nursery or postpartum nurse should first check this with a Level II or Level III nurse to verify the finding. Most of the time, this finding is benign and does not warrant testing. Only monitor to see if it gets any worse before moving forward. If the bulge worsens, a physician would require further testing to diagnose the cause. This is an important assessment finding which can be life-threatening if not found and treated quickly, but not a very common finding for the most part.

Bruising on the head or face

When a baby comes out of the mother forcefully *(via forceps or vacuum extraction)* or delivers very quickly, the head and face may sustain surface bruising on the skin. Any part of the baby's head or face that bumps against the vaginal wall or ischial spines in the pelvis can become bruised due to the rapid delivery. The forehead, nose, ears, cheeks, and head are all susceptible to this trauma. If your baby sustains this trauma, the bruising will generally subside within the next few days and resolve independently.

Birth trauma can also affect other body parts, including shoulders, arms, legs, hips, and feet. The bruising in these other regions will also resolve on its own. But be aware that with the additional bruising, especially if it is significant, your baby may develop jaundice with the additional red blood cells from the bruised sites. Your baby must break this down into bilirubin and eliminate it through pooping. If they cannot, they can become jaundiced and need phototherapy to correct it. This will need to be done before discharge. If the baby doesn't meet the need for phototherapy before discharge, be watchful of the baby having more jaundice over the next several days to two weeks. You'll need to let your pediatrician know if the baby's yellow coloring on the skin or whites of their eyes has gotten darker and more noticeable. Your baby may need another lab draw to determine if phototherapy is needed, which can be done at home. *(**This is discussed in greater detail further down in the section under "Skin Color Conditions" to "Color differences" then under "Jaundice.")*

Abrasions, scratches, and lacerations

Again, with rapid or forceful births, the scalp and face may sustain what appears to be scratches or abrasions. Most of the time, this will be more prevalent on the scalp as the head passes through the pelvis and scrapes against the ischial spines of the mother's pelvis.

Lacerations may be noted upon cesarean deliveries due to the scalpel sometimes nicking the head during surgery. This can occur, especially if the doctor moves quickly to deliver the baby due to fetal distress. There may also be lacerations found on the buttocks or upper legs if the baby is in a breach or side-lying position at the time of surgery.

Another laceration on the back of the skull can be from internal monitors screwed into the scalp's surface. This is done to more accurately monitor the baby's toleration to labor. This is usually only used when the labor nurse has trouble keeping the baby's readings on the monitor during labor. She has to discuss this with the obstetrician before it can be ordered unless it is on a standing order for the nurse to use when absolutely needed.

There also may be facial abrasions or lacerations from the baby himself due to long fingernails at birth. When the baby extends and flexes their hands close to the face, these sharp nails will score the skin and cause surface scratches. The pediatrician evaluates any of these abrasions or lacerations, and topical antibiotic ointment or steroid cream may be ordered to heal the site if needed.

Findings on the Facial Features

You'll look closely at your baby's face and various features as you study them in more detail. Anything we would consider "normal" might be concerning for you. Most everything you see in these sections is just short explanations compared to others you have read already. Sometimes less is more, and this is one of those times.

Eyes, ears, and face

- *Petechial hemorrhages* - These are due to the ocular pressure in the eyes and pressure on the face from a tightened nuchal chord or facial presentation during vaginal birth. Petechial hemorrhages may be found in or on the eyes, face, or scalp. Petechiae are little blood-filled spots on the surface of the eye or skin that will resolve themselves over time as the body breaks down these red blood cells and eliminates them.

- *Swollen eyes* - Tightened nuchal chords and antibiotic eye ointment are the two common causes of swollen eyes or eyelids. Over the next few days, the swelling will subside and resolve on its own. Just keep the eye area clean and look for any possible drainage. Your nurse will show you how to do this.

- *Eye color* - Most parents are already aware of the eye color of babies when they are born, which is usually a slate blue-gray color. But some darker-skinned babies, especially those with African, African-American, East Indian/South Asian Indian, Micronesian, Asian, Native American, Alaskan Native/Canadian *(Indigenous)* Indian, Mexican/Spanish descents, and others may present with dark-brown or brown-black eye color. Most lighter-skinned parents usually guess what eye color their newborn will eventually have. However, that can continue to be a guessing game for some over the next several years.

It is hard to predict the final eye color for the newborn, as eye color can change anywhere up to 6 years of age. Still, generally, the permanent color of the newborn's eyes will be determined by the age of 1 year. And— just because Mom and Dad have brown eyes, that doesn't mean the baby will too. Eye color is determined by genetics, so depending on the parents, grandparents, great-grandparents, or even further back, the eye color may have come from any one of them.

- *Milia* - Milia are white spots on the face and nose that look like little whiteheads and are made up of keratin and sebaceous *(oily)* materials in the facial skin. These are benign and will go away on their own without any additional treatment.

- *Preauricular pits* - These are small, pinpoint pits that are located on the upper front of the ear. They may be on one or both sides and mark the location of the sinus tract. Generally, these pits are benign and do not cause any problems. Still, they can produce cysts, become infected later, or be associated with potential hearing deficits. Your baby will have a hearing screening done before discharge.

- *Preauricular cysts or tags* - These cysts or tags are small mounds of tissue attached to the tragus, the little ear flap in front of the ear canal, or any part of the ear around it. They are also generally benign and do not cause any problems.

One or both of these preauricular malformations may be found during an assessment. A pediatrician may order a genetic workup to rule out potential congenital issues. But—if the cysts, tags, or pits are the only anomaly noted, they are considered mild cosmetic abnormalities.

Skin Color and Conditions

Pink, or pink undertones *(on darker-skinned babies)*, is the color we look for in newborns when assessing their well-being. This tells us the baby is providing sufficient oxygen for their body. Some other normal findings are benign, cause no other concerns during assessments, and are just noted during charting. However, at various times the skin may tell us there is some underlying issue that may need to be addressed and further evaluated. Follow-up care with a specialist or additional treatment may be necessary to help correct the problem.

Here we will address the color of the skin with various changes and what they mean, then follow with visible deviations on the skin surface and define what they are. Remember, some are normal and/or routine findings, but others may be concerning or even need prompt medical care.

Color differences

- *Acrocyanosis* - This finding is normally observed in newborns from when the baby is born and only lasts a few days after birth. If the extremities are cold, the hands and feet can take on a purplish or bluish tinge. This can be from exposure to lower temperatures around them or when the baby is held tightly around the arms and legs during breastfeeding. This causes the baby's capillary bed in these extremities to constrict and shunt blood to the major organs. Covering up the feet and hands can help to correct this issue by providing warmth around the extremities.

   When cold outside, we normally wear gloves, hats, and warm socks to keep our hands, head, and feet warm— otherwise, our extremities would get cold. This is the same principle for infants. Even though this phenomenon is common, it is important to keep those extremities warm for good circulation.

- *Circumoral cyanosis* - This is where there is a visible bluish tint to the skin around the mouth region, but not actually on the lips. It is a key concern for your hospital staff, and they need to know if the baby is showing these signs. Although this finding may be benign in most cases, this is a sign that there might be a hidden cardiac or pulmonary issue that needs immediate medical attention and intervention. If it is not evaluated and there is a health issue with your baby, it could be serious or even life-threatening if not treated.

  This is a temporary issue if the cyanosis around the mouth goes away. It may be due to an apneic *(stop breathing)* episode or airway obstruction that is or can be resolved. Suppose you see your baby continues having circumoral cyanosis. It may be accompanied by lethargy, limpness, poor feeding, irritability, or breathing issues. If the baby does, inform your nurse *immediately* so close observation and/or testing can be started.

- *Central cyanosis* - This observation is one where quick intervention is necessary for the baby's well-being. Cyanosis is where not only the extremities take on a purplish or bluish tinge, but the rest of the body takes this on too. This indicates to any healthcare worker that the baby is not breathing well and respiratory intervention is needed immediately.

  This may indicate a cardiac, respiratory, metabolic, or neurologic disorder, and further testing and intensive care would be necessary to find the underlying cause of the cyanosis. If you observe this with your baby, let your nurse know *STAT!!*

- *Skin mottling* - Cutis Marmorata is bluish, reddish, or purplish marbled *(blotchy)* skin, which is noted with mottling.

It can indicate the baby is cold or circulation is beginning to decrease along the skin's surface. If the baby is unwrapped for some time, wrapping the baby up in a blanket or increasing the room temperature can remedy this issue. However, it can also indicate, along with pallor *(paleness)*, that there is an underlying infection, cardiac issue, or poor circulation. Let your nurse know if you observe this in your baby so that additional medical diagnostic testing can be started if necessary.

- *Pallor* - This is not seen very often, but immediate medical attention is needed when it is observed. This can be due to a maternal hemorrhage at delivery, an abruptio placenta *(pulling away from the uterus while pregnant)*, placenta previa *(covering the cervix)*, and various other issues. These can cause anemia in the infant *(ie., low blood count, decreased hemoglobin, etc.)*, which can be life-threatening to the infant. Generally, it is known before delivery, there is a maternal issue that may threaten the baby's well-being. These newborns are immediately observed and tested quickly after delivery to determine what care is needed for a positive outcome.

- *Dusky skin* - Generally, dusky skin is observed in premature newborns or infants whose brains are "forgetting to breathe" frequently or for extended periods. When this happens, babies need to be on monitors and watched continuously by neonatal nurses. This is until the issue resolves on its own and close monitoring is no longer needed. This usually resolves when the brain's immature breathing center fully develops and starts functioning as it should.

- *Bruising on the body* - Bruising can be on other body parts, like bruising on the head and face. It will most noticeably be found on the shoulders and forearms, but some can be on the back, legs, or feet. Again, this can be from birth trauma. The forceful pulling or pushing down on the arms and shoulders during shoulder dystocia *(shoulders not wanting to deliver after the head is delivered)* or pulling and tugging the baby out during a cesarean section. Babies will sometimes have a presenting body part(s) that may be coming out along with the head, such as a hand or arm, which tightens the space even more during delivery.

Any bruising from birth trauma with the head, face, or other extremities will usually resolve quickly within the next few days. But, again, additional bruising can put the baby at risk for developing jaundice and may need to be treated. *(**See Jaundice below)*

- *Plethora (ruddiness)* - This is a medium to dark, beefy-red color of the infant's skin when not crying and can affect 1-5% of infants born. Babies who are ruddy or plethoric may indicate they have too much blood volume and increased hematocrit counts *(too many red blood cells)*. This can be due to many different issues:

  - Delayed cord clamping
  - Prematurity
  - LGA babies
  - Infants of diabetic mothers
  - Endocrine abnormalities
  - Uterine hypoxia *(decreased oxygen to baby)*

Other Newborn Observations

- Inherited diseases
- Genetic disorders
- Twin-to-twin transfusion syndrome *(blood moving from one twin to the other)*
- Placental insufficiencies *(not functioning as it should)* due to:
  - Post-date pregnancy
  - Preeclampsia
  - Primary renovascular disease
  - Maternal cyanotic congenital heart disease
  - Chronic or recurrent abruptio placenta *(tearing away from the uterine wall)*
  - Maternal smoking

The increased amount of red blood cells greater than 65% is called polycythemia.

Most babies *(79-90%)* will show no signs or ill effects of having this increased blood volume. The other 10-21% show one or more signs due to the increased blood volume:

- Vomiting or feeding poorly
- Lethargy *(limp, minimal movement)*
- Tachypnea *(continuous fast breathing)*
- Tachycardia *(increased heart rate)*
- Hypoglycemia *(low blood sugar)*
- Jaundice *(yellowing of skin and eyes)*
- Seizures

This may accompany other issues needing to be evaluated and monitored closely. Some complications may require intensive treatment.

With this finding, expect ahead of time your baby will more than likely become jaundiced and require phototherapy to correct it. Having excess red blood cells the body does not need; the excess will need to be broken down and eliminated from the body. *[***Pay close attention to the information below regarding "Jaundice."]*

- *Jaundice* - Here is a condition that most parents have heard about at one time or another. This condition is common in newborns and is evaluated and tested in each newborn in local hospitals. Still, some hospitals or birthing centers may only test newborns who are observed to be greatly jaundiced from head to toe and in the whites of the eyes. Darker-skinned babies are harder to observe visually, so blood testing should be done routinely on *all* babies to prevent any from "slipping through the cracks." Since this is a common condition observed frequently in newborns, this will be discussed in greater detail than the previously noted segments.

  Normally, the body breaks down red blood cells, turning them into bilirubin, and is filtered by the liver to be eliminated from the body mainly through the stool. If the baby has too few or no stools in the first few days, the bilirubin backs up in the liver and causes the skin to turn yellowish. *("Here's a really cute widdle pumpkin!" or "Look at that cute 'little suntan' the baby has.")* Gradually, the baby will begin to look jaundiced in the face first. It slowly moves down the body and increases in intensity and color. If the color gets darker yellow on the skin, the whites of the baby's eyes will also begin to turn yellow. When this happens, it is a good indication the bilirubin levels are too high and need treatment. This is called hyperbilirubinemia.

Lab testing is the first step in evaluating the intensity of jaundice. It helps to determine if further treatment is necessary. Blood is collected and tested for bilirubin; the results and the baby's age *(in hours)* are calculated to see if they fall in the treatment category. This helps determine if treatment is needed, if they need to recheck the bilirubin levels again soon, or if nothing needs to be done at this time.

If treatment is needed, three main types of phototherapy lights are used. The first is a banked light on a stand which can be placed angled above the crib and warmer. It provides one or two banks of light, depending on the light strength needed for therapy. Second is a BiliBed, in which the lights are inside the bed's plastic mattress and can offer moderate treatment. The third is the BiliBlanket. This electric light strip pad is placed against the baby's skin and wrapped inside a blanket.

Before the baby is placed under or above the phototherapy source, eye covers are placed over eyes. These covers are used to help protect the baby's eyes from phototherapy lights which can damage them. Once stripped down to their diaper, the baby is place under or on a light source. They will only be removed from the lights when feeding, which is usually limited to 30 minutes at a time, so the baby can get the maximum exposure to the lights during treatment. Periodically the pediatrician will order bilirubin levels to be checked. This will determine if phototherapy will continue or can be stopped.

If the baby is breastfeeding, then usually some formula is ordered supplemented with breastfeeding to increase fluid volume and help with increasing stool production. However, if the mother's milk is in supplementation may be unnecessary. Increased stool production and phototherapy will remove bilirubin from the baby's liver, thereby decreasing bilirubin levels. When you see the baby's stools after beginning phototherapy, they usually have a "glowing" green cast to them. So, do not be alarmed when you see this.

Phototherapy is a quick and easy fix for hyperbilirubinemia. However, jaundice puts the baby at risk of developing kernicterus. This is when extremely high bilirubin levels are deposited on the baby's brain tissue. If treatment for jaundice is not initiated promptly, hyperbilirubinemia can be toxic to the nervous system, leading to brain damage or death.

Hyperbilirubinemia is usually detected and treated in the hospital setting right after birth. Still, the condition can be slow to develop and happen after discharge. Keep an eye out for any of the symptoms noted above and contact your pediatrician immediately for further evaluation.

Your pediatrician may suggest indirect sunlight when the bilirubin levels are not elevated enough to be treated but the baby is visibly jaundiced. This can help break down lower bilirubin levels which may eliminate the need for phototherapy. Babies can develop jaundice up to 2 weeks after discharge from the hospital, so keep an eye on this and contact the pediatrician if it worsens.

- *Harlequin color change* - This is noticed when a baby is lying on their side. The visible top-side skin is lighter or paler than the side on which the baby lies, with a demarcation line running down the body's center. This is a benign *(non-harmful)* condition that is unknown why it happens; however, it can occur in 10% of newborns and generally resolves on its own. It can be scary to see this, but you can rest assured the nurse will continue to watch it and report it if it becomes concerning.

Surface Skin Conditions/Lesions

Here is where we discuss the more common visible surface skin conditions noted during the head-to-toe assessment at birth or that develop over the next few days. Again, some of these findings are benign and need no treatment. Still, others may need further evaluation or follow-up care with a specialist after discharge.

Certain skin conditions
You may find these skin conditions anywhere on the newborn's body. Some will be there at birth, and some may form sometime after delivery. However, all are very normal findings with new babies and are not concerning to the hospital staff.

- *Newborn rash* - Erythema toxicum neonatorum, or newborn rash, is the formation of small, reddened papules *(raised spots with a lighter or whitened center)* on the baby's body. These are usually found on the back, trunk, arms, and legs but may also be found on the face. This occurs in up to *72%* of newborns, ranging from mild to covering most of the body. Some parents are concerned their baby may have contracted chicken pox when they see this. This is not the case. It is thought to occur from the immature pilosebaceous glands activating *(hair follicles and oil glands)*, but it has not been proven. This benign condition usually resolves within 5-7 days without further treatment. I would recommend not putting baby oil on the skin for now, as this might worsen the problem.

- *Sucking blisters* - You may notice on the baby's hand or forearm it looks as if there is a blister or had been a blister, but it popped and is drying. It is not found on any other part of the baby's body, just in these areas. While the baby was still inside the womb, they had been sucking on their hands or forearms, creating sucking blisters. If the blisters break open in the womb, they will begin to heal, so you might see what appears as a drying-out blister at the site. Generally, these areas will resolve on their own without any treatment.

- *Dry, cracked, and/or peeling skin* - The vernix is beginning to disintegrate as a protective barrier for newborns who have been "overcooking" in their mom's oven *(more than 40 weeks)*. These post-term babies or even darker-skinned term newborns are at greater risk of dry, cracked, and/or peeling skin.

  The vernix disintegrates or breaks down when the baby has been in the womb too long. As this occurs, the baby is exposed to the amniotic fluid dehydrating the skin, which causes dryness, skin cracking, or peeling. Using lotion frequently on the exposed skin will help to rehydrate it.

- *Lanugo (body hair)* - Babies are born with soft, downy unpigmented hair covering their bodies. Some darker-skinned babies will have a larger-than-normal amount of this hair, which will be darker. The function of this hair is to aid the vernix by allowing it to "cling" to the hair and help protect the skin. This hair will often slough off within the next few days to a few weeks after birth.

Birthmarks or lesions

Several types of birthmarks could be noted during the head-to-toe-assessment after delivery. Stork bites, port-wine stains, Mongolian *(slate-gray spots)*, nevi, and freckles are some of the prominent birthmarks or lesions found. Some are pigmented *(having color)*, and others are vascular *(from blood circulation)* or from abnormal skin development. Here we will go over each one and discuss what, if anything, needs to be done to correct it.

- *Stork bites* - Nevus simplex or stork bites are pinkish-red, blanchable patches on the skin surface. They occur in 40-60% of newborns and may be singular or found in multiple areas of the baby. Common locations are the eyelids, forehead, and nape of the neck. Less common are the nose, lip, scalp, and back. These are largely benign and will fade within the next couple of years. However, on the nape of the neck, it may remain permanently.
- *Slate-gray spots* - Congenital Dermal Melanocytosis or slate-gray spots are generally found on dark-skinned newborns:
  - *Asians* – 85 to 100%
  - *Blacks/African Americans* – 80 to 90%

- *Hispanics* – 47 to 70%
- *Native American/Alaskan Indians* – 80 to 85%
- *Polynesians/Micronesians* – 90%
- *East Indians/South Asian Indians* – 80 to 90%
- *Latin Americans* – 46% (when associated with non-European descent)

However, less than 10% of white newborns can also present with this finding if they have European roots. *(**These were previously known as Mongolian spots, but the term has been changed for political correctness.)*

These slate-gray spots can appear more greenish-blue or brown and are most commonly located above or on the buttocks. In some instances, they may appear in the shoulder area as well. Mistakenly, these spots may look to an observer as bruising, which is not the case. However, there have been false reports of child abuse when seen in these areas of the body.

Slate-gray spots usually fade within the first year or two of life. Still, some remain up to age 10, and approximately 3% remain throughout adulthood.

- *Congenital melanocytic nevi* - Occurs in 0.2 to 2.1% of babies and appears as brown or black flat areas on the skin. However, there may also be raised areas. This type of birthmark has the potential for malignancy. Pediatricians will monitor these areas closely if they are small *(0.5 cm or less)* for additional growth in size. Medium-sized *(0.5 to 7 cm)* nevi will be referred to a dermatologist for evaluation. Large ones *(7 cm or above)* will eventually be removed by a dermatologist and then evaluated over time for recurrence.

- *Nevus flammeus (port-wine stains)* - Occurring in 0.3% of babies, these are dark red to purple in color and flat on the skin. These are readily noticeable and do not fade over time. In fact, they may deepen in color. Pulse dye laser therapy may help eliminate or reduce the visibility of these birthmarks and are best if treated by 12 months.

  Suppose these port-wine stains affect the eye area *(i.e., the trigeminal nerve's ophthalmic distribution)*. In that case, these babies are a risk for glaucoma. This might occur alone or with Sturge-Weber syndrome, which might cause mental deficits and need further evaluation. Babies not affected by Sturge-Weber syndrome are referred to an ophthalmologist for testing and monitoring.

- *Hemangiomas* - These are referred to as strawberry hemangiomas. The lesions may only be noticed as unmarked pale patches of skin and occur in 1.2 to 2.6% of babies. These are generally benign and require no further treatment. They may enlarge or become blood-filled raised areas on the skin but are usually still benign and will resolve on their own over time. Staff will monitor these blood-filled hemangiomas and will only intervene if it appears to be an issue needing to be addressed.

  If they compress the eye, airway, or vital organs, immediate evaluation is needed in the newborn period. Rare large or multiple hemangiomas can be life-threatening. They would be immediately evaluated and treated by the care team at birth.

Immature Body Systems

When babies are born at term, most parents believe their bodies will function just like they should, which is why they are surprised when certain things happen or come up in the days or weeks after birth. Just because they are good enough to come out of the oven doesn't mean they are "fully cooked." So here we will go over some of the more common systems that are affected and are not at full functionality.

Eyes

These take a long time to complete their transition. From changes in eye color to seeing the entire world as we see it, they have months and sometimes years to make necessary changes. For the most part, the eyes will be fully functioning and sending appropriate signals to the brain by 6-8 months of age.

The newborn can only see things in black, white, and gray and only see approximately 6-10 inches away from them. They also see things blurry because their brain hasn't yet fully processed what they are seeing. Light, shapes, and movement are all they can detect now, so bring your baby in close range with your face. Up close time is particularly good for your baby's eye development and facial recognition.

The muscles in the newborn eyes are not coordinated enough to control movement early on. You may see her cross her eyes or roll his eyes up into the back of his head. This uncoordinated eye movement will improve over time as the muscles strengthen. You will notice this when he starts tracking things and reaching out to them. This eye/hand coordination starts developing within two to three months of age.

Liver

One of the main causes of newborn jaundice is the immature function of the liver. The function of the liver is to filter out toxins and remove waste from our bodies, among other things. Still, the newborn liver cannot filter out things quickly enough. This puts them at risk for developing newborn jaundice when the liver cannot remove the bilirubin fast enough and transfer it to the intestines for removal.

Several common factors put the newborn at risk for developing jaundice:

- Premature or preterm births
- Significant bruising on the head or body
- Exclusive breastfeeding *(smaller quantities of colostrum)*
- Differing blood types in mother and baby
- Infections

Nervous system

Babies tend to jerk or startle easily, whether awake or asleep, and do not have full control over this. It is common in newborns' responses to the stimuli around them.

- *Benign sleep myoclonus* - This is where the baby jerks or flails their arms or legs during sleep but does not show signs of this when awakened. It happens periodically and is nothing to be concerned about.
- *Jitteriness* - is when the baby is awake and reacts to a sudden noise or their crib or car seat is bumped. This reaction is usually very brief in duration. They may also appear jittery when

in a full-out crying jag, such as when you change a diaper or bathe the baby. Whether awake or asleep, gently holding down the flailing limb and the jerking or flailing stops usually indicates an immature nervous system. If it continues, along with eye-rolling when holding them down, this can indicate some neurological issue needing further evaluation. So report this to your nurse if you see this happening.

Newborn babies may also be jittery for another reason. However, this is usually a little more prolonged and is noted when they are quiet or sleeping. This type of jitteriness may indicate the baby has low blood sugar levels *(hypoglycemia)*. This is one sign of hypoglycemia, so if you see this happen, let your nurse or doctor know. If you're unsure what type of jitteriness your baby has, ask. It's always better to be sure it is not from hypoglycemia or a neurological issue which would need treatment.

Gastrointestinal system (gastric reflux)

One of the most common occurrences with newborn babies is spitting up. Whether it's formula or breastmilk, it doesn't matter. The immature esophageal lower sphincter is associated with frequent relaxation, thus allowing for the formula or breastmilk to come back up easily. The newborn may spit up or vomit when burped or "spit up" without warning. As long as the baby gains weight, feeds well, and is not irritable, there is no cause for concern. Some babies are just "happy spitters" and will continue to do this for several months, usually stopping around 12 months.

Spitting up or vomiting substantial amounts of breast milk or formula can be associated with overfeeding. If we are eating food, it takes approximately 20 minutes for our brain to realize we are full and to stop eating. If a baby sucks down a bottle way too fast or continuously breastfeeds on a full breast without taking a break, they will over-distend the stomach. This can cause regurgitation because it has been over-filled, thus vomiting most of what was taken in, if not all. One way to eliminate this from happening is to slow down the feeding. That means taking the bottle out of the baby's mouth or disengaging the baby from the breast periodically to slow the feeding down. Only do this when your milk is in, *not* during the first few days when you are establishing breastfeeding.

Take this time to burp the baby well when you disengage them. It may take several minutes to relieve all the air— as they may take in a large amount of it because they are "snarfing" or gulping it down fast— so give it a little time. Also, by slowing the feeding down, the brain and stomach connection will kick in, and the baby will become full but not overfull.

Suppose your baby continues to have gastric reflux issues. In that case, your pediatrician may suggest a few things:

- Sitting the baby in a more upright position *(i.e., car seat)*
- Sitting in a non-moving bouncy seat
- Sitting in a non-moving swing

Do this for about 30-45 minutes after a feeding.

Any of these will allow the stomach to begin gastric emptying and reduce some reflux issues your baby may continue to have. If this doesn't help, there may be other underlying causes of this problem, and further evaluation by your pediatrician may be necessary.

Preterm or Premature Newborn

If you think the normal term newborn has immature body systems, it's even more so with ones born too early. Premature newborns are those delivered before 37 weeks, usually due to maternal issues such as:

- Infection of amniotic fluid or lower genital tract
- Preeclampsia
- Pregnancy of multiples
- Previous preterm delivery
- Problems with the cervix, uterus, or placenta
- Poor nutrition
- Smoking, drinking, or illicit drug use during pregnancy
- Diabetes *(gestational or chronic)*
- An interval of fewer than 6 months between pregnancies
- Underweight or overweight during pregnancy
- Multiple miscarriages or abortions
- Life trauma such as a death in the family or domestic abuse
- Physical injury or trauma *(i.e., car accident)*

The earlier the baby is born before its due date, the higher the risk of the previously mentioned issues and a host of others. So, keeping the "bun in the oven" as long as possible would be your obstetrician's goal for a better overall outcome. 39 weeks or greater is the goal, but we all know that is not always possible, as some women's bodies just cannot or will not do it.

Other Newborn Observations

For those still pregnant and reading this, please do not be tempted to "force" your doctor to deliver you earlier than you should. I know some of you are "tired of being pregnant" or want to plan the delivery around your schedule. Don't be tempted to act on this. There are several possible issues your baby may have to deal with if born too early. Will it be worth it in the long run for your baby to deliver early or worthwhile in the long run for just a few more weeks of discomfort? Just continue to read, and it might quickly change your mind.

Respiratory (breathing) difficulties

The most common issue for preterm or premature infants is breathing difficulties. Term babies are born with a substance called surfactant in their lungs. The earlier the baby is born, the more likely it will not have this substance, causing a lack of expansion and contraction of the lungs to move oxygen throughout its system. This causes Respiratory Distress Syndrome *(RDS)*; the earlier they are, the more likely it will cause further respiratory complications as they age.

Suppose the neonate is 34 weeks or less gestation, and the doctor has enough time before impending delivery. Or the labor can be stopped or postponed. In that case, the mother will be given one betamethasone injection and another 24 hours later. This steroid helps speed up the baby's manufacturing of the surfactant and to help decrease respiratory issues once the baby is born.

For those over 34 weeks, the baby is more likely to have some or most of the surfactant production. However, they are still at risk for respiratory issues. *Each* week of delayed delivery decreases the risk for respiratory distress, thus less treatment or intervention and fewer long-term effects.

Another factor at play is the risk of apneic episodes *(delay in breathing for more than 20 seconds)*. The brain centers that control breathing are also premature, therefore, not functioning as they would if the baby was a term infant. The delay in neurologic synapses *(brain communication)* does not signal the lungs to "take a breath," decreasing the oxygen supply to the body. Again, the earlier the baby is born, the greater the risk for apneic episodes and longer duration. *[**Respiratory issues for preterm babies also increase their risk for SIDS (Sudden Infant Death Syndrome). We will discuss at length under the section 'Other Topics for Discussion.']*

Feeding difficulties

When a preterm or premature baby is born, they are not driven to eat any time soon, as they are not supposed to eat by mouth yet. Or if they do, they get tired quickly from exerting energy to feed. Also, they have problems with sucking and swallowing coordination due to immaturity. This can make breastfeeding difficult, so in those cases pumping and providing breast milk for feeding can and would be beneficial.

For those who can breast or bottle feed their preterm or premature baby, limiting the feeding to 30 minutes can reduce fatigue and lessen the calories burned by feeding. If a baby cannot breast or bottle feed and needs nutrition, the nurse may place a nasogastric tube through the nose and into the stomach to deliver nourishment. When the baby is ready to breastfeed or bottle feed, they will be weaned from the nasogastric tube until they can take all feedings by breast or bottle. Usually, the baby will remain in the hospital until this happens.

Gastrointestinal (stomach/intestinal) issues

Since premature babies are not supposed to take their feedings by mouth yet, the immature stomach and intestinal tract may also have issues. Necrotizing Enterocolitis *(NEC)* is one of the more possible serious complications. The cells lining the intestines can become injured from the feedings, which can cause intestinal cells to die off. If this happens, it can cause the intestinal tissue to die. Babies receiving breast milk have a decreased chance of having NEC or other complications. However, they are still susceptible to this very serious one.

Hypothermia (low body temperature)

Due to the decrease in "brown fat" stores for heat production and the decrease in "white fat" for insulation, premature babies are at higher risk for decreased temperatures. They also lose heat more readily from the skin surface due to greater surface-to-body weight ratios. The more calories the baby uses during their feeding for crying, breathing, etc., then the greater chance of hypothermia. This can lead to hypoglycemia *(low blood sugar)*.

Because of the expending of calories to try and maintain adequate body heat, premature babies do not tend to gain weight very well. This is why they are kept in a warm environment, such as an incubator *(warming bed)* or skin-to-skin with Mom or Dad.

Hypoglycemia (low blood sugar)

Preterm or premature babies are at three times greater risk of developing low blood sugars. The abrupt loss of maternal-provided glucose during pregnancy is the main factor in hypoglycemia in preterm babies. Preterm babies also have decreased glycogen stores due to the abrupt loss and impaired ability to make glucose because of an immature pancreas. Due to quickly using up glycogen stores for energy, preterm babies can quickly become hypoglycemic. So monitoring of blood sugars begins within the first hour of birth and is continually monitored until glucose stores are adequate and remain so with feedings. This means the baby will be subjected to heel sticks frequently to draw a small amount of blood each time to check glucose levels until they maintain appropriate blood sugar levels on their own.

If a preterm or premature baby cannot maintain adequate glucose levels, they will be given an IV, and glucose will be administered. This will continue until they can wean off with feedings and maintain adequate levels on their own. Usually, D10 *(dextrose 10%)* would be given in a bolus, to begin with, and then a certain amount per hour based on the baby's current weight. This is usually a short-term treatment for hypoglycemia.

Cardiac (heart) issues

One of the most common heart issues for premature babies is PDAs, patent ductus arteriosus, the persistent opening of two major blood vessels leading from the heart. This often closes on its own with term babies. Still, with premature babies, it may not, which can cause too much blood to flow through the heart and cause complications, including heart failure, if left untreated.

The other common issue with a PDA is low blood pressure. Medications, changes in IV fluid amounts, and possible blood transfusions can help correct this.

Other potential cardiac issues can be associated with pre-term or premature births, such as cardiac defects to the structure and function of the heart. This can lead to other issues later in life, such as high blood pressure, heart disease, and heart failure.

Brain issues

If babies are born too prematurely, they are at greater risk for brain bleeds, especially if vaginally delivered. The additional intracranial pressure *(pressure in the skull)* during vaginal deliveries and the delicate brain structures of the early baby make them at risk for this.

Even if delivered by cesarean, these delicate brain structures and vessels can break, leading to an intracranial hemorrhage. Most small hemorrhages will resolve without issue, but others may have larger brain bleeds which can cause the cells in the brain to die. This can cause permanent brain injury. The larger fluid accumulation would require surgery to relieve the pressure large bleeds can cause, thus decreasing potential brain damage.

Blood issues

Anemia and jaundice are two of the most common blood issues a premature baby may have. Anemia can be caused due to lower blood volume. Repeated blood draws for labs or glucose checks can also put them at risk.

Jaundice in the premature newborn *(**discussed previously under the section "Skin Color and Conditions")* is caused by a very immature liver. It is not transporting the bilirubin to the intestines for removal through the stools. This causes the bilirubin to back up, which causes jaundice. Phototherapy would be necessary to help the body rid itself of the excess bilirubin, as the system cannot correct this on its own. More often than not, phototherapy is used for an extended period until the baby's liver matures enough to remove the bilirubin on its own.

Immune system

Premature babies are more susceptible to acquiring infections. This is due to the underdeveloped immune system in prematurity. With the inability to fight infections, preemies are at risk for developing neonatal sepsis, which can be life-threatening.

Visitors in the Neonatal ICU generally will be limited to parents and only if they are not sick. Strict hand hygiene and gowning will be required during visits. Only with preterm babies at lower risk will grandparents and siblings be allowed to visit— again if they are not sick and follow hand hygiene protocols.

Q&A on Other Baby Concerns

Here are some frequent questions or concerns parents have with their newborns post-delivery. Some are just the parents' thoughts but were incorrect in their interpretation. Again, most are normal and will resolve on their own and are nothing to be concerned with, but if you just aren't sure or your gut feeling is telling you something is wrong, *do not* hesitate to ask your nurse to check for you.

Q   *My baby's breathing is really fast, but it slows down again... Why is that? Is anything wrong?*

A   Babies do not breathe regularly like you, and I do— yet. They will breathe fast, then slow down, then speed up again. This is normal and is also why your nurse assesses the baby's breathing for a full minute instead of only a few seconds, as they do with you. We want the respirations to be between 40-60 per minute, but if you are unsure and think the baby's breathing is too fast, just ask your nurse to check. It's better to find out everything is fine than to worry about it needlessly. Then, suppose it continues to be fast and doesn't seem to slow down. In that case, this could indicate your baby is having some respiratory distress or possible infection and may need further evaluation. So, ask again if you are not sure.

Q   *I worry that my baby might stop breathing while he sleeps... How can I check on him without waking him?*

A   There are two things you can check without disturbing your sleeping baby. One is to place your hand on your baby's stomach. Babies are "tummy breathers," and this is one way to feel if your baby is breathing without disturbing them. Another thing is to look at your baby's skin color in the light. If the baby is *pink*, not pale, dusky, or blue— but *pink*, then your baby is breathing. I always told my parents, "A pink baby is a breathing baby."

Q *Oh... isn't that a cute little noise my baby is making... It sounds like my baby is humming or singing...*

A It may not be considered "cute" if your baby is "singing" or "humming." Sometimes babies might "hum" or kind of "whine" while they are breathing out. This may be due to a couple of things. The first may be due to the baby having a belly ache. Too much food or amniotic fluid in the gut may make your baby lightly "hum," "whine," or "groan," like you or I would do with a belly ache. It's uncomfortable or hurts— therefore, they make a little noise. Sometimes this lighter sound might also be the beginning of some respiratory issues. It's always better to check with your nurse, who can better determine if it is not concerning yet or if your baby needs to be watched a little closer.

If the noise is like a loud "humming," where you can hear it pretty well, it's a good chance your baby may have some respiratory distress. This would be the baby's attempt to open the lungs to breathe better. The alveoli *(ie., the lower portion of the lungs where oxygen exchange occurs)* are trying to collapse, which makes oxygen exchange harder. If this happens, the baby might require some interventions to correct this.

It's a good idea to ask your nurse to check this out whenever you hear it, whether light or loud. It's better to be sure your baby isn't having difficulty breathing than ignore it.

Q *My doctor/nurse said my baby has a heart murmur but didn't explain it... What does that mean?*

A When your baby is born, the circulation in the baby's heart changes, and the *ductus arteriosus* starts to close up. As it closes, the blood "swishes" through the hole as it tries to close, causing what is called a murmur. In most cases, this will resolve within the next day or two, and the murmur will no longer be detected with a stethoscope.

Sometimes the ductus does not close all the way, and the baby may have a murmur for months or possibly years. Usually, this is benign and doesn't cause any additional problems.

Suppose the murmur is loud and is noted at every assessment by each nurse and doctor assessing the baby. In that case, the doctor will write an order *(or there may be a standing order)* for the blood pressure to be checked to ensure they are within normal limits. If they are high, this can indicate an underlying problem with the heart's structure. Further evaluation with a pediatric cardiologist would be necessary.

If your nurse or doctor did not explain the heart murmur finding, this was likely a benign murmur. That's called a "soft" murmur, which will resolve without treatment. Some nurses and doctors have difficulty even hearing them, so you may not be informed by every care provider that there is one.

Q *I'm afraid I'll hurt the baby if I move the umbilical cord...*

A The umbilical cord does not have any nerve endings within the cord itself. It consists of a gelatinous substance called Wharton's Jelly and contains two arteries and a vein. As the cord dries, it will fall off, so there is no concern about moving the cord out of the way, like during a diaper change. The only surface where your baby would have nerve endings would be the pink skin area around the umbilical cord, which isn't moved enough to cause pain.

Q *Why does my baby's belly button around the cord pop out when he cries? My baby's belly button area is sticking out!!*

A This is more common in African-American, premature, or low birth-weight babies but can occur in any baby. The umbilical cord may pop out farther than most babies when your baby cries, sneezes, or strains when pooping. This is caused by increased inter-thoracic pressure *(pressure in the abdomen)* and separation of the rectus muscle in the abdomen. This is a common occurrence and usually resolves itself by age 4. However, it may need corrective surgery if it becomes tender, swollen, reddened, your baby is in obvious pain, or is vomiting.

Q *Why does my baby lose weight after delivery?*

A When your baby is born, additional fluid and meconium *(stool)* have accumulated throughout the entire intestinal tract. When they begin to urinate and stool *(pee and poop)*, they begin losing weight. Formula-fed babies generally lose less weight than breastfed babies due to the volume of nourishment they receive during feedings. Breastfed babies may only get a few drops to a few teaspoonfuls of colostrum versus the 10-30 milliliters of formula a bottle-fed baby gets at any feeding.

As long as your baby is *not* losing more than 10% of their birth weight, they are doing well. The weight loss will begin to slow down, stop, and then gradually trend upward again. The baby should return to their birth weight or higher by the time they are a week old.

Q *Why does my baby sound "congested"? Is she getting a cold? Why is he sneezing a lot?*

A No, your baby is not getting "a cold" so soon after birth. The congestion is most likely due to all the amniotic fluid they've been surrounded by in the uterus. Your baby sucked and swallowed this fluid and was "breathing it in," so it's normal to have some retained fluid in the nasal passages and upper airways. Your baby frequently sneezes to help clear the nasal passages, and the congestion will resolve over the next few days.

If the nose is clogged up, your baby cannot sneeze well enough to get rid of the congestion. If it is interfering with feeding, it might help if your nurse administers some saline nasal drops to help soften up the mucus. Then she would remove it with a nasal aspirator *(the little "sucky-thing")*. Once all the mucus is cleared out, the constant sneezing and congestion should resolve.

Q *Why is my baby gagging and spitting up stuff? I'm worried about my baby choking, especially when sleeping.*

A Your baby has been swimming in amniotic fluid for nine months. While inside, the baby practiced sucking and swallowing to get ready to feed after birth. Some amniotic fluid may still be in the stomach after delivery, especially if they deliver very fast vaginally or by cesarean section. This is due to not getting "squeezed" enough during birth, which helps to push out the excess fluid. And sometimes babies take a gulp of fluid as they deliver, which adds more fluid to the stomach.

This amniotic fluid does not digest. It sits on the stomach, turns to mucus, and upsets the stomach, causing your baby to throw up this fluid. It may be thick or thin, clear, whitish, or yellowish, and may even have red, pink, or brown *(old)* blood mixed in. Some indicators of your baby getting ready to throw up this fluid would be getting frothy or bubbly around the mouth. The baby might start gulping like they are about to throw up but don't want to, just like you or I would if we were going to vomit. They also might gag like they are choking on the fluid in the back of the throat. Any time you start seeing any of these indicators, there's a good chance the vomiting will begin. If you see anything that might concern you, just ask your nurse.

The scariest thing for parents when the baby starts to spit up this fluid is when their baby starts choking on it. Sit your baby upright or lean the baby forward and pat his back. *Do not* be overly gentle doing this; you want to help them spit up the fluid easily, but you also *don't* want to pound hard on the back. Keeping the baby upright for a little while, say on your shoulder or chest, will also help get your baby through this choking episode.

If any fluid is still in the baby's mouth or nose, gently use the nasal aspirator bulb *(the little "sucky-thing")* to remove the fluid. Depress the bulb first with your thumb, place it in the baby's mouth around the cheeks and front of the mouth, then slowly release the bulb as you move the tip around. Once you have removed some fluid, depress the bulb quickly into a blanket or burp cloth to remove it from the aspirator, and repeat if necessary. Always do the mouth first, then the nose, as you want to move from a "clean" area to a "dirty" area. Then be sure to clean the aspirator out with warm soapy water to be ready for the next time.

Sometimes when the baby is choking, *he will panic* because he spits up fluid in his mouth and through his nose at the same time. When he cannot breathe, he might stiffen up his body or go rigid, clamp his mouth tight, and get a panicked look on his face. If you cannot get him to open his mouth to take a breath, use your emergency call light to summon help quickly. The longer he goes without breathing, the more he will be deprived of oxygen and quickly start turning blue.

Once they experience this, parents get very nervous about continuously keeping their babies in the room while sleeping. If your hospital allows you to send your baby to the nursery to be watched while you are getting some sleep, you may rest more comfortably. However, if your hospital follows strict "rooming in," you must keep your baby with you. It is okay if you prefer to keep your baby with you and don't want to send your baby to the nursery. Have your spouse, significant other, or family member stay with you so you can switch off watching your baby while the other is sleeping. This way, your baby is continually monitored, and you can call at the first sign of intense choking. Rest assured, this issue should be resolved before discharge or within 24-48 hours after delivery.

Q *Why is my baby wide awake at night when I want to go to sleep?*

A Think back to when you were pregnant and the times when your baby was the most active. When you had settled down and were resting, especially at night, that was the time your baby started doing somersaults.

When you were up moving around during the day, you were "lulling" your baby with your movement. When you were resting, your baby woke up and started moving. This is still your baby's wake-sleep cycle and will continue for some time after birth.

If you mistakenly think you will get your baby on a schedule more in tune with yours— good luck with that! You will find your baby has other ideas when it comes to "play time"— possibly for a long while. If you do manage to make this work, then you are very lucky indeed, but— in reality— this does not happen very often.

Q *Why is my baby crying so much? I don't know what he wants…*

A There may be several factors that can explain why your baby is inconsolable and won't stop crying. Here's a list of several things which might be the cause of your baby's crankiness:

- I'm hungry, so feed me!
- My diaper is "dirty," and I don't like sitting in a mushy mess!
- I'm too hot, so take off the extra blanket!
- I'm too cold, so wrap me up!

- Something is poking me! *(check the diaper area, umbilical cord stump, and clothing)*
- I'm about to explode, so burp me!
- I'm overstimulated by all the visitors passing me around!
- I don't want to be put in the crib, so hold me!
- You are acting very nervous around me— and it's making me nervous!!
- I just scratched myself with my sharp nails— and it *hurts!*
- It hurts to pee since my "weenie" was whacked! *(circumcised)*
- I just want my Mommy!!

This is a list of the most common reasons for babies to cry until they get what they want or need. This is the only method of communication your baby has to "tell" you what is upsetting them. You just have to interpret what it is. Usually, if you work your way down this list, you will find the cause of the crying, and once you remedy it, your baby will begin calming down.

But there may be other factors that play into this as well. If the mother was a smoker or used drugs *(this is unfortunate, but it does happen)*, the baby has now been cut off from receiving nicotine or addictive drugs continually. So the baby gets irritable and frequently cries until they finish going through "withdrawal." This may require medical intervention if this is a matter of concern for the pediatrician.

No matter what it is, rest assured you will quickly start figuring out what the baby wants. You will interpret certain cries with certain issues based on the sound of the cry they are making.

Q *What are some of the ways I can try to quiet my baby when she's crying and won't calm down?*

A There is a method that has been successful in calming crying babies, and that is *"The 5 S's"*. These are *swaddling, shushing, swinging, side or stomach positioning* (but not during sleep time), and *sucking*. Each one can be very effective in getting your baby to relax and calm down.

Swaddling – This is the next best thing for babies to feel like they did when they were in the womb— all warm, cozy, and safe. By swaddling, your baby is wrapped fairly tight, which keeps arms from flailing around and startling them.

Wrap your baby tight but not too tight in a blanket, as you were shown in the hospital. Once you go home, do this only when your baby is fussy or during sleep time to help soothe them. Your baby shouldn't be wrapped like this all the time; they need to get used to being free from binding and relax in their surroundings. And *remember—* to lay your baby on their back for safe sleep.

Side or stomach positioning – This is a terrific way to soothe your fussy baby, but not during sleep time. Back sleeping is the only safe way for that. Holding your baby on their side, over your shoulder, or on their stomach across your forearm will help to soothe them in no time.

Shushing – This is also a great way to quiet your fussy baby. The baby was used to hearing the swishing of the blood flowing around them while in your womb, so naturally, the white noise of "shushing" will help.

Placing your mouth close to your baby's ear and using long, continual *"shhhhhh"* sounds will help to quiet them. Also, any other "white noise" with a continual sound will help to soothe your baby as well. Some CDs, MP3 products, or phone apps produce white noise specifically for babies, but if you don't want that, the *"shhhhhh"* by their ear will work just as well.

Swinging – This movement back and forth is another great way to calm your baby. They had been swung back and forth for months when your body moved during the pregnancy. So naturally, swinging your baby back and forth will make it like they are in the womb again.

Supporting their head and neck and their bottom, swing your baby a few inches side to side, back and forth. This will mimic the movements in the womb and help soothe a fussy baby.

Sucking – This is another way to help calm your baby when they are fussy. It is relaxing for some babies to continually suck, which helps to soothe them. Obviously, you cannot put your baby at the breast or put a bottle in their mouth every time your baby gets fussy. The alternative is to use a finger or pacifier if continual sucking is what they are craving.

These methods all work well, but some may work better than others. You just have to try them to find the perfect fit for you and your baby, and you can continue to use them when you go home from the hospital. But— be sure during this trying time of continuous fussiness *not* to shake your baby in anger or frustration!! Try remaining calm while trying any or all these methods, as your baby will pick up the calm vibe from you and attempt to calm down as well.

Q *Why does my baby cry whenever I put them in the crib?*

A Babies know what they like, and if they haven't been put down in their beds since birth, they generally don't want to be put down. They like those "nice warm arms" versus that "cold, hard bed." This is what we fondly call— "a *bed* allergy."

This doesn't mean you can never put your baby down. In fact, it's a good idea if you do. Let your baby cry for a little while in the crib and see if the baby can soothe themselves and fall asleep. Don't be tempted to pick them up at the very first whimper. Otherwise, they will quickly learn *that* is all they need to do for you to pick them up. Give the baby a few minutes, and if they do not seem to be relaxing and the crying is starting to escalate, then go ahead and pick your baby up. This may be a battle for a while, even after you go home, but babies will learn if given time.

Also, when your baby is rooming-in with you in the hospital, they are in close proximity to you. Your baby can hear you talking to others and smell you, so baby knows you're near, and then what do they want— *MOMMY!!* So, your baby will cry because the baby wants to be near and held by you or fed by you. That mother-baby bond is very strong, especially since you've been constantly together for nine months. So,

Dad, don't be upset if the baby doesn't necessarily want you right now. This is a natural survival instinct with the baby in the beginning.

When you go home, if your baby is placed in a room and you walk away, sometimes this makes it easier for them to relax and self-soothe. Once you are no longer within range of smell or sound, your baby can sometimes relax and fall asleep once all their needs are met.

Do not be tempted to put your baby in bed with you to co-sleep just to calm them down. This is a dangerous practice to get started as it has been shown that co-sleeping with your baby puts them at risk for SIDS *(Sudden Infant Death Syndrome)*. It is best to have a crib or bed to place the baby in, and it can be placed beside your bed, if needed, for easy access.

Q *My baby has very long nails... do you have nail clippers to clip them?*

A I believe most, if not all, hospitals do not have clippers or scissors to cut babies' nails. Cutting or clipping nails is considered a "surgical procedure" because of the potential for skin breakage and/or infection, so they do not provide this service.

However, if you have your own set or someone brings you a set while you are in the hospital, you can do this one on your own. Catch your baby while asleep, as the hands are more relaxed. While holding the hand, place your thumb on the tip of the baby's finger or thumb by the nail bed and gently pull the skin away from the nail. This will keep you from clipping the end of the finger or thumb. If you are too worried about clipping the nails, you can use an emery board *(usually comes with nail clippers)* and file the nails down. Use the same method described above to do this.

If this is not possible while in the hospital, most of the gowns or t-shirts provided for your use have hand covers built-in to them. This will help keep your baby from scratching themselves until you can do this at home.

Q *If I need to check my baby's temperature when I go home, how can I do that safely?*

A Checking a rectal temperature is not recommended anymore since there is a potential for perforating the bowel if not done carefully. After our first temperature check at delivery, done rectally, the nurses check the baby's temp axillary *(under the arm)* for all future temperature checks.

When you check your baby's temperature this way, place the thermometer in the baby's armpit in the center, and press the shoulder down snuggly to the body. This helps to make a good seal and get a more accurate temperature reading. Your baby may fuss when you do this because they either: 1) don't like the shoulder being held down, or 2) it is uncomfortable from the probe tip. It's okay to do this since it only takes up to a minute until the thermometer gives you a reading *(depending on digital or glass)*. If your baby is running a temperature of at least 100.4 and you call the doctor, tell them which method you used to take the temperature.

If your physician wants you to take a rectal temperature instead, here are the steps you need to take:

- Make sure your thermometer is clean. Either use alcohol and a cotton ball or wash with soap and water first.
- Use some petroleum jelly on the tip to make the entrance into the bottom easier.
- Remove the baby's diaper, push the feet towards the belly, and let the knees spread out to the baby's sides. Hold them down during the temperature check to keep the baby from wiggling around, just as you do during a diaper change.
- Place the tip of the thermometer in the rectum only about ½" to ¾" or until the metal tip is no longer visible.
- Once you have a reading on the thermometer, remove and replace your baby's diaper. Clean the thermometer.
- Give the information to the doctor— the reading and method you took for the temperature.

Suppose you're taking your baby's temperature to check for a fever. Your baby is wrapped in a blanket or has on several layers of clothing. In that case, this may be the cause of the baby's temperature. Be sure to unwrap the baby or remove a layer or two and wait about 20 minutes before taking the temperature again. The baby may have been overly heated from this and not running a fever. Removing clothing or blankets will not cool the baby down if your baby is running a temperature. If it is a true fever, you will get a more accurate temperature for the doctor.

Using an auditory *(ear)* thermometer on your newborn is not recommended. In fact, it's not recommended until they are at least 6 months old, as the ear canal is not big enough for an accurate reading. Also, temperature strips for the forehead and pacifiers with built-in thermometers are inaccurate, so do not rely on those either.

Feeding Your Baby During Your Hospital Stay

Nutrition and nourishment are essential for your newborn's optimal growth and development. To achieve this, you must start by feeding your baby on a routine basis— and around the clock. Most parents know this before the baby is born, so mental preparedness for routine lifestyle changes is already in place. But for those of you who are unaware, babies need to be fed every few hours— 1½ to 3 hours or on demand for breastfed babies and every 3-4 hours for formula-fed babies. This will continue for several months after you have returned home, so resting in between feedings is essential for your health and well-being. You're in for the long haul, but parents manage to make it through until the end— when babies start sleeping through the night, getting introduced to solid foods, and getting older.

Exclusive Breastfeeding is BEST... but It's <u>YOUR</u> Choice

Since help and education for breastfeeding will be provided during your hospital stay by nurses and/or lactation consultants, they will discuss the benefits for the mother and baby. They will do everything that can be done to make exclusive breastfeeding a reality or provide alternatives if this is not possible for you and your baby.

So much valuable information is available to mothers about breastfeeding and how it is *best* for their babies. Studies demonstrate that the pros of breastmilk far outweigh the cons. It provides nutritionally balanced meals for each stage of your baby's growth cycle. Antibodies are passed on from you if you have been vaccinated, so the baby becomes protected against many diseases they cannot fight on their own. Other benefits are better survival during the first year of life:

- Decreased risk for SIDS *(Sudden Infant Death Syndrome)*
- Reduced risks for allergies and asthma
- Reduced risk for obesity
- Improved baby's cognitive development
- Boosts the immune system

Mother's benefits include decreased risk for:

- Type 2 diabetes
- Ovarian cancer
- Certain types of breast cancer
- Rheumatoid arthritis
- High blood pressure
- Heart disease

Benefits for both mother and baby include skin-to-skin contact, which promotes bonding.

Several organizations agree that breastfeeding is *best*. The Centers for Disease Control *(CDC)*, the American Academy of Pediatrics *(AAP)*, the World Health Organization *(WHO)*, the American College of Obstetrics and Gynecology *(ACOG)*, the U.S. Surgeon General, and many others. So, hospitals worldwide are implementing protocols and procedures to prioritize "baby-friendly" maternity units to support breastfeeding. They provide information, education, and breastfeeding support from nurses, pediatricians, and lactation consultants.

The World Health Organization *(WHO)* and UNICEF joined in 1991 to promote the worldwide initiative *"Ten Steps to Successful Breastfeeding,"* where hospitals are launching the baby-friendly initiative. It has been demonstrated to increase breastfeeding initiation, duration, and exclusivity. Since the initiative began, over 152 countries have adopted this practice, which continues to grow.

Introducing breastfeeding exclusivity for at least 6 months, but preferably exclusive for up to a year and beyond. Breastfeeding exclusivity has improved with this initiative and has proven measurable impacts. Health-related costs are reduced and can be reduced even more nationally, up to $13 billion per year. This does not include the long-term benefits of reducing potential adult diseases acquired in childhood or decreasing parent-related work absenteeism. The benefits of exclusive breastfeeding are there in the *"Ten Steps to Successful Breastfeeding,"* utilized by hospitals worldwide that are making this happen:

"Ten Steps to Successful Breastfeeding"

- Written hospital breastfeeding policy that is routinely communicated to staff
- Train all staff in the skills necessary to implement this policy
- Educate all women on the benefits and management of breastfeeding
- Help mothers initiate breastfeeding within the 1st hour of birth

- Show mothers how to breastfeed and maintain lactation, even if separated from their babies
- Give no other food or drink other than breastmilk unless medically indicated
- Practice "rooming-in," allowing mothers and babies to remain together 24/7
- Encourage breastfeeding on demand
- Give no artificial nipples or pacifiers to breastfeeding infants
- Have established breastfeeding support groups available and provide referrals to mothers upon hospital discharge

Breastfeeding education is essential in providing parents with information on all the potential benefits of exclusive breastfeeding, along with ways to make this an important part of their lifestyle. Some mothers, at least here in the U.S., may feel overwhelmed with the thought of exclusive breastfeeding due to having other children to care for, a return to work after maternity leave, single parenting issues, fast-paced lifestyles, etc. Fathers may feel "left out" because of the continual bonding between mother and baby, wishing they could get in on the action. But help is available to make this a positive experience for all involved.

Lactation consultants are becoming more common in the hospital setting and pediatrician's offices to provide education, help with breastfeeding, and maintain continued exclusive breastfeeding. Nurses in the hospital setting are provided with educational opportunities to learn how to help mothers and babies initiate and establish breastfeeding. This also helps to effectively make breastfeeding work with most of their patients.

However, there are obstacles for some mothers with breast issues that will not allow them to breastfeed exclusively. Breast augmentations *(enlargement)* or reductions may affect breastfeeding with decreased milk supplies or scar tissue, not enabling them to provide enough or any milk for their infant. Inverted or flat nipples may never allow a woman to latch the baby correctly onto the breast. The shape or size of the nipple may make this difficult as well. Pain from sensitive, sore, or damaged nipples can be another factor. But there are ways around some of these issues which will allow babies to receive their mother's breast milk *(or even tiny amounts)* which is still beneficial for them. Do not despair— help is out there for these issues!

Breastfeeding, throughout the ages, has provided nourishment and nutrients to babies— and for those who could not or would not breastfeed, there were "wet nurses" used to ensure their baby's survival. The old adage, "… it takes a village to raise a child…" *could not* be truer here, and today it is still the same. *(**An old cliché but still true today!)* Breastfeeding is "natural." However, the caveat is that breastfeeding takes time, patience, and much effort. And it may not be easy!! With adequate breastfeeding education and support, mothers can be successful in exclusive breastfeeding.

However, one of the biggest issues with exclusive breastfeeding in the U.S. is maternity leave. The CDC even states maternity leave, or lack thereof, is a significant barrier to exclusive breastfeeding. The Family and Medical Leave Act provides up to 12 weeks of unpaid leave for maternity leave. However, most women cannot go unpaid for 12 weeks. And suppose there is not enough paid time off to cover this. In that case, it can be financially devastating for many families, especially if the mother is single-parenting. Yes, you can keep your employment open where you work, but you might not return to the same position when you go back if your employer must hire someone to take your place. Yes, you will still maintain your benefits while on leave— but you may have to pay some money into insurance premiums and other benefits. Some employers may step up and pay for some of your leave, but anything after is unpaid. Out of 41 countries in the World, the United States is the *only* country where laws do not make unpaid leave mandatory for employers to pay out. The lowest countries above the U.S. on the list have at least 8 weeks of paid leave. The United States is the richest country in the world— and paid leave is not mandatory!

Even after education about the benefits of breastfeeding and ways to make this successful for the long haul, some mothers still do not wish to engage in breastfeeding. Nor are they even pumping and bottle feeding. To those who still choose to formula feed your baby— it is *okay!*

Your baby will still thrive and undoubtedly do just fine. Many have throughout the years, but the protection from diseases by providing immunities and barriers to potential health risks will be lost. They can be prone to more illnesses during infancy, childhood, and possibly into adulthood. But, like anything, there is no guarantee this *will* happen— only that the risk is greater. It is ultimately *your choice* for you and your baby!

For those who choose *not* to breastfeed, you may run into nurses or lactation consultants who might try to *bully* you into breastfeeding. They may make you feel you are not being a good mother— a failure because you choose not to breastfeed— or tell you downright lies because you are not breastfeeding. Being made to feel guilty and belittled when you cannot or will not breastfeed— is *outrageous and unacceptable!!*— but unfortunately, it does happen to some mothers out there. There should be less judgment of mothers and more support. This has become a problem for some women because of the big push for hospitals to go "baby-friendly" and promote exclusive breastfeeding. Nurses and lactation consultants have been called "Breastfeeding Nazis" or "Breastfeeding Mafia" because of their bullying. *This must stop!!* This sheds a bad light on those who properly educate and support mothers who breastfeed but are willing to support the mother who decides this is not how she wants to feed her baby.

I will be the first to tell you that breastfeeding is best for your baby. I breastfed my babies, *but* only for "a short time." There was little support and education for breastfeeding when my older children were born— certainly a lack of resources readily available. Circumstances with my last one prompted me, at the time, to stop breastfeeding too soon— which I regret. I wish it could have all been different for me.

But *I did not* and *would not EVER* make a mother feel inadequate, bullied, or belittled just because she chose not to breastfeed. I *want* all mothers to love and enjoy their babies, and to me, that is the most important part! I do not want them to dread feeding their babies because their nipples are sore or torn up from breastfeeding. A baby with a "Hoover" vacuum mouth can cause their mom's toes to curl, their body to stiffen, and/or make them cry throughout the whole feeding time. I also do not want the mother to become more depressed with feelings of inadequacy, anxiety, depression, etc. One registered dietitian said it best in a September-October 2014 article for "*Food and Nutrition*" magazine titled "Besting Breastfeeding Bullies: A Case for Supporting, Not Shaming."

"Using formula to feed a baby is sometimes a conscious choice and other times a decision that's out of a mother's control. Either way, health professionals' roles are to provide less judgment and more support and encouragement— and, of course, science-based nutrition education free from personal bias."

~~ Kerry Neville, MS, RD

Whether you exclusively breastfeed or not, the ultimate choice is *yours*. And for those who decide to breastfeed— if you feel you are not providing enough nourishment for your baby until your milk comes in, you can choose to supplement with formula. It should not *only* be up to the doctor to deem it "necessary"— and "medically necessary" at that. You can do both if you choose. The most important part is feeding your baby— shouldn't it be "<u>Fed is Best?</u>"

Starting to Breastfeed

Feedings begin with "on-demand," meaning whenever the baby wants to nurse. The longest you should ever go in the beginning is 3 hours before feeding again, even if it means waking up your baby. One of the hardest things for parents is waking a sleeping baby. But babies must be fed frequently throughout the day to avoid potential issues down the road. If your baby is not getting adequate nutrition from feedings, they can have issues with the following:

- Hypoglycemia *(low blood sugar)*
- Decreased temperatures from expending calories to keep warm
- Decreased stools which can lead to jaundice

- Decreased wet diapers can indicate dehydration
- And various other issues

Suffice it to say, waking a newborn is important— even if you interrupt their sleep.

Colostrum and breastmilk are easily digestible food for your new baby. It digests *quickly,* which is why breastfed babies need to eat every 1 ½ to 3 hours— *and* on-demand, especially in the first few days. Colostrum comes in very small quantities and is richer and thicker than breastmilk. And because of the small quantities, your baby may want to eat more frequently or on demand. When your breastmilk comes in, 3 to 5 days for first-time moms and 1-4 days for subsequent babies, your baby will fill their stomach and be totally sated *(satisfied they are full)*. Once this happens, generally, feedings will be every 2-3 hours, and frequent demand feedings will be fewer and farther between.

While in the hospital, your nurse or lactation consultant *(if they have them on staff)* will assist you with breastfeeding. They will show you how to properly latch your baby to the breast, ensuring the mouth is wide, the tongue is down, and the lips flanged out *(ie., like a "baby fish mouth")*. Your baby must also get a deep latch, meaning they must take in not just the nipple but all or a lot of your areola, depending on its size. This is so important because your lower milk sinuses are right behind the areola. The baby must "massage" those sinuses to bring the colostrum or milk down from the upper milk ducts and stimulate milk production. If your baby isn't latched on deep enough, you won't get optimal stimulation or proper removal of colostrum or milk. And with improper latching, you will get soreness and trauma to the nipple as well.

Comfortable breastfeeding positioning

When working with breastfeeding mothers, I would have them get into a comfortable position for breastfeeding. I would instruct or remind them to always bring the baby up to their breast, not lean over to get the breast in the mouth. This way, the mother remained comfortable during the feeding and did not find herself stuck in an awkward position for 20-30 minutes. You always want to position the baby in a "tummy-to-tummy" position with you so the baby will be straight on the nipple. If the baby has their head turned to the side, the baby cannot stay in a straight line with the nipple. This would cause the nipple to be "pulled and twisted" just to keep it in their mouth. This is one issue that can lead to sore nipples.

- *Latching baby on* - I would have the mother cup the breast in one hand— in a "C" shape— and move their thumb on top— close to the nipple on the areola— with the fingers back close to the chest wall. I would have them use their thumb to gently draw the nipple upward *(toward the roof of the baby's mouth.)* Once the baby opened the mouth wide, I would have them "roll" the nipple and breast tissue into the baby's mouth, pressing it down on top of the baby's tongue. I would then have them hold it in that position until the baby latched on and began sucking. Then remove the thumb and support the breast in a relaxed "C." This helps to ensure a good deep latch and helps the baby know exactly where the breast is in their mouth.

By having the moms press the breast tissue and nipple down on the tongue, it would give the baby more surface area of the breast to latch on to. This would eliminate the issues of "finding" the nipple with their tongue, placing the tongue underneath it, and then getting a hold of it! If you only place the nipple in the mouth and nothing more, the baby will "search" around for it with their tongue and mouth, bobbing and fussing because they know it's right… there… they can smell it… they just… can't… get… a hold of it… and trust me when I say the baby can get *really* frustrated when they can't find it.

This also helps with getting that "baby fish mouth" you want the baby to have when latching on. By rolling the breast tissue and nipple in on top of the tongue, it automatically helps to bring the bottom lip down. Suppose the breast is just placed straight in the mouth. In that case, you run into the problem of having the bottom lip curl inward and not getting a proper latch— then having to reach under your breast and try pulling the lip down in those "tight quarters."

- *Positioning baby against the breast* - Once you have the baby latched on correctly, make sure that the tip of the baby's nose, chin, and *both* cheeks are *just* touching the breast and not pressed in too tight. Don't be afraid to hold your baby in this position during the feeding— and don't relax this firm hold. Your baby's nose is curved enough on the sides to allow them to breathe while latched without the worry of suffocation. This keeps the baby in a deep latch and does not let them "slide" down to the end of the nipple and lose the correct latch.

- *Positioning baby against large breasts* - For some women, you may have an overabundance of breast tissue. It can form around the nose and mouth *(**even if it's just touching with nose, chin, and cheeks)*, but you can use your finger to move some out of the way. *Lightly* press downward, toward your chest wall, on the breast tissue up against the baby's nose. This will allow airflow to the baby during feeding. But be sure not to press down too hard into the tissue. By doing this, you may block off a milk duct and not allow it to drain properly. Improper drainage of one or more milk ducts can lead to mastitis. And— if you *pull* back on the breast tissue instead of pressing down, you may stretch the breast tissue out. This could relieve the baby of some of that breast tissue and either— pop the baby completely off or cause them to slide down to the end of the nipple, which, in turn, can cause an incorrect latch—and later pain.

- *Taking baby "off" the breast* - If you need to remove your baby from the breast, slide your pinky finger into the corner of the baby's mouth. Place it between the baby's gums and twist your finger. This will help release the suction, and the baby will come off the breast easily. *DO NOT* try pulling your baby off the breast without doing this first. Your baby may not want to release the nipple and will continue to apply suction to the breast to maintain attachment. This can cause soreness and even tissue trauma, making future feedings difficult.

- **Mastitis* - is an infection of the breast which can cause fever, pain, redness, and swelling and will need to be treated by your physician. You _will_ still be able to breastfeed if you have mastitis.

Establishing Breastfeeding

Establishing successful breastfeeding between you and your baby takes approximately two weeks. Some think breastfeeding should be simple because "it's natural… so, therefore, it must be easy." I can assure you this is *not* necessarily the case. In fact, it is pretty rare for breastfeeding to be easy right from the get-go! You may have difficulty latching your baby to the breast because of flat or inverted nipples. Or you may have very dense breast tissue, which does not make it easy to compress it to get it into your baby's mouth. You may also have a baby who does not get the tongue down and wants to suck on the nipple as if they are "sucking on a straw." This can be very frustrating not only for you but also for your baby.

Positions for feeding baby

Positioning during breastfeeding is another obstacle for both mother and baby. Placing the baby on one breast may be awkward because the hold "feels" awkward to the mom. If the mom feels uncomfortable with the hold, the baby may sense this and not want to latch on that side. That will make getting the baby to latch on that side difficult until the mom is more comfortable with certain positions. It's a learning process for both mother and baby, so give it time if you struggle.

- *Cradle hold* - The *cradle hold* is the most common position people are familiar with. When envisioning babies breastfeeding— this is not the only possible hold that can be used. In fact, it's more difficult to learn to breastfeed for both mother and baby. This position makes it difficult to get a proper latch during the learning process. It also makes it difficult to fully visualize the baby's latch to ensure it is correct. (**This one should only be used after the baby is more adept at latching onto the breast.)*

   There are three other possible holds to use while learning to breastfeed— the *football hold*, the *modified cradle hold*, and the *side-lying hold*. The easiest by far is the *football hold*.

- *Football hold* - This is a good hold when just starting out to fully visualize the baby's position and latch in relation to the breast. It is also a great hold for mothers who have cesarean sections because it keeps the baby from lying on her already sore stomach. With this hold, the baby is placed in the mother's arms, like a football, with the mom's hand placed around the back of the neck and the baby's feet tucked under the arm. When the baby is placed at the breast, you can visualize the baby's whole face and latch versus half of the face with the *cradle hold*.

- *Modified cradle hold* - The *modified cradle hold* is like the *cradle hold*, except you are holding the baby with the opposite arm and opposite breast being used— instead of the same side. The baby is placed across the stomach, tummy-to-tummy, with the mom. The forearm is placed across the back, and the hand is around the back of the baby's neck. You use the hand on the same side of the breast to *cup* it in a U-hold instead of a C-hold, then latch the baby on. You can see more of the baby's face and position with this hold versus the *cradle hold*, but not fully like the *football hold*.

- *Side-lying hold* - The *side-lying hold* can be used when lying down. This one is especially good if you had a very extensive repair to your hoo-hah after a vaginal delivery. Sitting on your bottom may be uncomfortable, so lying down will make it easier. The baby is placed on their side facing you and latched onto the breast from this position. The downside to this position is you *do not* want to utilize it when you are very tired— *even just a little*. Breastfeeding is very relaxing, and if you are tired, you risk falling asleep during the feeding. This puts your baby at risk of suffocating against the breast when you fall asleep and cannot monitor the feeding and position. So, use this position cautiously, only when fully awake and not in danger of falling asleep.

Nipple shape and size

Nipple shape and size can also play a role in making latching the baby difficult. If the nipple is very large or wide in relation to the baby's mouth, the baby may not be able to latch on to the whole thing. Or the nipple may be all they *can* get in the mouth because there is no more room. If this becomes an issue, work with your nurse or lactation consultant. You may need to pump and feed until the baby gets big enough to latch on correctly, or they may have other alternatives for you.

If the nipple shape or size on one of the breasts is easier for the baby to latch on to than the other, the baby may resist being placed on the more difficult side. If the baby refuses to latch on the unwanted side, place the baby on the opposite side for a few minutes to calm them down if they're agitated. After a few sucks, remove the baby *(**release the baby's latch first with your pinky)* and place them on the unwanted side again. This might calm the baby down enough to get them to latch on and get a good feeding on the side they don't like.

Poor breast attachment

Other breastfeeding difficulties can include poor latching, tongue sucking or thrusting, not keeping the tongue down, not opening the mouth wide enough, wanting to suck like they are sucking on a straw, or wanting to push out all the extra breast tissue and latch only onto the nipple. Approximately 80-90% of newborn babies need some assistance or repeated assistance getting them to latch on properly, some more than others. Unfortunately, "babies did not 'read' the breastfeeding manual before delivery," so they are trying to figure it out once they get here. I told the mothers whose babies got latched on correctly right at the beginning that "this is ¾ the battle with breastfeeding." The rest of the feedings should make it a lot easier (**Review 'Taking baby "off" the breast' above under "Comfortable breastfeeding positioning" if baby is not latched correctly and needs repositioning.)

Just because a mother, and the nurse or lactation consultant, work with the baby, and the baby finally "gets it right," doesn't mean they'll continue to "get it right" every time. For every two steps forward, there may be one step back. Nursing is a learning process for both the mother and the baby, and any forward progress— is progress in the right direction.

Sore nipples

Sore nipples are a problem for breastfeeding mothers, and— *yes*, your nipples will get sore at the beginning and for a while until the tissue toughens up. Even if the latch is correct 100% of the time, this is a very common occurrence. This soreness can make putting the baby on to the breast somewhat painful— even make some mothers dread it. Your nipples have not been subjected to continuous suction for an extended period, possibly frequent latching off/on and incorrect latching. Your nipples can get sore, dry, cracked, blistered, and/or bleed. Some mothers have overly sensitive tissue on the nipples that might become severely damaged, like turning to "hamburger," which can make breastfeeding difficult— but this is uncommon. It may even cause them to stop because it becomes excruciating for them.

Think of the tissue on your lips and how easily your lips can get dry, cracked, and chapped. The tissue on your lips is the same type of tissue as what you have on the nipple, making it just as easily prone to drying, cracking, bleeding, etc. So don't be surprised if this does happen to you.

Be proactive with your nipples

One way to tackle dry, cracked, chapped, or bleeding nipples is to be proactive before it can get too bad. If you can express some colostrum or breastmilk after you've finished breastfeeding, you can rub this onto the nipples and areolas. Allow them to air dry before replacing your bra. There are healing properties in colostrum and breastmilk, so use whichever one you have. If you cannot express colostrum after a feeding, you can use a nipple cream after breastfeeding, such as Lansinoh® or Medela® Tender Care Lanolin. Neither one needs to be wiped or rubbed off before starting the next feeding. It is safe to put the baby directly to the breast without doing so, as it will not harm your baby.

Instant gratification

You may wonder why this is happening. Your baby has been nursing well but is suddenly popping off the breast after a few sucks. Then they *get* fussy after popping off. You get the baby latched on again, and the same thing happens— and they get fussy again. If your baby has been latching on well for a while, and suddenly this is happening— *do not* panic! When your baby gets latched on and starts sucking, they expect to "get something" for the effort. Even if the colostrum is in small quantities at the moment, babies are thinking in very *simplistic* terms, "I suck… I get something." They don't think like you or I would in *complex thought*, like "I have to suck for 2-3 minutes to get the colostrum to come down... and *THEN* I get something." This is why they get so frustrated. This is what's called "Instant Gratification." So, read on and see what you can do to help "fix" this problem.

Breast massaging

One thing you can do to help remedy the "instant gratification" issue would be to massage your breast before the baby latches on. Massaging your breast will move the colostrum down from the upper milk sinuses to the lower sinuses and out through the nipple. Place one or both hands at the top of the breast by your chest. Press downward on the breast to help compress the milk sinus and stroke with your hand(s) and/or fingers downward toward the nipple. You can also wrap both of your hands around the breast and slide your hands downward using your thumbs to massage the milk sinuses. Repeat this process over several minutes in different areas on your breast to move the colostrum down.

Expressing Colostrum

After the massage, place your thumb and forefinger on your areola with the nipple in between. Press inward toward your chest while spreading your fingers about 2-3 inches outward. Then grasp the breast where your fingers stopped and squeeze your fingers slowly together as you pull the nipple forward. You may need to do this a couple times before you start seeing the colostrum bead at the end of the nipple. If after this you haven't managed to work any colostrum down, repeat the process of massaging your breast for a couple more minutes and then working the nipple and areola again. This is very effective in getting the colostrum down to the end. When the baby latches on again, they will immediately "get something."

Some babies will keep popping off and re-latching onto the breast repeatedly. Others will show displeasure when they don't "get something" immediately— either screaming or crying loudly or pushing off the breast when flailing their arms— or both. Once the baby latches on after the "massage and squeeze" and "gets something," the sucking will get rhythmic and remain latched. Now the baby usually won't pop off the breast until done— and you and the baby will be happy again.

You may need to repeat this trick for each feeding until you feel your breasts tighten in a "letdown" reflex. When you start experiencing the letdown reflex, you will feel tightening in the breast tissue. Quickly you'll notice the colostrum *(or breastmilk)* is already at the end, dripping out and ready for them to nurse.

When your milk comes in

With some mothers, who have had previous children, their milk may come in during their hospital stay. This will be the engorgement period. For 1st time mothers, this will probably occur after you have returned home but may occur in the hospital. Remember, the average time for colostrum to change to milk is 3-5 days for new moms and 1-4 days for the pros. Your breasts will rapidly change, and you will experience an engorgement period.

The engorgement period

During this engorgement period, your milk production starts to increase greatly. This causes an overabundance of milk. This engorgement period is when your body determines how much milk to make based on your baby's feeding habits. This period lasts approximately 48 hours, and you may become *very* uncomfortable during this time. Your breasts will swell, get hard, heavy, feverish-feeling, and extremely tender to the touch. It will feel like you have a couple of "boulders" on your chest, which can be uncomfortable. But as previously stated, this only lasts about 48 hours— then you will start getting some relief.

When the engorgement happens, sometimes this becomes very difficult for your baby to latch on to the breast. All of the tissue in the breast swells and tightens— it may even flatten out the nipple more, making it difficult for the baby to get a good latch. If this does occur— don't panic! You may have to hand express or pump "a little off the top" to make it easier for your baby to latch on again.

Your nurse or lactation consultant can work with you to show you hand expression or set you up with a pump in the hospital to make this happen. If you use a pump, only pump for a minute or two to remove some of the milk. This will be enough to allow softening of the nipple and areola, which will allow the baby to latch on. *DO NOT* be tempted to pump or hand express the milk until you get complete relief. Remember the reason for the engorgement period—your body is trying to judge how much milk to make based on what the baby takes. Then over the next two days of engorgement, your body will adjust and produce only the amount the baby is removing from your breasts. If you breastfeed *AND* pump your breasts dry, your body decides, "Okay… I guess I need to make *THIS* much milk"— and it will. Then you will continue to produce larger amounts of milk right from the start—which is unnecessary in the beginning.

During your engorgement period, when you start feeling very uncomfortable and want *some* relief, put the baby on the breast and let them remove some of the milk. This way, the body is still making what the baby is taking away, and not more than what they need for the time being. Plus, your baby is getting the benefit of the milk's nourishment.

Down the road— starting in a few weeks— when your baby goes through growth spurts, they will demand to eat more frequently again, and you need to let them. With the growth spurts comes the need for your body to produce more milk for your growing child. And when more milk is needed, more breast stimulation is needed to produce a larger amount for your growing baby. This may continue for about 48 hours, the same as during the engorgement period, so your body will adjust to manufacturing the newer amount. Then your baby will slow the frequency of the feedings down again when they start receiving the amount of milk they now want. This will continue with each growth spurt they encounter until they start to take in more solid baby food and you start to nurse less frequently.

I so wish I knew then what I know now about breastfeeding. When I was breastfeeding my two older children, we didn't have lactation consultants available to help or give us information. We only had the nurse help the baby to latch on, then they would walk away. Plus, if the baby didn't nurse or did very little, they were given some sugar water—from a bottle. We couldn't afford the books available then to learn about breastfeeding. We were not told about La Leche League or any other outside help. We certainly didn't have the Internet, Google, Facebook, Twitter, and the like— well, the Internet *was* in the "early stages," its infancy. Still, we didn't have a computer or smartphones— and the World Wide Web *(WWW)* didn't have the vast amount of information it has now. Sounds kind of primitive, but that was the way it was.

I had a very small chest size when my oldest two were babies and they were breastfeeding. So, when each was going through a "growth spurt," I didn't realize it then. I thought my milk was drying up because the baby was nursing and wasn't getting fully satisfied. It never occurred to me that with the growth spurt, they wanted more food. And instinctually, they were trying to get more food by making my body produce what they wanted. Needless to say, I didn't breastfeed my first for longer than 6-7 weeks— when I went back to work. My 2nd had gotten about 3 months because I had gotten a handy-dandy little hand pump in my hospital "gift bag." That helped me to pump during breaks at work. I don't know why I stopped breastfeeding then. I guess I didn't want to do it anymore. The point is— if I had to do it all again, I would have made sure to breastfeed my babies for longer than they got. And I would have known that the more frequent feedings were to help produce more milk for them *and* that I was not "drying up." With all the education I have provided you *(**and others through lactation consultants, nurses, books, the Internet, etc.,)* you can have a great foundation to build upon for successful breastfeeding. So be sure and stick with it for *much* longer than I did. *(**I continue to regret that I did not breastfeed my babies longer.)*

Documenting feedings

While you are in the hospital, your nurse will ask you to keep track on a log of when you feed the baby and how long, and when you change the baby's wet and/or poopy diapers. This information will be documented on your baby's chart for the pediatrician to see, so the baby's progress can be tracked. Each time you attempt to feed the baby, and they are too sleepy to eat, document those as well. The pediatrician knows the baby will go through some sleepy periods in the first few days and will not feed, but they want to see that documented on the chart. This way, they know you are at least attempting to feed your baby and not just seeing a big gap between feedings. The doctor wants to be sure you are not just letting your baby sleep for prolonged periods without attempting or offering a feeding.

The hospital should provide you with a log to record everything. Note the time each event occurs and document what occurred. Some mothers will download an app on their smartphone to keep track of these things, and that's even better. Either way of documenting is fine, so just update your nurse when she asks. It is essential to monitor your baby's progress during the hospital stay to ensure they are well-hydrated and their systems function as they should. If they are not getting enough to eat to produce at least one wet diaper and one poopy diaper on day 1, then your baby is not getting the necessary nourishment needed. So supplementation may be in store. This includes 2 diapers each of pee and poop on day 2, 3 of each on day 3— and so on, until your milk comes in.

Supplementation

When your baby does not get enough to eat at the breast because you have very small quantities of colostrum or no colostrum production, the pediatrician will usually intervene with the order to supplement with each breastfeeding.

Some mothers have the mindset of exclusively breastfeeding— and *only* breastfeeding— from the beginning. This is acceptable by pediatricians; in fact, they encourage it. Suppose your baby is not getting enough to produce pees and poops, and there is too much weight loss *(remember, 10% is the threshold)*. In that case, intervention is needed to prevent other issues the baby might have from additional weight loss.

Banked breast milk

If you want to exclusively breastfeed and *do not* want your baby to have *any* formula, the pediatrician may write an order for banked breast milk. Sometimes they can do this based on the baby's need for an increased volume of milk due to your current lack of production. Usually, in the hospital, banked breast milk is reserved for preterm or premature babies with a greater need to receive this milk. Still, the pediatrician can order this for you if it is available and if there is a need. Ask the pediatrician if the formula is suggested and banked breast milk is not. Since your baby has a need, this shouldn't be a problem. But suppose banked breast milk is not currently available to your baby for the time being. In that case, the supplement will be done with formula. But do not fret— if you want exclusive breastfeeding, it is not possible at this time, and you have to use the formula for now— you can still exclusively breastfeed. Once you have gotten over the hump and started making breast milk, you can use this amount to supplement and decrease or eliminate the amount of formula or banked breast milk. *(**See "Supplemental Nursing Systems" below for methods of supplementing.)*

Formula supplementation

This usually is a short-time need for your baby either way. Once you start producing more colostrum or milk and the volume increases, the need for banked breast milk or formula will decrease. Your baby will produce more wet and dirty diapers— and slow down or stop weight loss. When your milk completely comes in, supplementation will no longer be necessary unless the amount of your breast milk production will never be enough. For example— If you're required to supplement with 30 milliliters, and you pumped 10 milliliters, use 20 milliliters of formula to make up the difference. As your breast milk volume increases, the amount of formula needed decreases by that amount until you can use just breast milk for the full volume. During this timeframe, your baby will continue to be monitored for however long the pediatrician deems necessary for your baby's well-being.

Supplemental Nursing System (SNS)

Supplementation *can* be done without the use of a bottle. A Supplemental Nursing System *(SNS)* is one method that can be used at the breast during feeding. This will give your baby more volume as your baby is suckling and stimulating your breast. Your hospital should have SNS available for use during the hospital stay, and your nurse or lactation consultant can help you set this up and demonstrate how to use this system. Suppose the hospital does not have a system available. In that case, a 10- or 20-ml syringe and a small neonatal feeding tube can be used as a substitute. With the push for more lactation education and the policies and protocols of hospitals changing to follow the World Health Organization *(WHO)* and UNICEF's "Exclusive Breastfeeding" initiative, your hospital should have this system available for you and personnel available to assist you. *(**See the section "Q&A on Other Breastfeeding Concerns" for information on more supplementation feeding methods— cup and spoon feeding)*

Nipple Damage from Breastfeeding

One issue with breastfeeding is the chance of problems with nipple soreness, cracking, blistering, bleeding, and/or extensive trauma to the nipple. You might even receive a "hickey" around the area of the nipple if the baby isn't latching in the correct spot. This can happen if you have flat or inverted nipples or very large breasts, making correct placement visually difficult. This may also come from:

- Putting your baby to breast incorrectly
- Baby not latching deep enough
- Baby sliding down to the end of the nipple when you relax your hold
- Not requesting help from your nurse or lactation consultant when you think you know what you are doing.

Some moms out there— and *you* know who *you* are— are either too embarrassed to ask for help *or* refuse help because they think, "I've got this." Help is there for you to hopefully avoid some or all of these issues— so don't be afraid to use it.

If you do have sore, cracked, blistered, bleeding, or damaged nipples, here are some ways to combat any of these problems.

Expressed colostrum or milk

Starting off, for sore nipples, the first line of defense— is expressed colostrum or milk. If you can express some colostrum or milk after the feeding and rub it into the nipple, this will help. It has natural healing elements, which help keep the nipple and areola soft and supple. Rub the expressed colostrum or breastmilk onto and around the nipple and areola. Let the breasts dry completely before replacing your bra, and do this each time after you feed your baby.

Lanolin ointments/creams

Initially, you may begin having soreness early on. Your baby may have "sucked you dry" after the feeding, and no colostrum or breast milk is left to express. Then Lansinoh® or Medela® Tender Care lanolin ointments should be available in the hospital. *(**If not, have someone go to the drug or department store and get some for you.)* Each ointment is easy to use and does not require you to "wipe it off" before putting the baby on the breast. The ingredients in these ointments will not harm your baby— but the baby might hesitate a few times when latching because your breast is "tasting a little different now." Eventually, the baby will get used to it and start latching again without hesitation.

Place a small bead of ointment on the pad of your clean finger and rub it over the whole surface of the nipple and areola. This will help to keep the nipple and areola supple and help with your soreness.

Hydrogel pads

If you start blistering, cracking, and/or bleeding, hopefully, your hospital has Medela® hydrogel pads to place on your breasts after feeding. These are extremely helpful too. These soothing gel pads are a wound healer and will help to heal your nipples while you are breastfeeding. They are especially good if you can place them in a refrigerator and use them when cold. This can give you additional relief with the added coolness. If you do not have a personal refrigerator in your hospital room, do this once you have returned home. You will be glad you did!!

These hydrogel pads are about 3" x 3". They can be cut in half *(horizontally or diagonally) or* in fourths to be placed on your nipples. Make sure your nurse uses alcohol wipes to wipe the scissor blades off really well before cutting them for you. (**We don't want any infections on wounds, which may be on the nipples.) Be sure to put your nursing bra on, as it will keep them in place between feedings. And— you can continue to use the Lansinoh or Medela ointments along with the pads. These pads are good for about 48 hours of use or until the gel starts disintegrating before needing to be thrown away.

(**Just a reminder— be sure and wash your hands each time you handle your breasts, at least before the feeding. This would be any time you handle the colostrum or breastmilk, ointment, or hydrogel pads and place any of these on the breasts. Remember, you have wounds now on your nipples, and they will be prone to infection from anything you transfer to them.)

All-purpose nipple cream

For those of you with extensive nipple tissue trauma where the nipple is really "torn up," there may be made available to you an all-purpose nipple cream. This is a prescription that only some pharmacists will fill. Still, a prescription can be ordered for you if needed by a lactation consultant or your obstetrician. They can let you know which pharmacies will fill it. However, with this nipple cream, there is an active steroid inside to promote healing, so it is not intended for long-term usage— just until the nipple(s) heals.

(**This nipple cream should be only used for about 2-3 weeks. If you still have a problem with your nipples not healing, follow up with the physician who ordered it for further recommended care.)

Nipple shells

Your hospital may have what is called "nipple shells," which are available for your use if you have very sore nipples. You don't want anything touching them— because it's irritating or hurts. The cloth from your bra may be too abrasive on your nipple, making you want to take it off. Nipple shells can help remedy this for you.

These nipple shells are made of a hard-plastic case on the outside. They have many holes around the shell and are cup-shaped like the breast. There is a pliable silicone covering underneath the shell with a large center hole to be placed over your nipple area for comfort. These will help to let air circulate around your nipple and not allow anything to touch it while it's sore. It will also help keep the bra from rubbing against the sore nipple. There are also two small crescent-shaped pieces of foam for placement on the lower segment of the shells— to catch any colostrum or milk leakage from your breasts.

Place one shell over the nipple and your bra cup over the shell to keep it in place, then repeat on the other side. This will help to give you some relief from your over-sensitive nipples. But there *is* a catch— you *might not* want to wear these nipple shells when sleeping, even with a bra on. They are hard and may be very uncomfortable to wear during sleep. Also, the shells may cause some suction when applied to the breast. As you sleep, the shells may move out of position and cause them to start a "hickey" on your breast elsewhere. Then you will lose the protection around your nipple. Just use a hydrogel pad at night to get some relief and protection, and then return to using the shells during your awake hours.

Breast Augmentation/Reduction

If a mother had surgery to enlarge or reduce her breast size, she might be worried breastfeeding would not be possible. The nurses or lactation consultants can help by working with the mother to determine if it is or is not possible. Putting the baby at the breast can help stimulate milk production if there isn't any structural damage from the surgeries. Pumping with a hospital-grade breast pump will accomplish this, too. Plus, the pumping can provide visible proof for the mother, nurse, and/or lactation consultant if milk ducts are open and transporting colostrum thru the breast. If drops or milliliters of colostrum are produced, breastfeeding can be established for these mothers. Continued monitoring during the hospital stay and after discharge would be necessary to establish how much milk is produced and if the mother provides enough volume and nourishment for the baby.

If enough milk is being produced for the baby— that's *Fantastic!!* The mother can provide exclusive breastfeeding for her baby and know her baby is getting what is needed. If the milk provided is insufficient for long-term breastfeeding, then what is produced can be given to the baby first. The donor breast milk or formula supplementation is given afterward. Mothers who *cannot* provide sufficient amounts, or any breastmilk, can qualify for donor milk instead of using formula to fill the gap. Some insurance companies may provide full or partial coverage if this is the case. Be sure to check into this option if you fall within this category.

Flat or Inverted Nipples

Some of you might not have the anatomical makeup for your nipple to draw out and stay out, or the nipple does not remain out long enough for the baby to latch on correctly. Don't despair— there is still hope! For mothers with flat or inverted nipples, some tools can be used to help with this. Flat or inverted nipples can be stimulated to pull out far enough, allowing the baby to latch on successfully. A breast pump used for a few minutes can help draw out the nipple. A latch assist and nipple shields can help as well. These three options have been successful for many moms out there.

Latch assist

A latch assist is a device that is like a very small meat baster or nasal aspirator— but made for the nipple. By depressing the bulb, placing the small "horn" over the nipple, and releasing the bulb slowly, you can bring about suctioning to draw the nipple out. Two to three times should be sufficient to draw out the nipple where you need it for the baby to latch on. If you do this, then attempt to get the baby latched on; the nipple might start to flatten out before you can get your baby to latch. You may need to use the latch assist a time or two again until you can get the baby latched on.

If this tool does not work for you, don't despair. There are other little gadgets you can use to make it work. You just keep trying different ones to find what works for you.

Nipple shields

There are nipple shields made of silicone in the shape of an everted nipple that can be placed over your nipple area, and the baby can latch on to this. This will allow the baby to suckle at the breast and stimulate some milk production. But this *does* have a downside. The nipple shields cover the nipple and some or all the surrounding areola with a thin but durable silicone. Your baby can suck and draw the nipple out somewhat but cannot compress the areola around the nipple as easily. Good compression on the areola is needed to compress the milk sinuses effectively to promote good stimulation and production. Usually, this is a temporary tool used by mothers whose nipples may start to evert *(stand out)* permanently later, and the baby can latch on effectively. So don't rely on this one for long-term usage. Remember, the goal is to get the best milk production, and nipple shields only give you some adequate production.

The goal will be to get the baby to latch on to your breast correctly without the nipple shield. Here's a good way to work on this so your baby can wean off this and directly onto the breast. Attempt at each breastfeeding to get the baby to latch directly on the breast first. Work with the baby for 5-10 minutes or until the baby gets really fussy— because they are hungry. Use the shield if it's needed. If not, and the baby latches directly to the breast, then chalk this up as a win! Continue this practice with every feeding until the baby exclusively latches onto the breast. Then you will have successfully weaned your baby from the nipple shield. But remember, sometimes this can be a "two steps forward, one step back" until your baby gets the idea, so don't get discouraged. It will all work out in the end.

Breast pump

This is for those of you whose nipples will not cooperate and stand out on their own, and you must continually use the nipple shield tool for each breastfeeding. Pumping the breast afterward would be necessary to help effectively stimulate adequate milk production. This may be cumbersome and time-consuming, but it can effectively ensure your baby gets breast milk.

If these methods are not a good fit for you, an alternative way to ensure your baby gets your breast milk is to pump and feed this to the baby by bottle. This might be a better alternative for some families, too. It will allow you to provide the baby with the best nourishment and allow the dad to feed his baby, thus letting him in on both the feeding and the bonding process. This goes, too, for anyone wanting to help by feeding the baby.

Pumping can be helpful for mothers who have no desire to put the baby at the breast. This might be for personal reasons or for mothers who are too anxious or stressed out with breastfeeding. Some mothers do feel this way, and that is *okay*. By pumping and bottle feeding, you can still provide your baby with the best nourishment available and cause you less stress in the end.

Pacifier Usage During Breastfeeding

Not giving babies a pacifier is strongly recommended in the beginning stages of breastfeeding. The reasoning is that the baby may have "nipple confusion" from taking the pacifier when breastfeeding. I like the wording "nipple preference" a little better than "nipple confusion." It has been called both.

When your baby is at the breast, you want the baby's mouth to open wide to get a large amount of nipple and areola for a good latch. If the baby uses a pacifier, they are generally not large enough nor in the right shape to mimic the baby latching onto the breast. The mouth must clamp down to latch onto a pacifier, mimicking a smaller latch. Then when your baby attempts to latch onto the breast, they may not open the mouth big enough. This is where the "nipple confusion" comes in. If you begin using a pacifier, it is not recommended until the breastfeeding is well-established, at approximately 3-4 weeks. This is the firmly held belief of the World Health Organization

(WHO), UNICEF, La Leche League International, and various other organizations.

However, according to SIDS research, using pacifiers during sleep time is encouraged because it *decreases* the risk of SIDS. So, what recommendations do you follow? A pediatrician, Dr. Clay Jones, from Newton-Wellesley Hospital in Newton, MA, wrote a very good article about this. He regularly contributes to the Science-Based Medicine blog, which discusses "issues and controversies between Science and Medicine." He discusses the above recommendations in the blog and breaks it down to further discuss "Is nipple confusion real?"

His thought is that it doesn't seem plausible. *(In other words, not reasonable, credible, believable, or conceivable.)* Babies will suck on anything, and they aren't all shaped like the breast. We talked about suck blisters previously, already on newborns' hands or forearms from when they were sucking on them before they were born. Dr. Jones also talked about babies sucking on hands or forearms. He listed various other items they suck on, such as blankets, hands, feet, or *anything* they can get into their mouth. And— he stated that they don't seem to alter their suck with the breast, so why would the pacifier be any different?

Another concern for breastfeeding, for the WHO, UNICEF, LLLI, and others, is that a pacifier would replace breastfeeding. They're concerned mothers might choose to offer "the pacifier instead of the breast, thus causing a delay in milk letdown from the breast and increase the likelihood of breastfeeding cessation." *(ie., breastfeeding ending, terminating.)* But then Dr. Jones also states that "a pacifier would not appreciably [noticeably] space out breastfeeding because a hungry baby is rarely soothed by one." I have found this true in my many years of nursing.

I have seen babies take pacifiers between feedings and "spit them out" after being repeatedly placed back in their mouths when they want to do— is breastfeed. With some, I have even witnessed them "shot-putting" them from their mouths. Then after they do breastfeed as "requested," the babies take the pacifier again after the feeding— without a problem. Some babies want to suck because sucking is comforting and soothing to them. Why deny that if a baby wants to constantly suck, even *after* a long breastfeeding session??

Before the "mandate" in hospitals was passed down about having "no pacifiers" except during painful procedures, babies were given pacifiers routinely between feedings to help soothe and comfort those who wanted to suck. Now some hospitals have gone to "locking down" pacifiers by putting them in their locked medicine machine/cabinet and can *only* get them out for painful procedures. If a parent wants to use a pacifier for the baby to suck on, they must bring their own.

If a baby wants to suck but is denied a pacifier? What happens then? Dr. Jones concluded that wouldn't the exhausted mother be more likely to offer formula when their baby is crying inconsolably than if offered a pacifier between feedings? Wouldn't the formula then be *more* detrimental for breastfeeding than the pacifier? Even in Dr. Jones's research, he found that the *"Cochrane Database of Systematic Review"* had a study of pacifier use in breastfeeding in 2012, and here was their conclusion:

"Pacifier use in healthy term breastfeeding infants, started from birth or after lactation is established, did not significantly affect the prevalence or duration of exclusive and partial breastfeeding up to four months of age. Evidence to assess the short-term breastfeeding difficulties faced by mothers and long-term effect of pacifiers on infants' health is lacking."

They then judged it to be of *"moderate-quality evidence"* and further stated:

"Until further information becomes available on the effects of pacifiers on the infant, mothers who are well-motivated to breastfeed should be encouraged to make a decision on the use of a pacifier based on personal preference."

> *Jaafar, S. H. (2016). Effect of restricted pacifier use in breastfeeding term infants for increasing duration of breastfeeding. Cochrane Database of Systematic Reviews (8), doi:10.1002/14651858.CD 007202.pub4

Even the *"Pediatrics"* journal for the American Academy of Pediatrics, which Dr. Jones also reviewed, concluded that:

". . . it raises serious concerns that restricting pacifier availability in the newborn period may even increase the likelihood that breastfeeding mothers will reach for formula."

> *Laura R. Kair, Daniel Kenron, Konnette Etheredge, Arthur C. Jaffe, Carrie A. Phillipi. (Mar 2013). Pacifier Restriction and Exclusive Breastfeeding. Pediatrics, peds.2012-2203; DOI: 10.1542/peds.2012-2203

So, should you or shouldn't you use a pacifier while exclusively breastfeeding?? I used to tell undecided parents my old mantra, "It's easier to take away a pacifier because you can't take away a thumb." If your baby has eaten well and continues to look for something to suck on, the decision is *entirely up to you*— as the baby's parents— to decide.

Pumping Your Breasts

You may start pumping your breasts while in the hospital. Whether it is due to a baby not wanting to eat for long periods and you need breast stimulation until they do. Or your baby is receiving specialized care in the nursery and unable to eat or even breastfeed. Your hospital should have a hospital-grade breast pump and the accompanying kit for personal use.

Starting to pump

Your nurse or lactation consultant should help you set up the pump at the bedside and demonstrate to you how to use the pump. Pump each breast for about 15-20 minutes per breast if pumping one at a time, *or* pump both for the same amount of time you would pump one breast. This will help to stimulate the breast when the baby is not at the breast to do so, therefore, helping you to initiate milk production. Be sure to pump every 2 ½ to 3 hours, or the same time frame you would put the baby to the breast— *around* the clock. If your baby would be breastfeeding at a certain time, then you should be pumping at the same time to keep up production for the baby until they can get on the breast later. If you will be going to sleep, set your phone alarm to wake you for the pumping session.

One thing you should do each time you pump your breasts— use some of your lanolin ointment before you begin pumping. Place it on the inside of the horn, which you place over your nipple. This will help lubricate the nipple and keep it from getting damaged from the friction of the nipple pulling in and out inside of the horn. I have seen some nipples get extremely damaged from using the pump without the ointment, so be sure to use it each time. And remember to wash your hands when handling your breasts or pumping equipment.

Cleaning your pumping equipment

After you have finished pumping, collect what you have pumped into another container for storage. Next, take apart the pump kit pieces and wash them in warm soapy water. Then rinse and lay the pieces out on a towel to dry— until you need them for the next pumping session. Your hospital may provide a container, dishwashing soap, and towels, so you can wash your equipment and keep it separate from everything else.

(**Be sure to read the subsections of the book "Baby Having Difficulty Feeding from the Nipple" through the rest of the subsections below. This includes "Overfeeding Your Baby Formula, under "So You Choose to Formula Feed Your Baby." Each section is relevant when using a bottle to feed your baby pumped breastmilk.)

Baby's Not Wanting to Eat

This is a common occurrence, usually on the first day following delivery. There are a couple reasons with many factors which might cause your little one to not want to eat, so we need to take these into account when breastfeeding:

Just too tired

Your baby has been through a lot this first day. The delivery was hard enough. But, many people were messing with the baby, bathing, giving shots, measuring, wrapping, and passing the baby around to a room full of visitors. This little kiddo hadn't been "touched" for 9 months, and now everyone "has to" get their hands on them. All this overstimulation can make your poor kiddo just plum "tuckered out." *SO*— sleep is the next solution. Eating… naaah, don't care about that right now. And that goes for almost all babies.

Trying to get a tired baby to eat is sometimes tough. Still, it's essential the baby gets *some* nourishment, even if it's just 5 minutes' worth of breastfeeding. That small amount will help, and any longer would be better— when they are more willing. You still need to wake the baby up if not waking on their own. You may need to try to "force feed," even just a little, by undressing and/or unwrapping baby, tickling feet or toes. This way, the baby will be more motivated to wake up and latch on.

(** See the Q&A section below after the "Breastfeeding Conclusion", where it discusses in more detail about waking your sleeping baby.)*

Don't want to eat because... BARF!!

Okay, your baby has now thrown up a mouthful or two of nasty, mucousy amniotic fluid that's been sitting in their stomach since they delivered. Remember the Q&A section on Baby, where we discussed the amniotic fluid? How it just sits on the stomach and doesn't digest— it just turns to mucous and upsets their stomach— and eventually they will throw it up? Well, that belly full of fluid makes it *really* hard to want to eat because the baby *is just not hungry!* How do you like it when someone tries to force you to eat more when you are already full??

Once the stomach empties out all the excess amniotic fluid, possibly old blood from the delivery, and undigested formula mixed with the mucous, the stomach will be empty again. Now the baby will be hollering to eat since the stomach is all stretched out and wants to get it filled again. Then you should have no problem with the little munchkin pestering you that they are hungry. And you will be happy to help your baby get what they are asking for.

Burping your Baby

Whether bottle feeding or breastfeeding, you should try to burp your baby several times during a feeding. Babies take in extra air that gets trapped in the stomach when they eat, so burping your baby during the feeding will help to get rid of this air. By burping the baby really well during the feeding, you help get rid of this air and potentially have a lot less spitting up since there will be less to bring up during each burp session.

With breastfed babies, they don't generally take in very much extra air. Yet some "little snarfers" really get into what they are doing and make a lot of heavy breathing or "popping" noises with their mouth while feeding. When they do this, the baby may take in some extra air, so burping is a good idea. You may have read in other places that "you don't need to burp a breastfed baby." Well— I tend to disagree with this little tidbit of information, and here's why. I had first-hand knowledge of some of the babies that had shown up in our nursery after a feeding. If a baby has not been burped previously during or after a feeding, they usually let you know quite loudly that a burp is in order. Those baby's shrilly cries and body stiffening up completely into a straight line is a good indication they need a burp. And that was the case in almost all of those babies.

When the body stiffens up, it's the baby's way of trying to "get away" from the pain the gas is causing them. The shrilly cry is an indication *they are in* a lot of pain. I've seen sleeping babies come back to the nursery and sleep peacefully for about an hour— then the screaming, crying— and stiffening up begins!! So, burp your poor breastfed baby between breasts for a couple minutes and after the feeding for at least 5-10 minutes. This way, you'll be sure to get out all the air possible.

However, some babies like to "hoard" their burps. So continue doing this for a longer interval between breasts and after the feeding to clear out excess air. You will be assured you have made your baby comfortable and satisfied.

It was always very difficult for me to get a baby to burp on my shoulder— like so many of us have seen done throughout the years. But, I found that sitting them up when burping seemed to work the best. So, this is the technique I used and also taught my parents to do:

- First, sit the baby on your lap sideways, in a sitting position, facing either the right or left, depending on which hand you will use on their backs to burp. *(**One side may be more comfortable than the other, so try whichever side works best for you.)* Then, place your first finger and thumb around your baby's chin for support and your third finger underneath the armpit and close your second and third fingers together. This helps you hold your baby steady since they like to wobble around. Next, lean your baby forward just a little and rest their tummy against the side part of your hand below the pinky finger. This will help to put a little counter-pressure against the tummy, which helps "push" up some of the gas.

- Once you have your baby positioned this way, take your other hand and pat your baby just enough that their whole body moves a little during each pat. This helps to "dislodge" or move the air bubbles around to the top so the baby can burp it out. If you pat too softly, you won't get the air bubbles to move around enough to dislodge them. And— you *don't* want to pound on their backs *really* hard because this isn't necessary, and you can possibly injure your baby doing this.

You know, for instance, when you pour some soda into a glass and "bubbles" cling to the sides, and if you bump the glass *just right*, the air bubbles will rise to the top, right? Well, this is the same idea when you burp your baby. You need the "right" amount of patting on the back to dislodge the bubbles to bring them to the surface of the stomach so they can come out when your baby burps.

- The second accompanying technique is to stroke your baby's back in an upward motion several times and alternate with patting the back. When you stroke the baby's back, firmly stroke it in an upward direction— from the waist to the shoulders. While doing this, gently lift your baby up just a little bit— maybe, an inch or less— and then set them back down. Repeat stroking and lifting about 10 times, then return to patting the back. Repeat back and forth on both until the baby gives you several good burps. This technique also helps to move the air bubbles around so the bubbles move to the top, and the baby can "burp" them out.

    (**This movement mimics rocking in a chair when my cesarean section moms had gas build-up. The movement helps to dislodge those extra bubbles you might miss if only patting the baby's back.)

- Now, some babies are a little harder to burp than others, and that's just normal. Sometimes you may get a *really big burp*— that would make *any* dad proud!! LOL! Sometimes, you may get only a little burp. So, continue to burp the baby for a little longer to ensure you're not leaving some gas behind. If you don't, they may let you know in about an hour or so when the gas pain is uncomfortable!! Thus, the stiffened up, shrilly crying baby...

- For the ones that are harder to burp, you may have to sit there and continue to burp your baby and stroke their back for 5, 10, or maybe even 15 minutes before you get them to burp. If you still cannot get a burp out, it's possible there may be no gas in the tummy, and you can stop for now. If your baby does wake up a short while later, start a shrill cry, and stiffen up, you can bet the gas was hiding in there and now needs to come out— so start burping your baby again. Usually, once the gas is gone, babies will go back to sleep rather quickly. Unless it's time to eat again— or the diaper needs changing— or they are awake now and want to stay up— you get my drift.

After the Feeding and Burping are Over...

Once you have completed feeding and burping your baby, and it's time for the little one to go to sleep, be sure and place a burp cloth underneath the chin and tuck it in and around the neck. Since most new babies spit up amniotic fluid and sometimes whatever they eat, placing the burp cloth there is a very good idea. That way, if the baby spits up, it doesn't get all over everything— their clothes, the blanket they are wrapped in, the blanket over the bed pad. This is just an easier way to eliminate a lot of changing bedding and wrapping blankets and clothing frequently— especially if they are spitting up a lot. Routinely doing this task will save you time and energy— time better spent resting between those feedings.

Breastfeeding Conclusion

Whether you are an old pro or just starting out breastfeeding, your nurses and lactation consultants are there to help you. Each baby is different; each baby's latch may start off differently. One child might be an easy breastfeeder, but the sibling is a big challenge. Your first or second baby may not have "figured it out" about breastfeeding, but you want to try with this one last baby. We want each breastfeeding mom to get it right every time and make each breastfeeding experience pleasurable and successful.

Q&A on Other Breastfeeding Concerns

Q *My baby is sleeping a lot and not breastfeeding, and I'm worried they aren't eating enough. What can I do?*

A It's common on the first day of life that your baby will be very alert for the first couple hours and then slip off to "dreamland." Your baby has been through a lot— with the labor and birth. Then any possible pain medications given during the labor or cesarean section might affect them a little. Plus, being passed around like a football to every visitor they encountered on the first day. Your baby is tired and in need of rest. They may also have a full stomach of amniotic fluid, just like we discussed in the section on *Q&A on Baby*. If the stomach is full of amniotic fluid, the baby won't have the urge to eat very much until the fluid is working its way out. *(**Just try eating when your stomach is already full…)*

It is important to attempt to wake your baby up to feed every 2-3 hours and every hour if you cannot arouse them to eat, even for 5 minutes. Change the diaper, sit your baby up and burp the baby or rub the back, and/or take off all the blankets and clothing down to the diaper. This will help to wake your baby.

Sometimes during the feeding, your baby will attempt to fall asleep as well, so there are a few things you can do to help keep the baby awake and feeding during this time. Use your fingertips on the back of the head in a "shampoo massaging" way, quickly and with a semi-light touch, but *not* slowly and rhythmically. Quickly will help keep the baby awake; slow and rhythmic will be soothing and cause the baby to fall asleep. The baby may pause for a second or two, which is normal. Do the shampoo massage again only when they stop sucking for 5 seconds or more to encourage the baby to suckle again.

Tickling the feet, ribs, or back may also help keep the baby awake and feeding. It will cause your baby to wiggle around when tickled and keep more interest in the sucking. You can also gently push your finger under the chin against the tongue a few times. Prodding in this location may signal your baby to start sucking again. And again, only do this when the sucking stops for a few seconds.

And last, try using a cold, wet washcloth against the exposed skin if the other methods do not work. Try wiping it anywhere, including around the face and on top of the head. It might be successful in getting your baby suckling again. I've been known to perform a few "wet willies" in the ears to see if it will accomplish our goal— which it did. So you can try this one as well.

About your concern with getting enough to eat, there are several things we check on frequently when assessing your baby. These will help to indicate if your baby is getting enough to eat to keep her hydrated. First, we check the number of wet diapers the baby is producing. In the beginning, there are fewer wet diapers for breastfed babies since he's not getting the volume yet for the 6-8 wet diapers expected after your milk comes in. This is normal and to be expected but will change once the volume picks up. Second, we check the mouth and lips for moistness. If it is dry, this indicates she might not be getting enough to keep her hydrated. She may need a little

Q&A on Other Breastfeeding Concerns

supplementation if the doctor feels it is necessary at that time. Last, we check the fontanels or "soft spots" on the top of the head to see if they are sunken in. This is another good indicator of dehydration; the baby will be supplemented if the doctor orders it.

Q *Now my baby wants to eat all the time... why the sudden change?*

A It's normal for them to eat that first day periodically. On the second day— after their "refreshing sleep" and spitting up the excess amniotic fluid, they will cluster feed to make up for what they didn't do the day before. This may last for up to 5-8 hours or more, with feeding for extended periods, then short breaks of 30 minutes or so, and then will quickly start up again. Once they get "caught up" on the missed feedings, they will generally slow down and eat every 1-1/2 to 3 hours as they should. This usually would be on the second day after not eating much on the 1st. Unfortunately— some babies may have different ideas about that!

Q *Why is my baby getting upset and pushing me away when I'm trying to get her to breastfeed? Does my baby not want me? Am I doing something wrong?*

A Babies will get upset when breastfeeding if anything is bothering them. They may not like the position they are feeding in, be mad because your breast isn't giving them "instant gratification. Maybe they're sitting in a dirty diaper and want it changed first. Or they don't like that nipple or that side to feed on. It can be any number of things. But you can be assured— that your baby loves and depends on you— and *wants* you no matter what.

When a baby is upset and frustrated, they flail their arms and legs around if they can. If they meet resistance, say like your breast, they may "push off" on your breast— but they *are not pushing you away*. When this happens, the baby may push so hard they pop themselves off your breast— then the real frustration and crying will begin! They are thinking, "What just happened to my breast… I want it back!!" They do not realize those arms are attached to them— *yet*. And so they don't realize they just pushed themselves off. They are just *mad!*

If your baby gets so mad that they are crying uncontrollably, get your baby to calm down by placing them on your chest. Cuddle, caress, talk softly and lovingly, and/or "*shhhhhh*," which will soothe your baby. Once you calm your baby down, you can re-attach them to the breast. If this continues, try to figure out what may be causing their frustration and fix it— then try the feeding again. *(**Remember to use the list given to you earlier on "Q&A on Your Baby" to "check off" what may be causing your baby's fussiness.)* Most of the time, I have found this is due to a poopy diaper that the baby wants changed before feeding. So, check this first if your baby continues to be fussy and will not latch back on.

Q Which breast do I start on? Why do I need to switch? Why can't I start on the same side each time? I get so confused…

A Breastfeeding aims to get equal stimulation on both sides, giving *each* breast equal milk production. When the baby starts to feed, they will be very vigorous with their sucking, creating *more* stimulation. Once they reach the second side, they slow down their sucking, stimulating that breast *less*. If you start on the same side each time, that particular breast will get more stimulation than the other one. Therefore, you will have unequal stimulation on your breasts.

When starting to breastfeed, you want to start on one side, then switch to the other for the rest of the feeding. The goal is 10-15 minutes of good sucking on each side, if possible. When you feed the next time, you want to start on the side you finished on *last*. This way, the 2nd breast gets more stimulation than the last time, and the 1st breast gets less. This is how you get equal stimulation. It would be best if you continued this practice throughout breastfeeding.

Now— if your baby is sleepy and you need to wake him *(like we discussed above)*, the new goal would be to get the baby latched on one side and *stay* feeding on that side. The reasoning is when you are struggling to get the baby latched on when they are sleepy, then you take them off to switch sides, you might not get them to latch back on. With the baby sleepy, you will continue struggling to keep them awake and suckling during this feeding. So it would be best to keep the baby on this side for the whole time. This way, you get a good feeding on the one side, and then you can start with the *other* breast the next feeding, thus again keeping the stimulation on both sides equal. When the baby becomes more awake and more demanding to feed, you can return to using both sides and switch accordingly.

Trust me, when your milk has come in a few days later, you will know which side you need to feed on first. One breast will be fuller, heavier, and more painful than the other, so you will *know* which to start with.

Q   *What is wrong? My baby is eating all the time, and I don't think I have enough to give him. Should I give some formula?*

A   Remember, when you are breastfeeding, your colostrum is in "a lot" smaller quantities than breast milk will be when it comes in, so, *yes,* your baby may want more than what you are giving them.

If your baby had a substantial amount of amniotic fluid in the stomach after delivery and has thrown up this fluid, then the stomach has been stretched out. So now the baby wants more to eat. Just think of it like giving the baby "dessert" when they want the "full meal deal." You are only filling up a portion of the stomach, not the whole thing. The solution would be to put the baby to breast "on demand" and continue to do so will help stimulate the breasts, and your milk may come in a little sooner.

You may be getting little to no sleep during this time because the baby demands frequent eating. Circumstances, such as "little to no sleep for an extended time," have been a problem— even before the delivery. *But,* to continue providing *exclusive breastfeeding,* you need to continue putting the baby to the breast to stimulate milk production. This is the appropriate way to go about it.

Now, if you are adamant that your baby is "starving" and you feel the need to give the baby formula— this is *your* decision.

Parents have insisted on going this route to satisfy the baby— if to get *some* sleep because they are extremely exhausted. If you do decide to do this, it would be best to limit the amount of formula to 10-15 milliliters during feeding time. This way, the baby will more likely wake up and nurse again in a 2- to 3-hour timeframe, following the breastfeeding schedule, than if you completely fill up the stomach.

If you supplement with formula, you may only have to do this occasionally when your baby wants more than the colostrum. Then again, if your baby likes having the extra food, they may demand to get it for every feeding— until your milk comes in. Every baby is different regarding supplementing with breastfeeding, so be prepared either way.

Q *If I do decide to supplement, how can I do this with breastfeeding? Do I feed with a bottle?*

A There is an alternative way to accomplish supplementing and breastfeeding at the same time *without* the use of the bottle. You may just be "shooting yourself in the foot" or "sabotaging the breastfeeding" if you introduce a bottle to the baby when you start breastfeeding. When the baby is at the breast, the baby must suck to get the colostrum to come out— so they must work at it to make it happen.

If you introduce a bottle, the nipple "drips" faster, and the baby does not have to work as hard to "get something." Then, when you put the baby back to the breast next time, the baby will expect the colostrum to "drip" just like the bottle, which may frustrate your baby. Then you have the problem of the baby wanting to refuse the breast because the baby must "work harder" for it— and they now *expect* it to be simple and less work.

One solution would be a Supplemental Nursing System *(SNS)*, which can be used at the breast while the baby is nursing. A breastfeeding syringe is filled with formula, and a feeding tube is attached to the syringe. The end of the tube can then be placed right next to the nipple before the baby latches on. If this doesn't work, it may be inserted into the side of the baby's mouth after they latch onto the breast. Your nurse or lactation consultant can help you set this up and show you how it's done.

The idea with this system is that the flow to the baby can be controlled, so they are only getting "a few drops" at a time when they are suckling— and *only* when they are suckling. If the baby gets the tube in the mouth— *just right*, they may be able to "suck" the formula out of the tube quickly. You can control that and pull back on the syringe plunger a little to control how much they take as they suck. This is how you control the flow of formula through the tube and *mimic* breastfeeding as it occurs now, which is different than when your milk comes in.

Another alternative with the tube and syringe can be finger-feeding the baby. If you want to breastfeed first and then give the supplement, you, the baby's daddy, or anyone else can do this. Your lactation consultant can demonstrate the positioning of you and the baby if you want to try this. You can control the formula given to the baby in drops or pull back on the plunger if the baby wants to suck it fast, just like we discussed above.

Another way to supplement the baby would be to spoon-feed or cup-feed the formula. Your lactation consultant will be

Q&A on Other Breastfeeding Concerns

familiar with these methods and can show you how to do them. If your nurse is familiar with these methods, they can help you too.

(**Not all nurses can work with SNS, cup, or spoon feeding. They may rely on the lactation consultants for this. But some nurses in some smaller hospitals may be familiar with these methods and can also help you.)

If you decide to decline any of these options and insist on giving your baby a bottle, you have one thing you can do to somewhat mimic the breast. This might help keep the amount your baby is sucking down to smaller quantities— *and* get the baby to slow down. What you can do is let the baby only take a couple sucks. Then you would remove the bottle from the mouth. Give your baby time to "pause" for 10-15 seconds, then give the bottle back to the baby, and keep repeating this until the baby *only* takes 10-15 milliliters. *(**If you exclusively breastfeed, I would discourage you from using this method, but if you insist, remember— it is your choice.)*

Also, remember, once you introduce formula to the breastfeeding equation, your baby may expect this at *"each and every feeding."* This may be until your milk comes in and the baby is receiving more volume to fill their tummy. This may last 1-5 days until your breastmilk comes in, so be prepared to go the short haul until it does.

Any unused formula the baby doesn't take during the feeding must be discarded after the feeding is completed. Don't worry about "wasting" the formula. It comes in 2 oz bottles, so it's not much to waste. And— be sure to wash the equipment thoroughly after the feeding so it's ready for use the next time.

Q *What is that dried white stuff around the baby's mouth?*

A Anytime you see this around your baby's mouth, you should be shouting, "Hallelujah"!! This is what is called a "milk mouth." It's more noticeable when the baby is getting a larger quantity of colostrum, or your milk is coming in. You may also hear your baby swallowing more frequently, which is another indicator of your baby getting more volume. When you are finished feeding, you can wipe off the dried stuff from around the mouth with a warm wet cloth. This is *definitely* a good thing!!!

Q *The pediatrician told me I needed to supplement my baby with formula. I want to exclusively breastfeed and not give my baby any formula. Why am I being "forced" to do this against my wishes?*

A The supplementation ordered by the pediatrician is generally done for a reason, not to undermine your desire to exclusively breastfeed. In fact, it's the total opposite. They encourage exclusive breastfeeding but may find your baby is not receiving a "sufficient amount" of colostrum. The pediatrician obviously has assessed your baby and, for one reason or another, has determined that, at the present time, your baby needs it. The lack of volume in the colostrum you produce is not adequate enough to avoid certain issues with beginning exclusive breastfeeding. This is strictly the pediatrician's concern for the baby's health. Dehydration, jaundice, low blood sugars, low temperatures, or losing more than 10% of birth weight. Any of these factors may be why the pediatrician ordered formula supplementation. The increased volume of nourishment for your baby will help remedy these issues, at least until your milk comes in.

You might have the option to ask if donor breastmilk could be ordered if you must supplement. Since you are not producing enough now, your baby must have something to correct whatever issue they are having. This way, your baby still gets just breast milk in addition to the colostrum you provide— and would be avoiding the formula, which you do not want your baby to have. This will be a "win-win" situation for both you and your baby if this is an option!

Q *What if I want to pump my breasts and feed this to my baby?*

A This is a great alternative for mothers who want to give their baby breast milk but do not want to breastfeed— or breastfeeding is not working for them. Your lactation consultant or nurse can set you up with a breast pump and demonstrate how to use it to start building up your milk supply for your baby. They can also give you information on storage options for the pumped breastmilk.

If you decide to pump your breasts to feed your baby, remember you need to pump every 2-3 hours, just as often as your baby would go to the breast. Pump for 15 minutes per breast or whatever your lactation consultant or nurse recommends.

So... You Choose to Formula Feed Your Baby

Choosing to feed your baby formula may have been an easy decision for you and your family. You may have already had a "not-so-great" breastfeeding experience with a previous child and *do not* want to go through that again... *EVER!!* You may be unable to breastfeed due to medications you *must* take, so you *cannot* breastfeed your baby. Maybe you cannot produce enough breastmilk, so why even start it again? Maybe your mother or grandmother strongly suggested you bottle feed because they had bad experiences, so don't even try! That it's not worth the hassle— and it's easier for others to feed the baby, too. Breastfeeding "disgusts you" or "gives you the willies." Don't want to think about the baby "nursing" from your breast because it's just "weird to you." Then some mothers know they are too anxious and don't feel they can do it or stick with it. There are countless reasons some mothers give for not wanting to breastfeed, and *that's okay*. It's your *personal choice* to do this if you want to, and no one should force you to do anything you don't want to do with your baby— including breastfeeding. This is your baby— are they going home with you to feed your baby for you? Are they going to raise your baby for you? You are the mother and/or father, and as your baby's advocate, you must do what is right for you, your family— and your baby's situation. This *is TOTALLY OKAY!!*

Formula-fed babies are fed a little differently than breastfed babies are. Breastmilk is easier to digest than formula, so with formula, digestion takes a little longer, so there are longer intervals between feedings. Babies need to eat every 3-4 hours versus every 1 ½ to 3 hours like their breastfeeding buddies. They generally receive a larger amount each feeding, so they also tend to be more satisfied after finishing. Newborns, within the first couple of days, usually start off with between 10-30 milliliters of formula. Then they gradually add "smaller amounts" of 5-10 milliliters a feeding if the baby seems hungrier. But some factors might come into play when bottle feeding your newborn, so we will review some of these possible scenarios.

Preventing Milk Supply from Coming In

Since you will not be breastfeeding your baby, you must wear a tight-fitting bra, such as a sports bra with a lot of support or a regular supportive bra, and wear it at all times. This will help to keep the swelling of the breasts down.

If you do begin to swell and get hard, you can use cabbage leaves to help reduce the swelling. Some properties in the cabbage help with the swelling. Just put one leaf on each breast inside the bra and leave them there until they become wilted. At this point, remove the leaves and replace them with new ones.

It would help if you also tried avoiding *any* stimulation to the breasts until the swelling has completely gone down. This includes letting the warm shower spray directly on the breasts, any additional "fondling" during sexual relations, or pumping breasts to relieve the pressure when you're not planning to breastfeed.

Staying away from pumping or hand-expressing the milk building up in your breasts is probably the hardest thing to avoid because you want relief from the pain and swelling. But when you stimulate the breasts and remove the milk for relief, the body automatically wants to replace the amounts you have removed to resupply you with milk.

It thinks you are feeding your baby; therefore, we need to replenish what has been taken. I know it's hard not to do this, but stimulation is a *no-no* if you want your milk to dry up.

If you have painful breasts due to the engorgement, you may take Tylenol® *(acetaminophen)*. This will help with swelling *(inflammation)*, heat *(antipyretic)*, and pain. Just be careful you don't take more than 4000 mg during a 24-hour period, as this would get into overdosing and cause toxicity within your body, damaging your liver over the long term. The newest recommendation is to use the smallest amount needed for pain relief and no more than 3,000-3,250 mg daily. However, if needed for this short duration, you may go up to 4,000 mg without any lasting effects. Also, when you go home, be sure the medications you were given in the hospital don't already contain acetaminophen. If it does, you don't want to add more to what you are already taking for pain relief. Percocet, Norco, and Tylenol 3 all have added acetaminophen, so don't take more if you already take any of these. Some others may as well, but these are the three main ones you generally take for pain relief after delivery.

(**This is also discussed in the Q&A portion at the end of this section.)

First Thing to Do Before Beginning to Feed

This one seems a little silly because most "ol' pro" parents know how to do this. It's just a reminder for some of you and new information for the newbies out there. That is— place a burp cloth under the chin and tuck it in around the neck. I know some of you think I am being ridiculous suggesting this to you, but you'd be surprised at even some of the "pros" out there *forgetting* this little step. Just because you may be starting back at square one with the new baby doesn't mean it hurts to have a few reminders on the "little things" you just may have forgotten since the last time.

Baby's Not Wanting to Eat

I discussed this at the end of the Breastfeeding section above. Still, these first two sections are just as appropriate with bottle feeding too, so I included it in both. Baby not wanting to eat is common, usually on the first day following delivery. A few factors might cause your little one to not want to eat, so they should be considered when bottle feeding.

Just too tired

Your baby has been through a lot this first day. The delivery was hard enough. But, many people were messing with the baby, bathing, giving shots, measuring, wrapping, and passing the baby around to a room full of visitors. This little kiddo hadn't been "touched" for 9 months, and now everyone "has to" get their hands on them. All this overstimulation can make your poor kiddo just plum "tuckered out." *SO*— sleep is the next solution. Eating… naaah, don't care about that right now. And that goes for almost all babies.

Trying to get a tired baby to eat is sometimes tough. Still, it's essential the baby gets *some* nourishment, even if it's just 5 mls worth of formula. That small amount will help, and any higher amounts would be better— when they are more willing. You still need to wake the baby up if not waking on their own. You may need to try to "force feed," even just a little, by undressing and/or unwrapping baby, tickling feet or toes. This way, the baby will be more motivated to wake up and latch on.

(**See the Q&A section *"Other Breastfeeding Concerns"* above at the end of the breastfeeding section, where it discusses waking your sleeping baby in more detail.)

Don't want to eat because... BARF!!

Okay, your baby has now thrown up a mouthful or two of nasty, mucousy amniotic fluid that's been sitting in their stomach since they delivered. Remember the Q&A section on Baby, where we discussed the amniotic fluid? How it just sits on the stomach and doesn't digest— it just turns to mucous and upsets their stomach— and eventually they will throw it up? Well, that belly full of fluid makes it *really* hard to want to eat because the baby *is just not hungry!* How do you like it when someone tries to force you to eat more when you are already full??

Once the stomach empties out all the excess amniotic fluid, possibly old blood from the delivery, and undigested formula mixed with the mucous, the stomach will be empty again. Now the baby will be hollering to eat since the stomach is all stretched out and wants to get it filled again. Then you should have no problem with the little munchkin pestering you that they are hungry. And you will be happy to help your baby get what they are asking for.

Don't seem to like the taste of the formula

At first, your baby may give you some "really funny" faces when getting some formula from the first feedings. Just keep in mind that your baby had not needed to take in *any* food before they were born. They are used to the amniotic fluid they have been sucking and swallowing for months, so they are used to that "flavor." So, now you are introducing a new "flavor," and it takes a few feedings for your baby to get used to the change.

Just keep offering the formula, even if they seem to not like it. Your baby will begin to get used to the new taste of the food and start taking it when offered.

Baby Having Difficulty Feeding from the Nipple

As discussed in the breastfeeding section, some of these little kiddos didn't come right out of your tummy knowing just how to suck right.

- The tongue might thrust outward. This pushes the nipple out of the mouth instead of using the tongue to draw it in.
- They may get the tongue back in the mouth but not bring it forward to latch onto the nipple correctly.
- They may not want to close their mouth around the nipple. That's because they have a big, wide-open breastfeeding mouth.
- The baby may suck on the nipple correctly but not yet coordinate "sucking and swallowing" together. So, the formula "pools" in the cheeks and then falls out of the mouth.
- They may have a very intense "gag reflex" with anything that barely touches the back of the mouth or throat. Therefore, they gag frequently with the nipple in their mouth.

These are just some of the problems you may encounter while feeding your new baby, so let's discuss some ways to help fix them.

Stroking the nipple down the tongue

This is for babies with difficulty grabbing onto the nipple and drawing into their mouths to suck. Take the nipple, insert it into the mouth, and "stroke" the nipple on the tongue— starting from the back to the front. This is one way to "train" the baby to place their tongue down instead of in the back of their mouth so they can grasp the nipple. You may need to repeat this method several times before your baby "catches on" to put the tongue down instead of back. Once the tongue is down, you can lay the nipple on top of the tongue, and hopefully, your baby will close their mouth around it, grasp it, and suck.

Using chin support

Using chin support is one way to help your baby close the mouth around the nipple so they can suck on it. You can do this by putting the bottle in your feeding hand and holding it with your thumb and first two fingers. This leaves the last two fingers to "anchor" against the bottom of the jaw and gently pull up— to help close the gap in the mouth. You may have to use gentle but firm pressure against the bottom jaw, especially if your baby doesn't want to close their mouth. Some want a "big, wide-open breastfeeding mouth" instead of a "smaller bottle one." These little kiddos have quite a bit of power in those little jaws, so sometimes it can be a little difficult to get them to close their mouths around the nipple properly. Just take your time and keep putting that gentle, firm pressure on the lower jaw, and your baby will start getting the hint.

You can continue holding your last two fingers under the chin to maintain chin support throughout the feeding. Once your baby gets used to sucking on the bottle correctly, this method will no longer be needed.

Using cheek support

This method is used for the little "chipmunk cheeks" who will only swallow a little formula. Then they like to hoard some formula in the cheek pockets and not swallow it all— then it dribbles out on the sides of the mouth. This one is a little more difficult to accomplish as it takes more coordination to pull it off. You may not be able to successfully achieve the correct hand position— but "we'll give it the ol' college try!"

First, you would need to get the nipple of the bottle into your baby's mouth for them to suck. Next, you "prop" the bottle against the web of skin between your thumb and first finger. This leaves your thumb and finger free to take and grasp the sides of the baby's cheeks and gently squeeze them together. This method helps close the mouth's sides and allows the formula to stay in instead of dribbling out when they suck and then swallow. This may be discontinued as they get better with the "suck and swallow" coordination. Then you can start holding the bottle the normal way.

Working around an intense gag reflex

A few babies out there seem to have a really challenging time breast-feeding or bottle feeding. That is because anything "too big" or "too long" getting in the mouth causes them to gag. If the nipple is too long, *they gag*; if too much formula sits in their mouth, *they gag*; if they're still trying to work up some amniotic fluid left in the stomach, *they gag*. Sometimes, you cannot seem to win in this situation. *(**I'm sure my mother had a tough time with this as I have a very bad one myself— and I still have a major problem with it!!)*

Fear not!! Your baby can get some of the formula down in the beginning, and when given a little time, will get better able to suck and swallow with coordination. Most babies, when sucking on a nipple, will take most or all of the whole nipple in the mouth when feeding. You would think the baby would choke on all that nipple, but most do just fine with it without any problem. But for your "little gagger," you must go slowly and take your time with the feeding.

One way you can help with this is to slowly push the nipple of the bottle in the mouth, but not to push it in all the way. Give your baby just a small enough amount of nipple he or she can grasp with the tongue but not have enough to gag on. This may make it easier for your baby to suck on the bottle without gagging.

Another idea is you can try taking the nipple out of your baby's mouth after a few sucks. This would allow your baby to take a breath or two and swallow what is in the mouth before getting too much formula, which might cause them to choke and gag. Once your baby has taken a few breaths and swallowed what is in the mouth, then you can re-introduce the nipple and repeat it throughout the feeding. As your baby's coordination improves, you can stop using this method or only use it when your baby "forgets" what they need to do again.

Forgetting to Breathe While Sucking on the Nipple

Every so often, I encountered one of those little munchkins who got so intense with sucking the bottle and swallowing that they forgot to take a breath. If this seems a problem for your baby, take the nipple out of your baby's mouth between 10-15 sucks. *Make your baby pause.* During that pause, your baby will then take some breaths and recover. After that, return the nipple to the mouth and resume feeding. Keep repeating this method each time throughout the feeding. This is another one where your baby should learn to breathe over time while sucking and swallowing. Then you can stop using this method. It just takes time for the baby to figure out how to simultaneously coordinate sucking, swallowing, and breathing.

Because you are stopping and starting frequently, your baby may gulp a lot when swallowing and recovering from taking a breath. They may also take in a lot of air while in the process. Burping frequently, say after about every 10 milliliters of formula, will help to get rid of that excess air earlier and lessen the chances of having a lot of spitting up. *(**See the section below on "Burping Your Baby.")*

Sucking Very Hard, Thus Sucking Down the Formula

Some little ones get a strong, coordinated suck going when sucking on the bottle— then they "wolf" down the formula too quickly. This is not a good thing since they might be overeating during feeding, then *throw up* a large amount of what they just ate afterward. You can use the same technique discussed above— take the nipple out of your baby's mouth between 10-15 sucks and *make* the baby pause. In this case, let your baby rest a good minute or two before giving back the bottle, even if your baby starts searching for it or crying. Some little ones don't like to wait when they are hungry, but if they eat too fast, they will bring it back up if they eat too much.

In between the pauses, sit your baby up and burp them. *(**See the section below on "Burping Your Baby.")* With this "fast food eating attempt," they might take in large amounts of air. So, getting the air out during those long pauses might keep your baby from spitting up a lot of formula when they burp.

Our brains are hard-wired with our stomachs and will send a signal to the brain when the stomach is full. If we eat too much too fast, we usually feel overly full *after* our stomach catches up to our brain. Eating slowly helps signal the brain when our stomach is full and tells us, "You are full," so we stop eating— or at least some of us do. This usually takes about 20 minutes of slow eating for this to occur. So, it makes sense that if the baby is "wolfing" down their food really fast— say in 5-10 minutes, the baby still thinks they are hungry— they continue eating *more*. Thus, throwing up a lot of formula afterward when they overeat.

Overfeeding Your Baby Formula

One of the problems with formula-fed babies is the potential to overfeed them. This is not necessarily the feeding amount but the frequency and amount of feeding together. Some babies may root for something to suck on sooner than they are due to for eating. The first thought of the parent is, "I guess the baby's hungry again, so I'll feed her again." This may be true that your baby is due to eat, but in some instances, it is not. This may not be a hunger cue if your baby starts a "requesting to eat" pattern every 1 ½ to 2 hours. If they're getting between 1 oz to 1-1/2 oz of formula per feeding in the first few days, that may be too much— unless the baby is larger-than-average and would have more room to eat. Your baby may have a tummy ache, and the only thing the baby would like to do— is to *suck!!* Since sucking is a comfort measure, and the baby's tummy hurts, your baby may want to suck for comfort. Offer a pacifier in between feedings to see if this is just what the baby wants.

If the baby spits out the pacifier and is still showing a hunger cue too soon to eat, holding the baby off with a pacifier until at least the 3-hour mark would be necessary. Try burping the baby to see if it's not just air causing their discomfort or using "the 5 S's" to soothe the baby. *(**Seeing "Burping Your Baby" in the next section and "The 5 S's" just before the "Feeding Your Baby..." section above.)* Do some skin-to-skin contact with your baby. See if any of these will work for you. If it doesn't— and the baby gets into a consistent pattern of eating "too much, too soon"— you begin to see thinner stools that start soaking into the diaper. Then your baby will begin to experience what we call "water-loss stools."

Water-loss stools are when the baby gets too much formula, and the body does *not* digest the larger, frequent amounts. The formula begins to "run right through the baby" and stops long enough to take some of the baby's body water with it. If this happens for a long time, the baby can start dehydrating from losing body water and become sick. To avoid that, if you start seeing water-loss stools in your baby and the baby is trying to eat too frequently, make the baby wait until it is time to feed again. That would be *no earlier* than 3 hours. And be consistent about holding the baby off. *(**I know it's really hard to make your baby wait, but it is important to do this to avoid the baby becoming dehydrated.)* Keep feeding the baby this way and make them wait a *full* 3 hours minimum before feeding again. When enough feedings have occurred, and the baby gets used to eating at 3 hours, your baby should be out of the clear. You should also see the stools become soft again and not soak into the diaper. If the water-loss stools continue to be a problem, be sure and let your nurse know so the baby can be evaluated for dehydration.

Burping Your Baby

Whether bottle feeding or breastfeeding, you should try to burp your baby several times during a feeding. Babies take in extra air that gets trapped in the stomach when they eat, so burping your baby periodically during the feeding will help to get rid of this air. By burping the baby several times during the feeding, you help to get rid of this air quicker. This would make for much less spitting up since there will be less to bring up during each burp session.

With bottle-fed babies, some can be "little snarfers," really get into what they are doing and make a lot of heavy breathing noises or "popping" noises with the mouth while feeding. The baby may take in even more air when they do this, so burping is a good idea. If babies don't get burped well enough, they let you know! I had first-hand knowledge of some babies that had shown up in our nursery after a feeding. If a baby has not been burped previously during or after a feeding, they usually let you know quite loudly that a burp is in order. Their shrilly cry and body stiffening up completely in a straight line is a good indication they need a burp. And that was the case in almost all of those babies.

When the body stiffens up, it's the baby's way of trying to "get away" from the pain the gas is causing them. The shrilly cry is an indication *they are in* a lot of pain. I've seen sleeping babies come back to the nursery and sleep peacefully for about an hour— then— the screaming, crying, and stiffening up begins!! With bottle-fed babies, they do take in quite a bit of air with their sucking. So, periodically burping them during the feeding is needed as well. And— for the "snarfers" who tend to try and eat fast, there should be several *extra* burps during the feeding session. However, some babies like to "hoard" their burps, too. Burping your baby more frequently and for a longer period after the feeding, you will be assured you have made your baby comfortable and satisfied.

It was very difficult for me to get a baby to burp on my shoulder like so many of us have seen done throughout the years, but I found that sitting them up when burping seems to work the best. So, this is the technique I used and also taught my parents to do:

- First, sit the baby on your lap sideways, in a sitting position, facing either the right or left, depending on which hand you will use on their backs to burp. *(**One side may be more comfortable than the other, so try whichever side works best for you.)* Then, place your first finger and thumb around your baby's chin for support and your third finger underneath the armpit and close your second and third fingers together. This helps you hold your baby steady since they like to wobble around. Next, lean your baby forward and rest their tummy against the side of your hand below the pinky finger. This will help to put a little counter-pressure against the tummy, which helps "push" up some of the gas.

- Once you have your baby positioned this way, take your other hand and pat your baby just enough that their whole body moves a little during each pat. This helps to "dislodge" or move the air bubbles around to the top so the baby can burp it out. If you pat too soft, you won't get the air bubbles to move around enough for the baby to burp the air out. And— you *don't* want to pound on their backs *really* hard because this isn't necessary, and you can possibly injure your baby doing this.

You know, for instance, when you pour some soda into a glass and "bubbles" cling to the sides, and if you bump the glass *just right*, the air bubbles will rise to the top, right? Well, this is the same idea when you burp your baby. You need the "right" amount of patting on the back to dislodge the bubbles to bring them to the surface of the stomach so they can come out when your baby burps.

- The second technique that goes with this is to stroke your baby's back in an upward motion several times and alternate with patting the back. When you stroke the baby's back, firmly stroke it in an upward direction— from the waist to the shoulders. While doing this, gently lift your baby up just a little bit— maybe, an inch or less— and then set them back down. Repeat stroking and lifting about 10 times, then return to patting the back. Repeat back and forth on both until the baby gives you several good burps. This technique also helps to move the air bubbles around so the bubbles move to the top, and the baby can "burp" them out. (***This movement is like when my cesarean section moms had gas build-up and rocked in a chair. The movement helps to dislodge those extra bubbles you might miss if only patting the baby's back.*)

- Now, some babies are a little harder to burp than others, and that's just normal. Sometimes you may get a *really big burp*— that would make *any* dad proud!! LOL! Sometimes, you may get only a little burp. Continue to burp the baby for a little longer to ensure you're not leaving some gas behind. They may just "let you know" in about an hour or so when the gas pain is uncomfortable!! Thus, the stiffened up, shrilly, crying baby…

- For the ones that are harder to burp, you may have to sit there and continue to burp your baby and stroke their back for 5, 10, or maybe even 15 minutes before you get them to burp. If you still cannot get a burp out, there may be no gas in the tummy, and you can stop for now. If your baby wakes up quickly, starts a shrill cry, and stiffens up, you can bet the gas was hiding there. Now it needs to come out— so start burping your baby again. Babies will return to sleep rather quickly once the gas is gone. Unless it's time to eat again. Maybe the diaper needs changing, or the baby is awake now and wants to stay up. Do you catch my drift? Oh, the vicious cycle!

After the Feeding and Burping are Over...

Once you have completed feeding and burping your baby and it's time for the little one to sleep, don't forget to place a burp cloth underneath the chin, tucking it in and around the neck. Since most newer babies spit up amniotic fluid and sometimes whatever they ate, placing the burp cloth under their chin is a good idea. This way, if the baby spits up, it doesn't get all over everything— their clothes, the blanket they are wrapped in, the blanket over the bed pad. This is just an easier way to eliminate a lot of changing bedding and wrapping blankets and clothing frequently— especially if they are spitting up a lot. Putting the burp cloth down routinely will save you time and energy— time better spent resting between those feedings.

Q&A on Bottle Feeding Concerns

Q *How much formula should I feed my baby?*

A In the beginning, you will want to feed your baby anywhere from ½ oz *(15 milliliters)* to 1 oz *(30 milliliters)*. On the first day, your baby may not take much if the tummy is full of amniotic fluid. It may be closer to ½ oz to ¾ oz *(15-22.5 milliliters)* or less. Once your baby starts getting rid of all the fluid, they will begin eating a little larger amount of formula to fill the void where the fluid was.

After the feeding and burping, if the baby is still rooting around and starts to fuss, give them another 5 milliliters of formula and stop. Burp your baby and then see if they are still wanting more. If they are, repeat another 5 milliliters, stop, and check again. When your baby is finished, record the amount of formula the baby took. Suppose during the time before the next feeding, the baby vomits up a large amount of formula. In that case, this is a good indication they over-ate during the last feeding, so back off 5 milliliters from what you gave the last time. If they eat that much again, wait and see if your baby holds it down this time. If your baby does, this would be the new formula amount to feed them for several more feedings— until they again "ask" for more. Over time, this will also continue as the baby grows and demands more to satisfy them.

Q *Can I use the same bottle the baby ate from for the next feeding? There's still a lot left in the bottle...*

A If it is within 1 hour of the baby's last feeding, the answer is "Yes." If it is longer than 1 hour, the answer is "No." Two answers are due to the length of time the formula has been left out. There's now a chance of bacteria starting to grow in the formula. That sounds "gross," and here's why… When your baby puts their mouth on the bottle, they introduce germs on the bottle's nipple, and the formula has now had contact with those germs. The formula has now been contaminated by the baby. If the bottle has been left out at room temperature for too long, there is a greater chance for bacteria to grow.

We all know parents hate to waste formula, especially since it seems like a lot to waste, but there is only 2 oz of formula in the pre-filled bottle. And— the bottle is meant for "one-time use only." So— don't be afraid to throw away what's left. It's safer for your baby if you discard the leftovers.

Q *Since I'm bottle feeding, how do I keep my milk from coming in?*
A You can do several things to help keep milk production at bay, but it's not guaranteed that you may not have some milk production or engorgement. Your body will naturally work to make milk when your baby is born. The key to helping suppress milk production would be to provide no stimulation to the breasts, or at least as little as possible. This means— *do not* put the baby on the breast to suckle— *even* for a few minutes. And certainly not just a few times for the "heck of it."

Some moms do this to give the baby some colostrum before solely going to formula feeding. They think, "Oh… I just give a little colostrum, so my baby can benefit from the immunities for a couple days, and then I'll bottle feed after." It is strongly suggested that you do not do this if you will be solely formula feeding unless you're adamant that the baby gets some colostrum. Any stimulation to the breasts can bring on milk production, so no stimulation would be more beneficial for you. Just remember, it is your choice. This is only a recommendation for your comfort.

If you decide to go ahead and breastfeed, even just a little, and then stop breastfeeding— be prepared for your milk to come in! However, if you put the baby to the breast for just a little of the colostrum, you might change your mind and decide to breastfeed. This would be great! So, be sure and utilize lactation consultants and nurses to help you with your quest for breastfeeding. They can also answer any questions you may have about changing back to bottle feeding in the future. If you want to go back to bottle feeding and your breastmilk is in, you may decide to pump and bottle feed it to your baby. This is a great alternative to feeding your baby formula, saving you a great deal of money that would be spent on formula in the long run.

Several things to do when you are not breastfeeding are:

- Wear a well-fitting support bra to decrease the chances of stimulation.
- Place ice packs on top of the breasts. This will help with breast swelling and constrict the blood vessels, which will help reduce the swelling and rapid blood supply to the breasts if engorgement is becoming a problem.
- Take a pain reliever, such as acetaminophen, to relieve breast pain. You may already be taking it during your

hospital stay, so you are covered, but if you aren't, just ask your nurse for some. If you have already been discharged from the hospital, be sure you have some at home to use if needed.

- Use clean cold cabbage leaves placed over the breasts and hold them in place with your bra. There are some enzymes in the cabbage leaves which help with milk suppression. Remove the leaves when wilted and replace them with new clean, cold leaves. The coolness of the leaves will help with comfort.

- Avoid warm packs, which increase the blood supply to breasts.

- Avoid direct shower spray of warm water to the breasts. This causes stimulation.

Contrary to what your mother or grandmother will tell you about pills to dry up your milk production, this method is no longer used. The medication used in previous years was found to increase the chances of heart attacks and stroke, so a prescription for this is no longer an option from your doctor.

Circumcisions (The "Boys Only" Club)

This controversial topic has two sides to the circumcision subject of the newborn male baby. It is thought by some, and this includes some medical professionals, that circumcision is an unnecessary elective surgery that is performed on the penis to remove the extra foreskin. With proper education from the parents on good hygiene and performance of good hygiene by the male child later on and into adulthood, there is no need to remove the foreskin. Then there are the others who decided that circumcision has definite health benefits or that due to religious or personal beliefs, circumcisions should be or will be performed.

In 2012, the American Academy of Pediatrics *(AAP)* posted a technical report in their *Pediatrics* journal on the subject of male circumcision. A task force was made up of members of the AAP, the American Academy of Family Physicians *(AAFP)*, the American College of Obstetrics and Gynecology *(ACOG)*, and the Centers for Disease Control and Prevention *(CDC)*. They concluded that factual, current, non-biased information regarding circumcision, along with post-circumcision care instructions, be provided to parents. This allows parents to make an informed decision about whether or not to have a circumcision performed on their baby. They also want benefits and risks presented to parents, so their decision can be weighed based on the correct information given. Information is also given regarding the need to provide educational material to all clinicians who care for newborn baby boys. This will enhance their knowledge base on education, care, and instructions given to parents. Whether or not to have their son circumcised is up to the parents and what they feel is in the baby's best interest— along with personal, cultural, or religious preferences.

According to the task force, the current recommendations are that the benefits of newborn circumcision *outweigh* the risks, and here are the findings:

- To prevent Urinary Tract Infections *(UTIs)*
- To prevent the acquisition *(contracting, catching)* of HIV or sexually transmitted infections
- To prevent the transmission *(passing on)* of HIV and sexually transmitted infections
- To decrease the risk of penile cancer
- That circumcision does not adversely affect the sexual function, sensitivity, or sexual satisfaction in the adult circumcised male.

Not all parents decide to have their boys circumcised. It may be for personal reasons, such as the father or other males in the household are not circumcised, and the baby will not be either. It could be because the parents do not believe the benefits outweigh the risks, deciding against circumcision. There may be many other reasons that help to make up the parent's minds regarding the refusal of circumcision. This is the parent's *right* to decide against the circumcision of their newborn baby boy.

Currently, most infant male circumcisions are performed today using what is called a Plastibell. This small plastic device is made in several sizes to accommodate the glans *(head)* size of the infant male's penis. This device helps to protect the glans of the penis until it is healed. Then the ring around the glans falls off after several days, and the penis finishes healing. For those who decide to proceed with the circumcision, here is some information on how the procedure is performed.

(**_WARNING:_ *This detailed information is graphic and is provided for parents who want to learn how circumcision is performed on their son. Anyone who doesn't want to know the details may skip the next four paragraphs.*)

The pediatrician or other clinician trained in performing the circumcision starts off by having the baby placed in a harness or restraint. This keeps both arms and legs down and out of the way during the sterile procedure. It also keeps him still so he cannot move around while the circumcision is performed. The baby may be given a pacifier and fed several drops of concentrated sucrose solution of up to 2 milliliters. Sucrose is found to have a pain-relieving effect for infants, like being given some Morphine or other pain reliever. It is used frequently during painful procedures such as heel sticks, lab draws, or in this case, circumcisions. The pediatrician, or clinician, will then use a local anesthetic to numb the penis. This is both on the top and bottom, close to his scrotum. They then wait several minutes before proceeding with the procedure to allow the anesthetic to take effect.

Once the anesthesia has taken effect, the pediatrician or clinician will use some small clamps to grasp the skin of the foreskin. Using sterile scissors, the pediatrician clips downward approximately ½ to ¾ centimeters. This will allow more room for the Plastibell to be placed over the glans *(head of the penis)*. Once the Plastibell is in the correct position, a small piece of sterile string is half-knotted loosely and slipped over the glans. When the string is in the correct position to follow the groove on the ring to accommodate the string, the string is then tightened very tightly and tied in a knot. That allows it to cut off blood flow to the upper foreskin tissue. The remaining foreskin tissue is then clipped off around the upper portion of the Plastibell ring around the glans. Once this is complete, the plastic positioning piece used by the pediatrician or clinician is snapped off, and the head of the penis is checked for bleeding after the procedure.

Circumcisions (The "Boys Only" Club)

After completion and the bleeding is minimal or non-existent, the baby is removed from the harness or restraint, diapered, and returned to the parents for continued comfort care. Instructions are then given to the parents for the care of the circumcision until it is healed. Within the next couple of days, if you notice a black ring around the Plastibell ring area, this is normal and not to be concerning. This is the remaining tissue in and around the outer ring where the string has cut off the blood supply. This necrotic *(dead)* tissue will fall off when the ring falls off.

Eventually, over 5-8 days, the necrotic tissue and the Plastibell fall off, leaving a completed circumcised penis. Any remaining edges of the circumcision site may need to heal for another day or two. During the healing period over those 5-8 days, parents or caregivers should look for bleeding, redness, swelling, foul odor indicating infection, or tightening of the ring around the top of the glans. If you notice any of these during your hospital stay, notify your nurse so it can be assessed and treated if needed. And, if you have returned home, notify the pediatrician or primary care physician who will be taking over the baby's care, so that prompt medical attention can be obtained.

Two other devices are still used to remove the foreskin— the Gomco and the Mogen clamp. With these devices, the clamp is placed around the glans of the penis snuggly, and the foreskin is then clipped off. With this method, there is generally a potential for more bleeding. But pressure applied with gauze and the clinician's fingers to the site will usually stop the bleeding. There may be a need for silver nitrate or Gelfoam® gauze tape used to stop the bleeding from the circumcision site if the pressure to the site is unsuccessful. These procedures also leave the head of the penis exposed and raw around the site of foreskin removal, which has more detailed care instructions than with the Plastibell device.

*(**These devices are being used less and less by clinicians who now favor using the Plastibell device.)*

Care of the Circumcision Site

Depending on the type of device used for the circumcision, the pediatrician, nurse practitioner, or postpartum nurse would give certain care instructions to the parents upon completion of the procedure. Be sure someone goes over these care instructions with you and does not just give you a handout. It's important to have verbal education along with paper instructions. The handout should be a reference in case you have forgotten something about the education you were given over the care. Also, if you have forgotten any of it once you have gone home. If you do not get education regarding the care of the circumcision site while in the hospital, you at least have this book to refer back to.

Plastibell

This is an easier type of circumcision to clean, as there is no need to use a lubricant with this device. When changing the diaper, you need to take care with cleaning around the Plastibell with a diaper wipe or soft washcloth with warm water. The best way to clean around the Plastibell is to take your index finger, place it on the side of the shaft, and move the shaft aside slightly. The maneuver essentially shields it with your finger and keeps the wipe from coming in contact with the tip of the glans *(head of the penis)*. Then wipe all along the diaper area on that side and clean thoroughly. Repeat the process on the other side to protect the glans again. Once you have cleaned the entire diaper area, place a new diaper on the baby loosely so the diaper doesn't come in much contact with the exposed tip of the glans. *(**Tape the diaper snugly around the waist, but make sure the diaper is "baggy" around the site of the circumcision.)*

If there's stool in and around the Plastibell ring, here's what you'll do. First, follow the cleaning instructions above to remove as much of the stool as possible from the diaper area. Be sure and leave the dirty diaper under the bottom during this so the diaper can catch any water that flows off your baby. Take a washcloth full of warm water and squeeze it out *over* the top of the Plastibell. This will help rinse out inside the ring and remove the stool without wiping on the sensitive glans. Repeat with another washcloth or two full of water, if necessary, to remove all the stool. Then once the ring is clear, clean around the back portion of the diaper area, as discussed above, remove the old diaper and replace it with a new one.

Mogen or Gomco clamps

The procedure from these two clamps leaves the glans *(head of the penis)* raw and exposed. During the healing time, the glans of the penis will likely stick to any surface coming in contact with it, i.e., the diaper. The glans must be well lubricated to prevent it from sticking to the diaper from some healing drainage and possibly "small amounts" of oozing blood. It can be done with a water-soluble lubricant, such as Vaseline®, and be covered with a small amount of gauze.

Once the whole diaper area is cleaned, gently wash off the exposed glans with a soft washcloth and warm water to remove any remaining urine or stool during cleaning. Or you can clean it like discussed in the previous section on *Plastibell*. *(**Leave the dirty diaper underneath and* *rinse by squeezing warm water from a washcloth.)* Then take a 4 x 4 square of gauze with a pea-sized to grape-sized amount of Vaseline® and lightly rub the gauze together. *(This is, so the Vaseline® is covering a larger area on the gauze.)* Then place it gently over the glans of the penis. Carefully pull the diaper between the legs and fasten it around the waist snugly. But— be sure the diaper area around the circumcision site is "baggy," so there is very little pressure from the diaper against the penis. When making the next diaper change, remove the soiled 4 x 4 gauze, clean the bottom area, and apply a new 4 x 4 with Vaseline® on the glans. Repeat this process for the next 24 hours, then only apply the Vaseline® on the glans before replacing it with a clean diaper while the site is healing. This you will do for the next couple of days. You may see blood spotting on the diaper, but anything less than quarter-sized is okay.

Drainage or oozing from the site

With either procedure, there may be a small amount of oozing or bleeding from the site. As long as it is less than quarter-size, it is normal. You may also notice yellow drainage, especially on the tip of the glans. Unless this has a foul odor, this is *not* an infection. This is *normal* healing drainage. It will dry in and around the site and go away when it is close to healing completely. You may even notice a pinkish salmon color on the glans as well. These are uric crystals from the concentrated urine and are also normal. (**Refer to the section "Diapering Your Baby" under 'Some "Oddities" Found in the Diaper' regarding the pinkish color found on the diaper.)*

Your son may have the procedure in the hospital a few days before discharge, but some are done the morning before discharge. Either way, be sure and watch for any heavier bleeding than normal. If you

Circumcisions (The "Boys Only" Club)

are in the hospital, let your nurse know if you find blood spots that seem to be soaking in the diaper and are larger than a quarter-sized. The pediatrician may order some silver nitrate to be placed on the bleeding site or need to come back in to correct the issue. If you have gone home and noticed the site bleeding more than it should, contact the pediatrician for further instructions— either to come into the office or an urgent care facility.

Watching for the 1st post-circumcision void

After the circumcision, your son may be a little fussy and need extra comfort from you. Over the next several hours, you need to keep a close eye on your baby's diapers and report when you have the 1st urine after the baby's circumcision. This is very important information for the pediatrician. They want to be sure your son can urinate after the circumcision, so report it to your nurse so she can document this on his chart.

Don't be surprised if your son does not pee for a long time— it may be closer to 12-15 hours before your baby has the 1st one. There are a couple reasons why there may be a delay in your son beginning to urinate again. First, you are breastfeeding, and the smaller amount of colostrum may delay having much output— and he doesn't want to pee— *BECAUSE IT HURTS!!!*

Now that your poor little guy had his "weenie whacked," he will pull the pee back whenever he starts urinating. This is because the tip of the glans is raw, and the concentrated urine is hitting the area— and *IT STINGS!!* So— you may find a couple tiny spots of pee, but not a whole lot. This would not count as a wet diaper— yet. Over the next several hours, your son will continue to pee and pull back again— until he cannot hold it any longer! When he does have that first pee, he will have a very large wet diaper that might have very dark urine in it. Now— you can report this void to your nurse.

Yay! The penis still functions as it should, and your son shows he can urinate after the circumcision. He may still hold back on urinating again for the next few diapers until the stinging and soreness lessen. Once it subsides, he will urinate again without it bothering him.

Crying or sleeping... which one is it going to be??

After a baby boy has been circumcised, I found that the baby usually reacts in one of two ways— either *eating* or *sleeping* through the pain. The ones who *sleep* through their pain also become difficult *again* to wake up and feed when it's time to eat. During that time, use the same techniques described under *Q&A on Breastfeeding* for your sleepy baby by waking up your baby to feed. Again, it's hard to wake a sleeping baby, especially if it makes him feel better. But we both know he needs to keep on his feeding schedule as much as possible. Now, for little ones wanting to *eat* through their pain, this is like a "cluster-feeding phase" on day 2. They want to be "permanently attached" to the breast or suck on anything to help soothe them. Sucking, remember, is a comfort measure for babies, and when they are in pain, such as with a circumcision, they sometimes want to suck— *a lot!*

We talked about pacifiers earlier under *Q&A on Breastfeeding*, so using one now for your baby's comfort is still *your* choice. Suppose you decide to allow the baby a pacifier. In that case, the one used during the circumcision may still be available for you in your son's crib. If it was discarded after the circumcision and your hospital does

Circumcisions (The "Boys Only" Club)

not give any extra out, have someone purchase some for you and bring them in if you want one for him. This way, he'll get the comfort he needs, and you won't feel like your nipples will fall off!!

And— if you are bottle feeding, don't be tempted to put a bottle in the baby's mouth whenever he cries. This can lead to overfeeding. If your baby is overfeeding, this can lead to water loss stools, as we discussed in the section, *"So… You Want to Bottle Feed Your Baby."*

Other Topics of Discussion

This section will review several issues concerning parents or healthcare workers. We will review things such as SIDS, co-sleeping, rooming-in, and some general topics for me to address regarding you and your baby. This information is not only for you during your hospital stay; it is also beneficial information for you after you have returned home.

Sudden Infant Death Syndrome (SIDS)

Parents worry about this most concerning issue after their new baby arrives. SIDS can strike at any time within the first year of life but is most prevalent in the first few months of age. The death of an infant with SIDS is unexplainable, meaning they cannot come up with a cause of death. The cause is unknown but is thought to be a defect in the brain that controls breathing and waking from sleep.

One factor of SIDS is believed that babies are subjected to asphyxiation *(smothering)* or strangulation *(choking)*. This is in their sleep environments, whether bedsharing or in their own cribs. Yet there is no definitive proof of the actual cause of death upon the coroner's autopsy. Without proof of strangulation or asphyxiation, most coroner's death certificates are filed as "unknown" or "unspecified."

"Although SIDS rates have declined by more than 50% since the early 1990s, SIDS remains the third-leading cause of infant mortality and the leading cause of post neonatal mortality (28 days to 1 year of age)."

> SIDS and Other Sleep-Related Infant Deaths: Expansion of Recommendations for a Safe Infant Sleeping Environment Pediatrics Nov 2011, 128 (5) e1341-e1367; DOI: 10.1542/peds.2011-2285

Several risk factors have been identified which may contribute to SIDS. They have identified actions you take to lessen the chances for SIDS to affect your baby. *The most* important measure for parents to follow is placing the baby on the back to sleep.

A combination of physical and sleep environment factors can make your baby more vulnerable to SIDS. Still, each child is different, so any combination of these can contribute to SIDS.

Physical factors

- *Brain defects* - Some babies have problems that make them more vulnerable. This is because the breathing and sleep-arousal centers of the brain are not fully mature or functioning properly.

- *Low birth weight* - Premature or Low Birth Weight babies have a higher risk for SIDS. Again, this is because the brain is likely very immature in development. These babies have little or no control over automatic responses to breathing or heart rate.

- *Respiratory infections* - Babies that have recently had a respiratory infection are at greater risk for SIDS, contributing to breathing problems.

Environmental factors

- *Sleeping on sides or stomachs* - Babies may have more difficulty breathing in these positions than on the back.

- *Sleeping on a soft surface* - Fluffy pillows, comforters, or blankets can block the airway, especially if the baby turns over on their stomach to lie face down. Baby can re-breathe carbon dioxide they are exhaling, which also contributes to SIDS.

- *Bed-sharing* - Even though co-sleeping is recommended to reduce the incidences of SIDS, bed-sharing is *not*. Babies cannot move away from a person's body if their face gets buried against them. Since this increases the risk of SIDS, it is *not* recommended for a baby to sleep in any bed with parents, siblings, or family pets.

- *Overheating* - This is another environmental factor that may contribute to SIDS. These babies cannot move away from a person's body or unwrap themselves from a blanket if they get overheated.

Infant risk factors

- *Sex of baby* - male babies are at a slightly higher risk for SIDS than their female counterparts

- *Age of baby* - baby is most vulnerable between 2-4 months of age

- *Race* - it is unknown why, but non-white babies are more vulnerable to developing SIDS

- *Family history* - siblings or cousins of the baby who have died of SIDS increase this baby's risk of having issues too

- *Second-hand smoke* - babies who live with smokers are at a higher risk for SIDS

- *Prematurity* - this also puts your baby at risk for SIDS

Maternal risk factors

Risk factors that put a baby at risk for SIDS are:

- Under the age of 20

- Smokes cigarettes

- Drinks alcohol or uses drugs during the pregnancy and/or after

- Has inadequate or no prenatal care.

Prevention

- *Back to sleep* - Always place the baby on the back to sleep, not the side or stomach, for the first year of life. Don't be concerned with trying to keep your baby on their back. Especially if the baby starts to roll on their own

- *Don't always assume* - Other caregivers may place the baby on the stomach or sides to sleep. So, let your wishes be known to everyone. They must place the baby on their back to sleep at all times.

- *Don't overheat your baby* - Outfit your baby to stay warm with several layers and without a blanket. As a substitute, you can place the baby in one outfit and place a blanket over their body around the waist. Tuck the blanket in on both sides of the mattress to keep it from coming loose.

- *Don't place blankets in the crib/playpen* - When the baby starts moving around in bed more frequently, *forego* placing a blanket around them. Just dress them in several layers. The blanket becomes dislodged easier when tucked in and easily becomes a smothering hazard.

- *Have your baby sleep in the same room* - Ideally, the baby should sleep in the same room with you but in their own crib or sleep surface. Do not place them in bed with you—bed-sharing is *not* "safe" sleeping for your baby, as this puts them at risk for suffocation.

- *Breastfeeding your baby, if possible* - Breastfeeding for at least six months lowers the risk of SIDS-related deaths.

- *Bare baby crib* - It is recommended that when outfitting your baby's crib, you do not place anything in the crib with the baby. This is to protect them. Stuffed toys, bumper pads, loose blankets, baby hats, and pillows should not be placed in the crib. Babies, as they get older, become more active when sleeping and can move around in bed more. Their faces can get tangled in the blankets or "snugged up" to the bumper pads, stuffed toys, or pillows. This causes them to re-breathe the carbon dioxide they exhale, contributing to SIDS.

- *Don't rely on baby monitors* - Some baby monitor companies will advertise the safety of using monitors to reduce the risk of SIDS. The American Academy of Pediatricians discourages using monitors or other devices as ineffective at preventing SIDS. You *can still* use the baby monitor for other needs but don't rely on it for SIDS prevention.

- *Pacifier usage* - Offer the use of a pacifier to your baby. If they're not interested, don't force it. And, if the pacifier falls out of the mouth while sleeping, don't replace it.

- *Immunize baby* - Evidence supports that immunizing your baby decreases the risk for SIDS. However, there is *no* evidence that it puts them at risk by immunizing them.

Co-Sleeping

This differs from bed-sharing in that the baby sleeps in the same room with you, just not in the same bed. According to the American Academy of Pediatricians, co-sleeping in the same room reduces the risk of SIDS by as much as 50%. Separate sleep surfaces are safer than bed-sharing. Should you, or shouldn't you? Is it helpful or harmful? There are definitely two sides to this coin, so we will weigh the pros and cons found about the subject of co-sleeping.

Benefits of co-sleeping

- Learn your baby's feeding cues and can attend to baby quicker; more convenient
- Synchronizing sleep cycles together between mom and baby
- Babies fall asleep easier and go back to sleep easier after waking up
- Helps lead babies to more nighttime sleep over time
- Gives parents a sense of more intimacy with their baby, especially if they are apart during the daytime *(or nighttime if you work nights)*

Cons to co-sleeping

- Less sleep for mom. Baby makes all kinds of noises during sleep, and moms wake up to every little noise
- Less sleep for the baby since moms tend to pick up the baby during first noises *(super-attentive)*, which may make things more difficult for you and the baby to get more sleep

- Less intimacy with your partner. A noisy baby may make getting "in the mood" or concentrating on your partner's needs very difficult

Bed-Sharing

This is a big ol' hot topic of discussion and debate among parents, advocates, and the healthcare community. There are many advocates and studies done about the positive aspects of bed-sharing. Still, there are several out there concerning the dangerousness of it. Which ones are right? Did they do a measurable study, or were the results not conclusive? According to the American Academy of Pediatrics, infants at greater risk for SIDS are between 0-3 months with bed-sharing. Here's a list of recommendations of what not to do when bed-sharing if *you* do decide bed-sharing is the way you want to go:

- No smoking around your baby. This increases exposure to second-hand smoke and puts the baby at risk for SIDS.
- Avoid alcohol, drugs, or over-the-counter medications which might cause you to fall asleep and not awaken easily.
- Do not bed-share on a sofa, recliner, or chair. Risk for baby to suffocate/smother accidentally or become entrapped between cushions, parents, armrests, back of the sofa, etc.
- Do not place the baby on top of a pillow, head on a pillow, or around one. Increases risk of suffocation/SIDS.
- Make sure there's no bedding bunched up around the baby's face.
- Do not swaddle baby while bed-sharing. Increases the baby's

risk of overheating from blankets and parents radiating heat and increases the risk for SIDS.

- Moms and dads, bundle up your very long hair. Increases risk for wrapping around baby's neck.

- Do not bed-share if the parent(s) are obese. Increases the risk for mom and/or dad not to be able to feel how close the baby is to the body, increasing the risk of suffocation.

- Do not breastfeed your baby lying in bed, on a reclining chair, or on a sofa if you are tired and in danger of falling asleep.

Rooming-In During Your Hospital Stay

There seems to be a differing of opinions with regards to rooming-in during your hospital stay. It is shown that rooming-in is beneficial for breastfeeding in general. Babies are put to the breast quicker for feedings, increasing the number of breast feedings and allowing for feeding on demand. Bonding is also established and continued with rooming-in, which benefits the mother-baby couplet. It is also proven that babies are less likely to develop newborn complications and have less risk for SIDS.

Although rooming-in has become the norm in the hospital setting, there should still be some leeway in the hospital policies allowing exceptions. Alison Steube, MD, an assistant professor of Obstetrics and Gynecology at the University of North Carolina School of Medicine, puts rooming-in in the correct perspective. "*Rooming-in should be the norm, but flexibility is needed to individualize care when circumstances require it,*" she said. What is being said here is that "Yes," rooming-in is good and should be done routinely in the hospital setting. However, certain situations need to be "*taken into account*" or addressed, which might benefit some separation time between mother and baby.

When babies remain in the room continuously for several days, some issues happen more frequently with rooming-in than not:

- Baby knows you are near "at all times." They can hear you talking and smell you in the room, so they know you are nearby. If the baby wants to be held "at all times" or put to the breast continuously, this might interfere with the mother's sleep. Suppose she is already sleep deprived before entering the hospital. In that case, it gets even worse after the baby is born with continued rooming-in. Mom then goes home even more sleep-deprived, and "anything goes" if it will allow for some sleep.

- Sometimes, sending the baby to the nursery for a few hours can allow the mom some much-needed sleep. She might otherwise not get this with her baby continually fussing. With rooming-in and mom having sleep deprivation, there is an increased risk of mom falling asleep with the baby in her arms and dropping the baby. There have been countless hospital incidents with babies being dropped from the bed to the floor. Also, many documented accounts of these incidents have been made since the "Baby-Friendly Initiative" was introduced into the hospital setting.

- Baby develops a "bed allergy" to sleeping in the crib, even if it is next to mom. Baby falls asleep while being held or finished feeding, then when placed back into the crib, begins to fuss and cry until held again. This is what we lovingly call a "bed allergy." Baby "wants those nice warm arms versus that cold hard bed." Therefore, they will fuss every time you put them back into the crib. They may fuss and root around for food, then when it's offered again, the baby falls back to sleep, is put back in the crib, and the process starts all over again. This can be extremely exhausting— at least until your breastmilk comes in, but it may not stop— even then.

- Baby wants only mom to hold them and will cry until they get what they want. Doesn't matter who attempts to quiet or soothe the baby. The baby fusses, cries, or gets downright angry until mom holds them again. Sorry, Dad, but the baby has been with mom continuously for nine months, so naturally, mom is *the* #1 person the baby wants "right now." Unfortunately, this could lead to unsafe co-sleeping on the mom's part because of the exhaustion she's experiencing due to all the baby's demands.

- From sheer exhaustion, the mom might be tempted to place the baby in bed with her, essentially bed-sharing, which puts the baby at risk for SIDS.

- Mom may become sick after delivery, and her caring for the baby may not be possible at this time. She may need additional medical support and rest to recuperate, and caring for the baby might put her at additional personal risk.

- Mom may fall asleep just from breastfeeding due to the cathartic effect of the natural oxytocin release, which causes sleepiness and relaxation.

Some hospitals across the country are reviewing or changing rooming-in protocols. This is due to documented cases of falls or near-falls of infants when mothers had fallen asleep holding them.

Unfortunately, not all hospitals are doing away with this practice and continue to require babies to room-in with their mothers. If the hospital you deliver at *does not* allow the baby to go to the nursery, insist on someone watching your baby for you so you can rest. Especially if you have no family or friends around you to help. In times of exhaustion, sleep deprivation, narcotic pain management, etc., continue to force the issue with your nurse, nurse manager, house supervisor, and so on up the ladder, if necessary. You have a *right* to have a safe environment for you and your baby, especially when you are at risk of falling asleep while holding/nursing your baby. The other part of your argument can be about going home *too exhausted* to cope. You've been through a lot in just a few short days and deserve to rest while having staff watch your baby for you. Going home exhausted will not help you recover well and leads to baby blues or postpartum depression quicker than otherwise normal. So, insist on the staff helping you out so you can have a much better transition to home life with your new baby and family.

Anxiety Around the Baby

Your baby is crying, and you don't know what to do. What is the baby crying for? Sometimes parents get really anxious around their babies, especially first-time parents. This frequently happens with new parents because they constantly learn or have questions or concerns about many things. It's also normal behavior with experienced parents, which can be an issue when they are anxious around the baby.

Babies sense when the person is holding or near them but anxious or tense. If they sense this, they may get tense and distressed just because *you* are. Then they start fussing or crying even more, which gets you even more anxious or tense, and the baby gets even fussier— and so on and so forth!

It may seem hard to do when you start feeling this way but try to remain calm and soothing during this stressful time for your baby. This will help them to start relaxing and winding down. Talking to the baby soothingly, no matter what words are coming out of your mouth, can not only help calm the baby down but also help calm you down.

If you cannot calm down around the baby, it's okay to step out of the room or even out of the house if you have returned home, to help you calm down. If you are still in the hospital, step out of the room if someone is there to watch the baby. Or you can ask for some help from the nurse. It's not good to continually be around a baby who is distressing to you until you can calm yourself down. You'll keep "feeding" off each other and escalate the situation, which could put you in the perfect position to cause harm to your baby. (**Which I know you don't want to do— but situations like this can be a precursor to child abuse.)

If the anxiety around the baby does not subside, it might be beneficial for you to talk to your doctor. They can assist you by finding something to help manage your anxiety. You may need medication to help you get "over the hump" until things smooth out for you. Don't be reluctant to enlist help from family, friends, or other caregivers. They can take over for a little while so you can get away for some *"me time,"*— which will also go a long way in helping to reel in the anxiety.

Your Discharge from the Hospital

Several things must be finished before you are discharged from the hospital. Filling out the birth certificate, the baby having labs and hearing screenings, and car set check needs completing. Once these tasks are completed, or anything else you must do, you can take your newly expanded family home.

Birth Certificate/Affidavit

Your hospital will give you a form to fill out for the birth certificate, which will be filed with the state after your discharge. This will need to be completed before you go home. You may have a form that will be the original sent to the state, or you may have a worksheet to fill out, and the hospital secretary will type it up for you. In this digital age, hospitals usually provide a worksheet for parents to fill out. Then a unit secretary produces a state-issued typed copy for parents to review before the final filing. The typed copy is returned to the parents to ensure everything on the birth certificate is correct. They must initial and sign the copy before the secretary submits it to the state. This ensures no errors are on the birth certificate, which can be difficult to correct once the state has processed it. *(**Red tape… and lots of it!)*

Suppose the parents are not married, which happens with increasing frequency in this day and age. In that case, an affidavit is also produced to accompany the birth certificate when it is filed. This is signed by both parents in the company of two hospital witnesses, as this is a legal document.

Sometimes, there are incidents where the baby's mother is still married to her husband— but the husband is not the baby's father. When this happens, it can be easily remedied when all parties are aware of the situation and cooperative. There is a section on an affidavit for the husband to fill out stating he is not the father of this child and gives up all rights to this baby. This has to happen because, in many states, if the husband and wife are still married at the time of the baby's conception or birth, the husband is automatically declared the baby's father. This is regardless of actual paternity. The affidavit is a legal document where the husband can easily declare he is not the father, and the baby's father can declare he is.

In the situation the husband would be required to sign over his rights to the baby, but is not cooperative, absent, and/or will not sign the affidavit, you would need to go through other legal means. This is when you contact an attorney to get a court order. Then the father can be legally declared the father on the birth certificate, and the husband declared not the father.

Again, ever state is different on their requirements. If your state doesn't handle it this way, ask you nurse how you should proceed. If she is unsure or doesn't know, contact your local Division of Family Services or an attorney on how to proceed.

Paternity Testing

There may be a dispute over who might be the baby's father. The father denies paternity, or there is a question as to who specifically the baby's father is if the mother had several partners. At some time, a paternity test will need to be completed to determine paternity. This is helpful for the mother to know who would be financially responsible for the baby— especially if the mother and father are no longer together. It is also helpful to determine the baby's lineage for a medical history that might affect the baby later on— heart disease, diabetes, and a host of other diseases or disease processes.

Some hospitals in the United States do not do in-house paternity testing at the time of delivery or any time during your stay but may help you collect blood or buccal *(cheek)* swabs for private DNA tests. Then some hospitals will charge for DNA testing, which may cost much more than testing through other services. Some insurance companies may cover this cost, but you need to check with the company first to be sure.

If you find yourself in this situation and do not know if you can do this at the time of delivery, check with your obstetrician or the hospital directly to see what options are available or how you can get testing done for your baby.

Car Seat Check

Before your baby can go home, the car seat you will place your baby in must be checked to be sure it is safe to transport your baby home and anywhere needed in the future. This is a necessary national safety feature most, if not all, hospitals today complete before dismissal.

The hospital staff checks your car seat to make sure it is up-to-date and there are no pending recalls. This is done with the National Highway Traffic Safety Administration *(NHTSA)*, the country's national registry. If there are recalls on the make and model of the car seat, you will be notified by your nurse. If the recall is significant but might have a workaround, you may still be able to use the carrier safely. But you can choose whether to use the car seat or purchase a new one. For instance, some recalls were because the carrier and base were not staying latched, which could cause them to separate upon impact in a crash and put babies in danger. In this event, your carrier could still be used without the base. Once the manufacturer replaces the latch mechanism, the carrier and base can be used together again. Many different recalls can be found on the registry. If the recall is significant and cannot be repaired, a new car seat must be purchased before discharge.

Car seats are good for 6 years, so any older ones could risk your baby's safety. If left in the car outside continuously, they would be subjected to heat and cold for several years. Because of this, the plastic frame of the car seat begins to become brittle after 6 years. It can break easily, thus not providing a safe and secure seat for your baby in the event of a car accident. Also, even mild-impact crashes at 35 mph will require the replacement of the car seat.

It is also good to check and ensure the car seat is registered with your current residence. This is so you can be notified of any recalls later if one is on the seat. You can usually register directly with the manufacturer on the company website. If not, you can send the registration card in by mail. Be sure to contact the manufacturer if you move when you are still using the car seat or will be before the expiration date. *(**Some parents may move in between children and still be using the original car seat from the first child but forget to make the change with the manufacturer.)*

It is important *not* to purchase an unknown car seat from a garage sale, consignment shop, or thrift store. Even though parents want to save money when purchasing baby needs, the car seat is one you *do not* want to compromise on. You will have no idea whether that car seat has ever been in a car accident, plus you have no way of knowing if the seller is being honest about whether it has or hasn't. If it had been in one, you are now compromising your baby's safety, as car seats are only good for one accident before they must be replaced. If, by chance, you get one from a trusted source, say, a family member or close friend, the decision is up to you if you want to use it. When you want to save money on baby things, such as baby clothes, blankets, toys, etc., by all means— do so. Those things can be safely reused— but please don't do it with a car seat.

As part of the safety, car seats are also checked to see if anything is "added on" to the carrier. Baby toys, cushioned or padded backings, headrests, and anything that did not come with the car seat are considered an "add-on" and not recommended to be placed on the car seat when in use in the vehicle. These "add-on(s)" have not been crash-tested with the car seat, therefore, can compromise the *safety* of the car seat itself. Most infant car seat carriers today already come with a padded back and headrest, which are okay. These have been tested by the manufacturer for safety with the car seat.

Added cushioned back and headrests that did not come with the car seat are *not* recommended. It is safer not to use these since they have not been tested. However, you may receive this as a gift, and if so, thank them kindly, but ask if you can exchange it for something else you need for the baby. If you let the gift giver the reasons "why," they should understand and be okay with the exchange. If you do not have a back with a headrest, a safe option would be to use a couple of baby blankets rolled up and place them on both sides of the baby inside the carrier. This way, if you are in an accident the blankets will "fly" out of the car seat and not compromise the baby's safety within the car seat.

Toys attached to the car seat handle for the baby to play with can become projectiles within the car in the event of an accident, harming your baby or any other passenger in the vehicle. If you are carrying your baby in the carrier, say to the pediatrician's office or the store, you may attach the toys during this time. But be sure to remove them when placing your baby back in the car— before you drive away. We only want your baby to stay safe.

Screenings for the Baby

Several screenings take place before your baby is discharged from the hospital. Bilirubin levels, hearing screening, PKU testing, and CCHD testing are performed right before discharge. We will go over each one to give you a better understanding of why these are performed on your baby.

Bilirubin levels

As discussed in the *"Skin Color and Conditions"* section under *Jaundice*, labs are drawn on all babies just before discharge or within 48 hours of birth. By testing all babies before discharge, we are ensuring no babies are missed that may have become jaundiced enough to now require phototherapy. Some babies do not become visibly jaundiced enough to alert their caregiver that the bilirubin levels may be too high and need to be treated. Or, their skin color is dark enough, which may make it difficult to visualize any jaundice. Testing every baby before discharge helps to eliminate the chance for a jaundiced baby to be dismissed before phototherapy is initiated— especially when vitally needed. Remember, if bilirubin levels become too high and are not treated, this can be deadly to your baby. *(**Refer to "Jaundice"* *under the 'Skin Color Conditions' then "Color changes" above.)* As a reminder—jaundice can slowly develop up to two weeks after delivery. So be mindful of watching for the signs of yellowing skin from the face down to the feet. Also, watch for the yellowing of the whites of the baby's eyes. Contact your pediatrician if you notice these after you have been discharged.

Critical congenital heart defects (CCHD) testing

This very simple screening, completed within 5-10 minutes, can help detect whether your baby might have a congenital heart defect. An otherwise healthy-looking baby may have a cardiac issue that can worsen over time if not treated promptly. Therefore, the test is performed prior to discharge.

A pulse oximeter is wrapped around the palm of the right hand and the right or left foot of the baby when they are quiet or sleeping. This detects the oxygenation of the blood, like the one placed on you during your hospitalization. After a few minutes, we will get a reading of the blood oxygenation levels of your baby. If your baby is showing a negative result for a cardiac issue, the readings are 95% or higher, with less than a 3% difference between both readings. They would have a positive result if they saturate less than 95% or if there is a significant difference of 4% or more. This could indicate your baby may have a cardiac issue, and further testing would be needed.

When the testing is done and a baby shows a positive result, the nurse or practitioner will usually retest after an hour. This is to ensure the baby does not have a "false" positive result before jumping right into testing. False positives can result from a baby's cold hands or feet, a crying baby, or improper pulse oximeter attachment. The baby would be re-screened in one hour and a 3rd time if the 2nd screening is also positive. If there are 3 positive screenings and your baby is not immediately symptomatic of a cardiac issue, the pediatrician will refer them to a neonatologist or pediatric cardiologist for further testing. If the screening result is less than 90% or greater than a 3% difference and the baby is symptomatic, immediate testing and treatment will be initiated. When hospitals cannot provide the needed care for babies, in this situation, they will be transferred to a tertiary pediatric care center. There they can get immediate additional testing, and treatment can be performed.

This is a quick, easy screening for several major cardiac issues, but it is *only a screening*. This does not guarantee there is not another possible cardiac issue that may not be detected early on. This screening only tests seven major cardiac issues requiring immediate testing and treatment. Still, some other cardiac issues could also be detected but might not need addressing immediately. Your nurse or physician will go into more detail about your baby's situation and only act promptly if there is cause for concern.

Hearing screening

This screening is used to detect if your baby may have a hearing problem. If that is the case, the screening can help jump-start the process early for follow-up with a pediatric audiologist. Early detection of a hearing problem benefits your baby's language and communication development. Treatment can begin earlier rather than later by further testing and pinpointing your baby's hearing loss. Instead of having a frustrated 2-year-old who cannot communicate with those around them, you can get a hearing problem detected well before that age. Then treatment can be started *before* communication can become a problem.

Hospitals use two testing methods for hearing screenings— OAE (*otoacoustic emissions*) and ABR (*auditory brainstem response*). OAE is tested using a small probe placed in the ear. Sounds are transmitted into the probe, and a response of the hair cells of the cochlea is measured. When hearing is detected, these hair cells in the inner ear send signals to the brain through nerve pathways. With ABR testing, electrodes are held in place with sticky tabs on the skull, and "sound" is transmitted into the ear. It records the baby's response to the sound through brain waves, and the response is measured. Both screenings are easy to complete and do not harm the baby.

Again, this is a *screening*— so one failed hearing screening does not necessarily indicate your baby has a hearing problem. Sometimes OAE testing is done too early, or the baby may still have some fluid or vernix in the ear canal. Either one can cause a false "failed" test. Re-testing is usually done to determine if the first test is accurate before a referral to an audiologist is made.

PKU (phenylketonuria) testing/state testing

This blood test is performed to detect whether or not your baby's body can break down the amino acid *(phenylalanine)* found in protein feedings. If the phenylalanine cannot be broken down and continues to build up in the body over time, it can cause several developmental and mental issues. This is an inherited disorder passed on from *both* parents to their children. (**Both parents are carriers of the gene.) If only one parent passes on the gene, the baby then becomes a carrier but does not have PKU.

How the testing is done— a nurse places a few drops of your baby's blood *(from a heal stick)* on a special paper for testing. This paper is then sent to the state agency lab for testing to be completed. If the results show a positive result for PKU, your pediatrician or PCP will provide further diagnostic testing to determine if the initial testing results are accurate.

If your baby does have PKU, you will be notified by the state agency completing the testing. The state agency may pass the results directly to your healthcare provider *(pediatrician or primary healthcare physician)*. Then the doctor's office would notify you of the results. They will provide or refer you for additional testing to determine PKU severity. Then dietary changes will need to be made specifically for your baby. Along with dietary changes, routine frequent blood testing will be performed to test phenylalanine levels. These will continue throughout your child's lifetime.

There are several other tests the states run along with the PKU test. According to the US Department of Health and Human Services' National Institutes of Health, all 50 states and Puerto Rico test for a minimum of 29 different health conditions— some states test for more. For instance, in Missouri, where I live, there are 70 different ones tested for. This gives physicians a jump start on treating or managing these other health conditions and having good long-term outcomes for all babies.

Blood testing/typing

Generally, babies are not routinely tested to determine their blood type before discharge from the hospital. However, babies whose mother is Rh-negative will have the cord blood tested to see if the baby shows up Rh-positive. This is to let the obstetrician know whether the mother needs a RhoGAM® or Rhophylac® shot when she is Rh-negative. This is so she has no blood-related issues with her next baby.

If a baby is found to be O positive when the blood is checked, there is a Coombs test run. If the Coombs test returns positive, the mother's antibodies can attach themselves to the baby's red blood cells and cause them to break down more quickly. Thus it can cause even more red blood cells for the liver to break down into bilirubin and for the body to get rid of, putting the baby at greater risk. This can cause two things for the baby— anemia and jaundice. So when the lab results come back with the baby's Coombs and the baby is positive, it will alert the nurse to watch your baby closely. Your baby is at greater risk of developing one or both issues. She will look for these symptoms:

- Yellowing skin and eyes
- Hypotonia *(limp arms and legs)*
- Lethargy *(sleeping too much, little to no activity)*

She will then notify the pediatrician, if needed, for a treatment plan. Your nurse should educate you about blood testing and watch for the same signs, which can be treated while the baby is still in the hospital. Your baby's nurse should also educate you to watch for this once you go home, as the baby can develop jaundice after discharge. If not, then at least we discussed it here. *(**See "Jaundice" under "Skin Color Conditions", then scroll down to "Color Differences.")*

The "OTHER" Topics

This section may become what I look at as potential problems, and you may find yourself faced with any of them during your hospital stay. These are not care-related issues, per se, but they can impact your recovery or when you go home. Or— they might be just a few minor issues that might bother you or your spouse/significant other. Let's discuss a few potential issues and see if being proactive can make a difference.

Visitors, Visitors, Visitors...

Everyone has been anticipating the baby's birth for some time now and cannot wait to see the little bundle of joy, which is great, wonderful, and spectacular!!! And, of course, you as parents want to show off our prodigy with the *entire world* (or at least with everyone you know. . .) However, visitors sometimes do not think to call before they show up to ensure you are ready for them. They may not even check if it is convenient for you to receive them. They show up and expect you to welcome them with open arms— and you do! "Oh, what's one more visitor." Go ahead— and let them in— but trust me when I say— you may *regret* it later.

Think in advance, long before you head to the hospital, about how this might all go. If you are scheduled to be induced or have a cesarean section on a pre-appointed day, you may not be able to fall asleep. Your brain doesn't want to shut down the night before because you anticipate the coming event and may get behind on much-needed rest. How about— if you start going into labor or your water breaks, you may be in for several long hours before your baby arrives. Heaven forbid any of this happens in the early or late evening or after you have just gone to bed for the night. And this is all after you have been up since early morning.

Suppose you're already exhausted and have multiple hours added to your schedule with your labor and/or delivery. In that case, you are already starting to get way behind. Next, you will have broken sleep, taking care of yourself and taking care of and feeding your newborn— *if you can sleep at all.* Now that you are adrenalin rushed with all your excitement about having your baby. Add some more hours for all the visitors to come in and see you and the new baby. They don't all come in at once. NO-O-O-O... they come in one... right after... the other, so it's continuous for hours on end. Kinda seeing where I am going with this??

When the exhaustion finally hits you, it hits you hard!! But you don't get any reprieve because now the baby is:

- Not sleeping very long and keeping you awake
- Demanding to breastfeed
- Crying because she wants to constantly be held and doesn't want to lie in her crib
- Crying because he needs a diaper change
- Crying because his little penis hurts from the circumcision
- Crying for something to constantly suck on
- Crying because they have a tummy ache from the formula,
- Crying because they need to burp

The list can go on and on and on. Add to it the new guidelines for many hospitals for babies rooming in with their mothers, and you *can't* send your baby to the nursery so you can get some sleep. Now your pain meds aren't working very well because you are exhausted and can't get any sleep. Again, the list can go on and on *ad nauseam.*

Will all those well-meaning visitors deal with what you are now dealing with when they go home later??? Have some of those visitors who have children forgotten how restrictions on visitors in the past allowed them to get some sleep? How about sending the baby to the nursery when they wanted— and feeding them sugar water bottles after breastfeeding when babies were still hungry? With all the changes over the years from *then* to *now,* your parents, grandparents, or older visitors may have forgotten or don't know that it's not the same for you as it was for them. Heaven forbid they don't care. Or your younger visitors think this is entertainment time— and you and the new baby "are the entertainment!!" Now they come in and stay, and stay, and stay… and STAY… *FOR HOURS!!!* They think it's party time… so let's party!

It's *okay* to limit your visitors. Tell them not to come to see you and the baby right away. In fact, don't even tell anyone when you are heading to the hospital. This is your special time with your spouse, significant other, or support person. Take your time to enjoy this event without sharing it with everyone in person— just yet. Share it on social media, emails, FaceTime, Skype, or whatever you have— but only when you are ready to. In fact, have your spouse/significant other/support person do this for you so you can rest.

You need this time to adjust to your newborn and new family, so take all the time you need. And— if any of your family and friends become offended that you have put them off, for the time being, just remember— they all waited nine months to see the new baby. Just. Like. You. It will not hurt them to wait a while longer for you to rest and adjust to your new family. I always say, "If they get *mad*… they can get *glad* in the same pants they got *mad* in." It is your right to say, "No visitors— I need some sleep," or "We are having a rough time today— can you come back tomorrow?" Don't feel as if it is your responsibility to "entertain the masses" and cater to their wishes and whims. In reality, shouldn't it be the other way around? They should be thinking of you and your baby's and family's needs— and cater to you all instead.

So, with that said, think long and hard before you let every Tom, Dick, and Harriet visit you in the hospital. Once those few potential sleep intervals between the baby's care and your care are gone while you are in the hospital— they are gone for good. Then in a few days, you head home, and you will be so sleep-deprived you cannot tell if you are coming or going. Oh, you'll survive it— other people managed to do it— but is it worth it in the long run???

Sick Visitors

Regarding your visitors— don't allow them to visit you while sick!! This is considered a "well" floor at the hospital, so you don't want them to expose you and your newborn to cold, flu, chicken pox, etc. (**And— *the hospital staff certainly do not want to be exposed either.*)

During the official flu season, visitors with any signs or symptoms of the flu will not be allowed to visit. It is recommended that only essential persons to the mother's well-being be there. This follows the CDC guidelines during the flu season, which runs from October thru the end of March, to prevent transmission to the mother or baby. Also, children approximately 13 years or younger will not be allowed in unless they are siblings with no signs of illness. Since children come in constant contact with other children and can contract or pass on the flu easily, they will not be allowed to visit. (**Generally, this ban does not take full effect unless there is a documented local influenza virus outbreak. However, some facilities might impose the ban regardless.)*

But— this does not only mean the flu. This covers *anything* that could be passed on to the mother or baby. It can be anywhere from a simple cold to any highly contagious virus. Parechovirus, COVID-19, RSV *(Respiratory syncytial virus)*, influenza, and rhino/enterovirus *(common cold)* numbers are rising. They have been more prevalent for newborns and young infants in 2022. This is partly due to the lifting of the masking bans within the past year. And also due to decreased quarantining when the outbreaks of COVID-19 began waning. There has been a vast surge in hospitalizations of infants and children since early 2022 as these diseases flourished. Adults have also been affected, as our body's immunity levels have taken a nosedive due to protection via masking. Once those masks came off, our bodies were trying to rebuild our immune systems. So we passed around bacteria and viruses right and left, infecting those around us, including the most vulnerable people.

As a mother, you want what's best for your baby and yourself. Rightly so! So, placing a "no visiting" or "minimal visiting" ban on your family and friends may be what you need to do for now. This is to protect yourself and your newborn(s); they should understand that. But if you allow the visitors, we want all our patients to be protected. So be vigilant in screening your visitors before they come to visit. If they are sick or have been in contact with anyone sick, do not let them visit you or the baby until they are well. They certainly should not bring children with them showing signs of illness or have been exposed to other children who have been ill. Coughing, sneezing, congestion, nausea and vomiting, diarrhea, fever, spots on the skin, rashes, and sore throat are all signs and symptoms of illness. It doesn't matter how minor the symptoms may be. If someone visits you and shows any of these signs, ask them to leave. If you do not wish your sick visitor to leave, they must wear a hospital facemask and wash their hands. It would be best if the sick individual stayed at the perimeter of the room. Do not let them get close to you, your baby, or your significant other. You don't want them to pass anything to *any* of you.

For the health of you and your new family, it's important to be aware of any sick individuals coming into the hospital. If they are thinking of you and your new family, they should not be coming to the hospital if they are sick or showing signs of sickness. They expose you and your family and the nursing staff/doctors, exposing the other mothers and babies on the unit, along with their families. Also, once you have returned home and if you allow visitors at that time, be sure anyone who will hold the baby washes their hands thoroughly. And— NO kissing the baby. This includes you, your significant other, and any children in the household, which can be very hard for you all to do. RSV *(Respiratory syncytial virus)* has been transmitted by something as simple as a touch or kiss. This is so innocent and unintended by anyone who would come in contact with the baby— especially wanting to show their love and affection. Be sure everyone is washing their hands and cleaning surfaces in high-traffic areas.

(**Parents, I hesitate to remove this particular section from the book. One day, hopefully soon, there will not be so much of a national issue with the numbers of very sick infants and children due to weakened immune systems. People will start building up immunities again and lessen, but not eliminate, the transmission of major viruses and bacterial infections. RSV, influenza, parechovirus, etc., continue to be prevalent in infants and small children hospitalized because it is so contagious and devastating

to these little bodies. Be your baby's advocate in making sure anyone coming in close contact with the baby to wash hands and refrain from kissing them. They have to build up their own immunities, which will take a long while, so protect your little bundles. Hopefully, this will cease to be an issue one day, and we can return to a "new" norm with visitors again, like before the pandemic hit.)

Inexcusably Pushy Visitors

It's only natural that people want to come to the hospital to see you and the new baby. They've been waiting a long time, too, waiting "with bated breath," but sometimes people get a little overzealous in their quest to see this new baby. Grandparents can be the most exasperating when it comes to their grandchild.

I was all for visitors coming to see mom and baby, but when it came to ignoring what was being asked of them or getting rude to the nursing staff— that's where I drew the line. I couldn't tell you how many times I would run across the patient's mother, aunt, sister, or best friend who insisted that they were to be in the delivery room with the soon-to-be-mom. In reality, the soon-to-be-mom had no intention of having other people in the room beside the dad. I even called security on some people because a situation escalated, and the visitor verbally abused staff. Unfortunately, today, we are a society of "*ME, ME, ME.*" Some people think, "If I want something, I can get it without following the rules— *and* if I complain long and loud enough, I will get what I want no matter what!!"

One of the many issues we face in the hospital is family members or close friends *pushing* their way in to be with mothers and fathers-to-be during the baby's birth. Or to access the patient's room before recovery is complete because they can't seem to wait any longer. Unfortunately, in today's society, we have a lot of people out there who don't know *limits* or *boundaries*. They will try to push their way into the delivery room or take over in the days after the delivery. They think they can bully others, such as nurses, doctors, or other hospital staff, into letting them do what they want. This is regardless of the rules or regulations the hospital has in place. Those rules and regulations are in place to provide a safe delivery environment and maintain the health of the mother and baby during their hospital stay.

Family and friends tend to forget they are in a hospital setting during the birth and recovery of a baby. In the normal course of a hospital visit, they wouldn't push their way into the post-surgical area after a loved one's surgery, would they? No— they would wait until the hospital staff would tell them it was okay to "come in now" once everything was completed. What makes delivering a baby any different? I'll tell you— a new baby is now involved, and according to these types of people, they think "all bets are off," and they don't have to abide by any hospital's or nurse's or doctor's rules.

If you want others in the delivery room with you *(except during a cesarean section)*, there may be a limit to how many can be there. The decision would be up to the hospital's protocols, and also with the doctors, on the specific number who can bear witness to the event. If you do not know what will or won't be allowed— ask your nurse, and she will tell you. When you know what is okay and what is not, you can decide who you want to be with you and your significant other— *or* if you want *no one* to be present. Be sure and share those wishes and rules with everyone who might be there waiting for the delivery. This way, they will already know what is expected of them.

And speaking of decisions— regardless of what others want, it is ultimately your decision if *you* even want them in the room with you! Trust me when I say some may try and bypass all the rules *or* your preference— and sneak into the room anyway. I have seen this happen repeatedly. Sometimes they get away with it because the staff's attention is focused elsewhere. Still, there are times when they are prevented from making entry into your room, and disorderly conduct begins. Hospital staff will have no reservations about contacting security if a scene is started on the unit, especially today. With all the media news on violent hospital patients and visitors in the past few years, the hospital staff has been assaulted and severely injured because of them. So the staff is becoming increasingly intolerant of misbehavior. The staff's safety and the safety of other patients, including you and your baby, are now at the forefront of hospital care.

When it comes to visitors— and that means everyone except the persons wearing a matching band to the baby— they don't really matter to the nursing staff. Don't get me wrong— the staff is very cordial to the visitors and laughs and jokes with them when they are present. Still, they can be disruptive to you and your baby's recovery. The only people that matter to the staff are you, the baby, and the father/significant other. They are here to ensure you and the baby are healthy, and things are going well for you all as a family until you are discharged. You and the baby are our #1 priority, not the visitors, so whatever you decide to do during your stay is all that matters.

Let your staff know if you don't want visitors while in the hospital. If you don't want certain people to come, tell those people in advance of your hospital stay so they know ahead of time not to come. This is supposed to be a very happy and exciting time for you and everyone involved, and nobody wants to take away the enjoyment of anyone during the birth of your baby. Just be sure everyone waiting for the birth knows there *are* ground rules, just like in any other hospital setting. We expect them to be followed without causing any undue stress on you, your support person, or the staff. So— let's all get excited and have a happy and healthy delivery, and everyone can celebrate!!

Passing the Baby Around "Like a Football"

This was briefly touched on in the Q&A section on *"Other Breastfeeding Concerns."* Still, I felt it was another area needing to be discussed in a little more detail. This also concerns you having visitors and everyone wanting to hold the baby.

This is a common thread among most babies from many years of observation. Visitors come in to see you and the new baby, and the first thing they all *(or most)* want to do is "get their hands on the baby." Grandma wants to hold the baby; Grandpa wants to hold the baby. Uncles and aunts, brothers and sisters, etc., want to hold the baby. But what happens when everyone, or nearly everyone, holds the baby for— say— 10 minutes each? Finding that out would be for the parents later that evening or nighttime. That's when you might find your little one has gotten pretty fed up with the day's events— in the form of crying their little heads off. Why are they doing that, you ask? Well, here's a little secret— the baby is *overstimulated*.

One of my favorite nurses and colleague had a really good analogy. She used to tell this to all her patients, and I began doing the same in my nursing practice. She used to say, "Imagine every person who came in the room and held the baby gave you a hard hug for about 10 minutes each. You would be sore— and irritated, wouldn't you? So that is just what would happen to the baby, with everyone coming in to hold them." There's a lot of rationale and insight behind those statements, so let's break it down just a little bit.

First of all, your baby had not been touched for roughly nine months. *(Give or take a little.)* They've been in your womb all nice, warm, and cozy; haven't had anyone "touching them" or "messing with them" that whole time. Then they are born and encounter a lot of stimulation— just in the first few hours. That includes the nurses assessing routinely, changing diapers frequently, bathing, measuring, etc. Then comes the doctors— and the visitors. With an immature nervous system, all the visitors and staff have now overstimulated this baby. Not just a little— quite a lot. So— what does the baby do to try to release some of the pent-up stimulation? *Cry*— uncontrollably. The second line of thought is that the baby is *sore* from all the holding. Those 10-minute "hugs" have made their little body sore *everywhere*, so they now hurt all over. That would be like you just worked out for the first time in a while, and now you're sore all over. The same principle is there.

Nothing like having a crying baby that makes your first night into parenthood difficult. Here you are, already exhausted and looking forward to getting a little sleep after your very busy day— and you must try and calm your baby down. But— to no avail. If you find yourself in this mess, just remember *"The 5 S's", Swaddling, Shushing, Swinging, Side or Stomach, and Sucking.* Start working your way down this list to see which one might help you out. Hopefully, one of them will.

Unfortunately, there is nothing that can be done about all of the staff handling the baby frequently— but you can control the visitors. My recommendation to combat this from happening to your little one would be to limit the number of people holding the baby and limit the amount of time those designated people hold them. Just inform everyone that only a select few will hold the baby briefly. If they ask why, tell them. They should honor your wishes if you explain what was discussed here. Again, the truth is that not one person visiting will be dealing with the baby later tonight if they get cranky and cannot be consoled. You will be. You must be your baby's advocate and your own since this can affect you both. If a visitor gets upset they can't hold the baby, even after you have told them why you are limiting it, then you can use my old adage, *"They can get glad in the same pants they got mad in."* And here's one I used with my little ones when they were babies, *"Don't wake a sleeping baby."*

Babies need to get acclimated to their new surroundings, their new world. But this needs to happen a little at a time, not hitting them like a tidal wave. Let them adjust slowly— and after a few days, they may tolerate being held a little more than they have been.

Social Media

After the delivery and recovery are completed, you share your news with everyone. Dad may tell those waiting at the hospital or with text messages if not present. However, you may have to relay your instructions to family and friends on the social media platforms they can or can't use. Also, what information they can or cannot pass on to others.

During the excitement, everyone else wants to share the news of your baby's birth, but do you want that to happen? Shouldn't you be the one to decide if you want that information posted on Facebook, Twitter, Instagram, Skype, or what have you? Or if you want to be the ones to post it out there yourselves? Or if you even *want* to post it at all? Since this is your "special" newsworthy event, I believe you should be the one to post or decide where or if you want it posted.

This might be another thing you need to discuss with your family, friends, and associates about your personal decisions to post anything without your permission— even through texts. Be sure to share those choices with everyone unless you are okay with anyone or everyone passing on the good news.

Generational Pictures

When your baby is born, you may have your parents, grandparents, great-grandparents, or even great-great-grandparents around. It would be so great to get a photograph of all the generations you can get together with you and your new baby. But be sure to only do this once your pediatrician believes it is safe. Life is short, and with elderly family members, we don't know when their time will come when they will no longer be with us. The sooner you can safely get the family together for a generational picture, the better— and you will be glad you did!! This will be a valuable piece of family history that can be passed down through the family, so you don't want to miss the opportunity to capture this special moment, if possible.

I have been researching my family history for several years now. I treasure all the pictures I have captured, and those passed down or shared with me. Family is very special, and photographs can keep those memories alive for a long, long time.

Hospital Gifts

Suppose you still insist on having visitors in the hospital and have a lot of the gift-giving kind. In that case, I highly recommend you tell them *not* to come bearing gifts— at least not while you are in the hospital. Family and friends are always well-meaning when they bring something for you, your baby, or the baby's siblings, but they tend to forget "one tiny little thing." Who must haul all of the gifts, flowers, etc., home?? Do they?? No— YOU do!!!

I cannot count how often parents were inundated with so many gifts and flowers needing to be taken home. When it came time to load their vehicle— there wasn't any room to get mom or baby or both in it!! Some parents realize this issue early on and have the dad start hauling things home; when going home to take care of other kids and/or pets or stay home. Or they have enlisted the help of family or friends to take some things home while they are still in the hospital. Some parents have left the plants, flowers, and leftover goodies for the nurses to enjoy, and that is certainly not the intention of the gift-giver. They don't buy them for *us* to enjoy— they buy them for you. So, ask your visitors if they insist on gifts to please bring them when they visit you at home later or send them to your residence if they cannot come to see you anytime soon. This way, you have one less stressor upon discharge and can get home safely without impairing your driver's visibility.

A Note to the Fathers/Significant Others

When writing this second edition, I realized I had forgotten to include the fathers/significant others for the new role in their baby's life. I missed it completely in the first edition. So I sincerely apologize for the omission and have added this little note to you all.

Of course, if you haven't been around babies very much, or not at all, you can feel just a little bit intimidated, overwhelmed, and helpless. Nothing is in your control throughout this whole ordeal. This can be

The "OTHER" Topics

with the *whole nine-month* process. The mother goes to doctor visits, through the labor/delivery procedure *(whether vaginal or cesarean section)*, to the actual delivery process and what comes after. Now here's your new baby, and you might start feeling more anxiety, fear, intimidation, helplessness, etc. If this is the first time, you may have never held a newborn baby before. You may think, "If I pick up this baby, will I break him/her?" "How did that big baby come out of my wife in one piece and not be broken?" "What can I do now?"

All I can say is— *no*, you won't break your baby unless you handle them too roughly. Over the years, I've told my parents that their baby was more resilient than they thought. "Your baby could probably "bounce" on the ground a lot better than any of us, and it not hurt them. But— I do not recommend testing that out." Or "Think about what your baby just went through to be born and how well they tolerated it." That seemed to help calm them a little bit more.

You can help your wife/significant other by caring for your baby in many ways. Ways that will not only help take some of the baby care load off of her but will allow you to bond with your baby. First and foremost— Dads, get your hands dirty! Get in there and start changing diapers, putting on clothes/taking them off— and I promise you will do a great job at it sooner than you think. *(**If you have forgotten or missed it earlier in the book, review the "Diapering Your Baby/Changing Clothes" section for a refresher.)* Secondly, if the mom is nursing the baby for now, the time will come when you can help feed your baby, which may have to wait until the baby is older. But suppose mom is pumping to feed from a bottle, or you two have decided to feed your baby formula. In that case, you can jump right in to help with the feedings and spend some valuable bonding time with your baby.

Speaking of bonding time— do you realize one of the best things you can do during bonding time is to start doing skin-to-skin with your baby? Not just holding your baby— but doing skin-to-skin right there in the hospital— even after you go home? Place your baby in only a diaper on your bare chest and wrap a blanket over their back. This will allow them to get to know you by smell and sound. They will hear your heartbeat and feel comforted and secure, just like your baby does with mom. Now your baby will know both of you and feel even more safe and secure— and you can be a big part of your baby's life and feel good about it.

Dads, or significant others, can be a big part of their baby's life— from the beginning and throughout their lives. Initially, it may seem scary or intimidating but don't hesitate to jump in there and get your feet wet with your new baby. Nothing warms a mother's heart more than seeing their partner getting to know their baby by feeding them, changing diapers, and bonding with them in any way they can. I've seen it time and time again, watching my parents interact with their baby. When Daddy gets involved— Mommy smiles.

It's the "Little Things..."

Everything we do as nurses or practitioners is to make sure you and your new baby have a great start to your new life ahead. We want you to be educated, informed, and comfortable with your care and your baby's care. Unfortunately, your time in the hospital is *very short*— and there's a lot of information and teaching to pack into those short two or three days. Remember what I stated at the beginning of the book that you are *lucky* if you remember even 25% of the information we gave you during that time??? Well— that's very true!! That time will go by so fast you won't know "which end is up," and then you are left to go home with this new baby.

During your and your baby's hospital stay, if you have questions about anything concerning you— *don't* hesitate to ask your nurse or doctor. Never be embarrassed to ask questions about anything, even if you feel it might be a "stupid question." There are *"no stupid questions"*!! Anything you aren't sure of, just ask— and don't let anyone you ask "make" you feel bad *for* asking. If you have a question and want clarification to understand, just ask! That's it— end of story!!! Also, don't hesitate to ask a question a 2nd, 3rd, or 4th time if you forget the original answer. Remember— 25% may be the only amount of retention of information for you during your stay— and that's not a lot.

Here's another piece of advice directly from me to all of you. Whatever hospital you may be in and wherever you live, you may have some issues with your nursing care or certain ways things are done. You have a right to be treated with respect and have a voice in how your and your baby's care will go. If you don't want to breastfeed— *don't*. What are they going to do— let your baby *starve*?? They can't bully you into breastfeeding if you do not want to. That is your choice—not theirs.

If you want to use a pacifier for your baby, go right ahead. You can decide if you don't want to take narcotic pain meds. That's okay. If you want to get some sleep and want your baby to go to the nursery for a little while, just ask.

This book is filled with recommendations and suggestions. There's also a lot you may or may not agree on. Remember, these are recommendations and suggestions— not "hard and fast" rules, only advice. We do want what is best for you and your baby, but you are the ultimate deciding factor of how and when you may use this advice— or *if* you even use this advice.

Don't be scared— you'll do just fine. Just listen to your "gut instincts." If something is not right, or you're concerned with something you don't think you can wait on, call your obstetrician or pediatrician— whichever the case may be. If it is after office hours, call if you cannot wait until the next business day. An obstetrician, a pediatrician, or any other doctor is on call 24/7. They can help you work through a problem, issue, or concern. They can also help decide if you can wait until the next business day to be seen or need to go to urgent care or the emergency room.

And just so you know, us nurses rely on "gut instinct" in our practice, and it serves us well. It lets us know something "just isn't right" so we can act on it. So, *please* don't ignore it when it happens to you, whether it's about you or your baby! Please, don't let doctors "poo-poo" your concerns away if you think it's more serious but they are not taking you seriously— and you think there is more to the problem. They often look for a more common diagnosis than rare ones. Mothers especially know when something just isn't right. Countless articles on people who kept pushing and pushing to find answers, and their persistence paid off in the end. They got the answers they were looking for. So, be your baby's and your own personal advocate.

Last... But Not Least

Here's the last bit of cautionary advice— *beware of the Internet!!* With the vast amount of healthcare information— and misinformation— on the Internet, you may not find the right or exact answers to your questions— and a lot of information is also *outdated*. Stay away from blogs written by just anybody. Mostly these are just opinions or someone's personal accounts. Don't Google something and take just anyone's opinion as gospel. Make sure you are looking for reputable and reliable sources when researching any healthcare questions you may have. Government health websites, scholarly journals or articles written by healthcare professionals, government organizations such as the Centers for Disease Control *(CDC)*, university studies, etc. Look for credentials from the author of a publication, website, or blog. I had patients ask healthcare questions about certain things that were either incorrect or outdated information, and I asked where the information came from. Usually, it was from an outdated or inaccurate source. Sometimes it's from a personal blog. *(**Again, personal perception or opinion. Not necessarily researched accurately— if at all.)* So be diligent in your searches online— look for the *best* sources.

Conclusion

I hope you found this book informative— if not a little bit entertaining, too. This has been a labor of love and caring on my part. It is *so important* to me— to see that every mother is completely informed about her hospital care. And that every parent is completely informed about their baby's care. There is so much information and education to be provided. Unfortunately, there's only so much time during your hospital stay to give you this information. Because of that, I felt the need to provide this book. As stated at the beginning of the book, there are books galore about pregnancy, breastfeeding, baby care, infant loss, etc. Still, there wasn't anything out there about the hospital stay itself. So— here you have a book to read *before* your *"Big Day"* and one to return to during your stay. If you can't remember what you read about a "particular situation" that has come up, you now have a reference book to help you get through.

Unfortunately, this ol' body has fallen apart over the years, and I had to move away from the bedside. Because of this, I found a very familiar avenue to continue educating patients— through my writing. This book started my jumping-off point in preparing myself for nursing "away from the bedside." From there, I will continue writing on the one topic I know and love best— POSTPARTUM. I'll continue writing articles and blogs on my website, Mom Baby RN (mombabyrn.com). I will have open discussions and surveys and have the readers make requests for info they would like me to post on. This site is not up and running yet but will soon be available by mid- to late-2023.

I might be adventurous, branch out, or try my hand at podcasts down the road. I may even have short informational videos to view, so check out YouTube if you want to follow me there. Just keep checking back if you're interested in following me on my new journey.

Lastly, I would like to thank you for purchasing my book and ask if you would please leave a review on whatever website you purchased the book from. If you purchased yours at a campus bookstore or any other brick-and-mortar store, please leave a review on Amazon or you can leave an email review at: mombabyrnc@gmail.com. This will allow me to determine if changes need to be made to the book to make it better for my readers. Good luck to each and every one of you on your journey forward with your new little one(s)!!

Acknowledgments

I want to thank my former nursing educator guru and former nurse manager, Kim Dishman. You helped nudge me along to do more with my nursing career just in the first few years I had known you, and I thank you for doing that. I wouldn't have had the guts to do this without your encouragement and enthusiasm for my ideas. Who would have thought I had it in me?? To my previous partners-in-crime— Gloria Theno, Amy Horton, Sheila Green, Elizabeth Murphy, Terry Jackson, Cindy Robinette, Terri Jenkins, and Amber Tenay whom I had laughed, cried, bounced around ideas, and had each other's back with over a lot of years. We had been together so long that I truly valued your opinions— and trusted you *explicitly*. To my newer nurse buddies just before I left postpartum— Sara Gena, Kerry Davenport, Linda Grossglauser, Bree Fallon, Monica Bailey, and Michelle Andrews. Without everyone's continued support, honest opinions, and thorough review of my transcript, I would have done a severe injustice to this book. Some of you have moved on or retired, but you know what?? *You* all *still rock!!!*

And last… but *not* least to my family.:

To TJ and Jessica— thank you for helping support my going back to college and my nursing career from the beginning. I know I spent a lot of time missing games and activities while you were growing up, but I did it to make life much better for you— I hope it was.

To Jenna— my youngest, who came along after the career change. You got the most significant benefit of that life-changing career move— and you might not have graced us with your presence if I hadn't done it. Returning to school with two kiddos was an immense struggle, but it allowed us to have three. So, I'm delighted you came along when you did!

To Bobby, my husband and best friend— although you may have thought this idea was silly and your wife couldn't possibly be an author, I say— ha, ha, in your face!! LOL! No— *really*, thanks for supporting me through the many months it took to write the 1st Edition. And thanks for allowing me the time to put this book together again a second time. I have put off many things to re-write this book, so I appreciate the patience. (Maybe we can go to Maui together now??)

~~ Karen

About the Author

Karen Brewer is a mother-baby nurse who had been working over the past 20 years for a health system in the Greater Kansas City area. She is passionate about her career as a registered nurse specializing in mother/baby care postpartum and wants the utmost care for her patients, as well as for other patients out there. Even though she has left the bedside, caring for her postpartum patients, she continues to educate through her writing. By educating this way, she feels her reach to women and families far exceeds the teaching she provided at the bedside. This is her new mission and the next step in her nursing career.

While not finishing college the first go-around (a business major that didn't go as planned), she worked a state government job and started raising a family. Soon she realized this was not the path she wanted to continue, so she went another route and returned to school when the older two were very young. Changing directions and completing her nursing degree became the turning point of her new career and her family's future.

She is married to her college sweetheart, Bobby, and has three adult children, two married and one soon-to-be. She also has beloved "puppies," Gordy and Molly, and a calico cat, Lilo. She lives in Kansas City, Missouri.

Please Help by Giving Back

Many Thanks for Reading My Book!

I really appreciate all of your feedback and

I love hearing what you have to say...

so...

I could use your *honest* input to make

the next version of this book and my future books better.

Please take two minutes now to leave a helpful review on Amazon

letting me know what you thought of the book:

amazon.com/author/karenbsnrncmnn

OR leave a review on whatever book site you purchased the book from...

OR you can send it directly to my website:

mombabyrn.com/reviews

Thanks so much!!

~~ Karen Brewer

References

AAP Media. (2014, July 14). Bed sharing remains greatest risk factor for sleep related infant deaths. *AAP Pressroom Media Center*. https://www.aap.org/en-us/about-the-aap/aap-press-room/Pages/Bed-Sharing-Remains-Greatest-Risk-Factor-for-Sleep-Related-Infant-Deaths.aspx

Abboud, T. L., Moore, M., Zhu, J., & Kimball, S. (1987). Epidural butorphanol or morphine for the relief of post-cesarean section pain. *Anesthesia & Analgesia, 66*(9), 887-893. https://doi.org/10.1213/00000539-198709000-00015

ACOG Committee on Obstetric Practice. (2017, March). *Delivery of a newborn with meconium-stained amniotic fluid* (ACOG Committee Opinion; Research Report No. 689). https://www.acog.org/Resources-And-Publications/Committee-Opinions/Committee-on-Obstetric-Practice/Delivery-of-a-Newborn-With-Meconium-Stained-Amniotic-Fluid

ACOG Committee on Obstetric Practice. (2017, August). *Opioid use and opioid use disorder in pregnancy* (ACOG Committee Opinion; Report No. 711). https://www.acog.org/Resources-And-Publications/Committee-Opinions/Committee-on-Obstetric-Practice/Opioid-Use-and-Opioid-Use-Disorder-in-Pregnancy

Agrawal, R., & Elston, D. M. (2017, June 30). *Diaper dermatitis*. https://emedicine.medscape.com/article/911985-overview

American Academy of Pediatrics. (2012). Breastfeeding and the use of human milk. *Pediatrics, 129*(3). http://pediatrics.aappublications.org/content/129/3/e827#ref-24

Antipuesto, D. J. (2011, February 9). Difference between caput succedaneum and cephalhematoma. *Nursing Crib*. http://nursingcrib.com/nursing-notes-reviewer/maternal-child-health/difference-between-caput-succedaneum-and-cephalhematoma/

Assessments for newborn babies. (n.d.). http://www.stanfordchildrens.org/en/topic/default?id=assessments-for-newborn-babies-90-P02336

BabyCenter Medical Advisory Board (Ed.). (n.d.). *Baby sensory development: Sight.* Baby Center. Retrieved September, 2016, from https://www.babycenter.com/0_baby-sensory-development-sight_6508.bc

Ball, H., & Blair, P. S. (2017). Health professionals' guide to: "Caring for your baby at night". In *UNICEF* [PDF]. https://www.unicef.org.uk/babyfriendly/wp-content/uploads/sites/2/2011/11/Caring-for-your-Baby-at-Night-A-Health-Professionals-Guide.pdf

Bartick, M., & Reinhold, A. (2010). The burden of suboptimal breastfeeding in the united states: A pediatric cost analysis. *Pediatrics, 125*(5). http://pediatrics.aappublications.org/content/125/5/e1048

Baskin, L. S. (n.d.). Neonatal circumcision: Risks and benefits. In C. J. Lockwood, J. G. Bartlett, D. Wilcox, & K. Eckler (Eds.), *UpToDate.* https://www.uptodate.com/contents/neonatal-circumcision-risks-and-benefits?source=search_result&search=circumcision&selectedTitle=2~90

Baskin, L. S. (n.d.). Patient education: Circumcision in baby boys (beyond the basics). In C. J. Lockwood, D. Wilcox, & K. Eckler (Eds.), *UpToDate.* Retrieved March 9, 2017, from https://www.uptodate.com/contents/circumcision-in-baby-boys-beyond-the-basics?view=print

Baxley, E. G., & Gobbo, R. W. (2004). Shoulder dystocia. *American Family Physician, 69*(7), 1707-1714. http://www.aafp.org/afp/2004/0401/p1707.html

Bed-sharing. (n.d.). https://www.marchofdimes.org/baby/co-sleeping.aspx

Berens, P. (n.d.). Overview of postpartum care. In C. J. Lockwood & V. A. Barss (Eds.), *UpToDate.* Retrieved September 14, 2017, from https://www.uptodate.com/contents/overview-of-postpartum-care?source=search_result&search=shivering%20postpartum&selectedTitle=1~3

Berghella, V. (n.d.). Cesarean delivery: Postpartum issues. In C. J. Lockwood & V. A. Barss (Eds.), *UpToDate.* Retrieved October 3, 2017, from https://www.uptodate.com/contents/cesarean-delivery-postoperative-issues

Blank, S., Brady, M., Buerk, E., Carlo, W., Diekema, D., Freedman, A., Maxwell, L., & Wegner, S. (2012). Male circumcision [PDF]. *Pediatrics.* http://pediatrics.aappublications.org/content/pediatrics/early/2012/08/22/peds.2012-1990.full.pdf

Bodenlos, K. L., Maranda, L., & Deligiannidis, K. M. (2016). Comparison of the use of the EPDS-3 vs. EPDS-10 to identify women at risk for peripartum depression [3K]. *Obstetrics & Gynecology, 127*, 89S-90S. https://doi.org/10.1097/01.AOG.0000483802.69290.1b

Boyd, K. (2017, May 22). *Baby's vision development: What to expect the first year* (S. N. Lipski, Ed.). American Academy of Ophthalmology. https://www.aao.org/eye-health/tips-prevention/baby-vision-development-first-year

Breastfeeding report card [White paper]. (2022, August 3). CDC: Centers for Disease Control & Prevention: Breastfeeding: Report Card. Retrieved February 21, 2023, from https://www.cdc.gov/breastfeeding/data/reportcard.htm

Brown, T. (2015, October 6). *Breastfeeding support on upswing in many US hospitals.* https://www.medscape.com/viewarticle/852227?src=trendmd_pilot#vp_2

Caput succedaneum. (2015). In K. G. Lee, D. Zieve, & A.D.A.M. Editorial Team (Eds.), *Medical encyclopedia: MedlinePlus.* https://medlineplus.gov/ency/article/001587.htm

Caput succedaneum vs cephalohematoma. (2015, March 4). Health Research and Funding. https://healthresearchfunding.org/caput-succedaneum-vs-cephalohematoma/

Care for an uncircumcised penis. (n.d.). Healthy Children: The American Academy of Pediatrics. Retrieved June 19, 2017, from https://www.healthychildren.org/English/ages-stages/baby/bathing-skin-care/pages/Care-for-an-Uncircumcised-Penis.aspx

Checa, A., Holm, T., Sjodin, M. O. D., Reinke, S. N., Alm, J., Scheynius, A., & Wheelock, C. E. (2015). Lipid mediator profile in vernix caseosa reflects skin barrier development. *Scientific Reports.* https://doi.org/10.1038/srep15740

Chordee. (n.d.). In J. Robinson (Ed.), *WebMD.*

Coco, A. S., & Silverman, S. D. (1998). External cephalic version. *American Family Physician, 58*(3), 731-738. http://www.aafp.org/afp/1998/0901/p731.html

Colvin, J. D., Collie-Akers, V., Schunn, C., & Moon, R. Y. (2014). Sleep environment risks for younger and older infants. *Pediatrics, 134*(2). http://pediatrics.aappublications.org/content/134/2/e406

Co-sleeping and bed-sharing. (n.d.). Retrieved May 21, 2017, from https://kellymom.com/parenting/nighttime/cosleeping/

COVID-19 pandemic. (2022, December 27). In *AAP publications: AAP news: COVID pandemic.* The American Academy of Pediatrics. Retrieved January 2, 2023, from https://publications.aap.org/aapnews/news/1362/COVID-19-pandemic?autologincheck=redirected

Dahlke, J. D., & Magann, E. F. (2015). Immune and non-immune hydrops fetalis. In R. J. Martin, A. A. Fanaroff, & M. C. Walsh (Eds.), *Fanaroff and Martin's neonatal-perinatal medicine* (10th ed.). http://www.umm.edu/health/medical/ency/articles/hydrops-fetalis

Dancel, R., & Price, D. (2012). Evaluation of newborns with preauricular skin lesions. *American Family Physician, 85*(10), 993-998. http://www.aafp.org/afp/2012/0515/p993.html

Dekker, R. (2013, August 23). *Friedman's curve and failure to progress: A leading cause of unplanned cesareans* (I. Ali & E. Wilson, Ed.). Evidence Based Birth: Evidence That Empowers. Retrieved March 17, 2023, from https://evidencebasedbirth.com/friedmans-curve-and-failure-to-progress-a-leading-cause-of-unplanned-c-sections

Dekker, R. (2014, March 18). *Evidence on: The vitamin K shot in newborns.* https://evidencebasedbirth.com/evidence-for-the-vitamin-k-shot-in-newborns/

del Castillo-Hegyi, C. (2015, April 18). *Letter to doctors and parents about the dangers of insufficient exclusive breastfeeding* [Letter]. https://fedisbest.org/2015/04/letter-to-doctors-and-parents-about-the-dangers-of-insufficient-exclusive-breastfeeding/

Demerol. (n.d.). Drugs.com. https://www.drugs.com/demerol.html

Demerol injection. (n.d.). Drugs.com. Retrieved December 27, 2017, from https://www.drugs.com/pro/demerol-injection.html

Diaz-Tello, F. (2016). Invisible wounds: obstetric violence in the United States. *Reproductive Health Matters, 24*(47), 56-64. https://doi.org/10.1016/j.rhm.2016.04.004

Dilaudid. (n.d.). Drugs.com. Retrieved December 27, 2017, from https://www.drugs.com/dilaudid.html

Duthie, E. A. (2020, December 1). In-hospital newborn falls associated with a sleeping parent: The case for a new paradigm. *AAP Publications, 10*(12), 1031-1037. https://doi.org/10.1542/hpeds.2020-0112

Eichenwald, E. C. (n.d.). Overview of cyanosis in the newborn. In L. E. Wilseman & M. S. Kim (Eds.), *UpToDate*. Retrieved May 26, 2016, from https://www.uptodate.com/contents/overview-of-cyanosis-in-the-newborn

Eidelman, A. I., & Schanler, R. J. (2012). Breastfeeding and the use of human milk. *Pediatrics, 129*(3). http://pediatrics.aappublications.org/content/129/3/e827

Facts about critical congenital heart defects. (n.d.). Centers for Disease Control and Prevention. Retrieved June 27, 2017, from https://www.cdc.gov/ncbddd/heart-defects/cchd-facts.html

Facts about hypospadias. (n.d.). Centers for Disease Control and Prevention. https://www.cdc.gov/ncbddd/birthdefects/hypospadias.html

Facts about jaundice and kernicterus. (n.d.). Centers for Disease Control and Prevention. Retrieved November 7, 2016, from https://www.cdc.gov/ncbddd/jaundice/facts.html

Feldman-Winter, L., & Goldsmith, J. P. (2016). Safe sleep and skin-to-skin care in the neonatal period for healthy term newborns. *Pediatrics, 138*(3). http://pediatrics.aappublications.org/content/early/2016/08/18/peds.2016-1889

Fentanyl injection. (n.d.). Drugs.com. Retrieved December 27, 2017, from https://www.drugs.com/pro/fentanyl-injection.html

For babies receiving donor milk. (n.d.). Three Rivers Mother's Milk Bank. http://www.threeriversmilkbank.org/recipients/

Fuloria, M., & Krieter, S. (2002). The newborn examination: Part I. emergencies and common abnormalities involving the skin, head, neck, chest, and respiratory and cardiovascular systems. *American Family Physician, 65*(1), 61-69. http://www.aafp.org/afp/2002/0101/p61.html#sec-1

Garcia-Prats, J. A. (n.d.). Neonatal polycythemia. In D. H. Mahoney, L. E. Wiseman, & C. Armsby (Eds.), *UpToDate.* Retrieved September 19, 2016, from https://www.uptodate.com/contents/neonatal-polycythemia

Geller, D. (n.d.). *Is it normal for my baby's genitals to be so swollen?* https://www.babycenter.com/404_is-it-normal-for-my-babys-genitals-to-be-so-swollen_9940.bc

Gibson, E. (n.d.). *Premature infant* (E. Gibson & U. Nawab, Ed.). Retrieved January, 2015, from http://www.merckmanuals.com/professional/pediatrics/perinatal-problems/premature-infant

Gozen, D., Caglar, S., Bayraktar, S., & Atici, F. (2014). Diaper dermatitis care of newborns human breast milk or barrier cream. *Journal of Clinical Nursing, 23*(3-4), 515-523. https://doi.org/10.1111/jocn.12047

Granberg, C. (n.d.). *Hypospadias.* Mayo Clinic. Retrieved October 25, 2017, from https://www.mayoclinic.org/diseases-conditions/hypospadias/symptoms-causes/syc-20355148

Grant, G. J. (n.d.). Adverse effects of neuraxial analgesia and anesthesia for obstetrics. In D. L. Hepner & M. Crowley (Eds.), *UpToDate*. Retrieved June 28, 2017, from https://www.uptodate.com/contents/adverse-effects-of-neuraxial-analgesia-and-anesthesia-for-obstetrics?source=see_link&sectionName=Shivering&anchor=H18#H12560398

Grosse, S. D., Riehle-Colarusso, T., Gaffney, M., Mason, C. A., Shapira, S. K., Sontag, M. K., Van Naarden Braun, K., & Iskander, J. (2017). CDC grand rounds: Newborn screening for hearing loss and critical congenital heart disease. *MMWR: Morbidity and Mortality Weekly Report, 66*(30), 888-890. https://www.cdc.gov/mmwr/volumes/66/wr/mm6633a4.htm?s_cid=mm6633a4_w#suggestedcitation

Grosse SD, Riehle-Colarusso T, Gaffney M, Mason CA, Shapira SK, Sontag MK, . CDC grand rounds: newborn screening for hearing loss and critical congenital heart disease. *MMWR: Morbidity and Mortality Weekly Report* 2017;66:888–890. DOI: http://dx.doi.org/10.15585/mmwr.mm6633a4

Guidance for the prevention and control of influenza in the peri- and postpartum settings. (n.d.). Centers for Disease Control and Prevention. https://www.cdc.gov/flu/professionals/infectioncontrol/peri-post-settings.htm

Havaei, F., Astivia, O. L. O., & MacPhee, M. (2020). The impact of workplace violence on medical-surgical nurses' health outcome: A moderated mediation model of work environment conditions and burnout using secondary data. *International Journal of Nursing Studies, 109.* https://doi.org/10.1016/j.ijnurstu.2020.103666

Healthwise, Inc. (n.d.). Childbirth: Epidurals - topic overview. In J. Robinson (Ed.), *WebMD*.

Heart murmur. (n.d.). Health Children: The American Academy of Pediatrics. Retrieved November 21, 2015, from https://www.healthychildren.org/English/health-issues/conditions/heart/Pages/Heart-Murmur.aspx

Hepatitis B vaccination. (n.d.). Centers for Disease Control and Prevention. https://www.cdc.gov/vaccines/vpd/hepb/index.html

Hill, D. L. (2012, May 11). *Erythromycin ointment.* Healthy Children: The American Academy of Pediatrics. https://www.healthychildren.org/English/ages-stages/prenatal/delivery-beyond/Pages/Erythromycin-Ointment.aspx

HIV transmission. (n.d.). Centers for Disease Control and Prevention. Retrieved June 6, 2017, from https://www.cdc.gov/hiv/basics/transmission.html

Hoath, S. B., Pickens, W. L., & Visscher, M. O. (2006). The biology of vernix caseosa. *International Journal of Cosmetic Science, 28*(5). https://doi.org/10.1111/j.1467-2494.2006.00338.x

Hoeger, P. H., Schreiner, V., Klaassen, I. A., Enzmann, C. C., Friedrichs, K., & Bleck, O. (2002). Epidermal barrier lipids in human vernix caseosa: Corresponding ceramide pattern in vernix and fetal skin. *The British Journal of Dermatology, 146*(2), 194-201. https://doi.org/:10.1046/j.1365-2133.2002.04584.x

Horli, K. A. (n.d.). Diaper dermatitis. In M. J. Levy, J. E. Drutz, & R. Corona (Eds.), *UpToDate*. Retrieved September, 2017, from http://www.uptodate.com/contents/diaper-dermatitis

Horsley, T., Clifford, T., & Barrowman, N. (2007). Benefits and harms associated with the practice of bed sharing: A systematic review. *Archives of Pediatrics and Adolescent Medicine, 161*(3), 237-245. https://doi.org/10.1001/archpedi.161.3.237

Hundt, G. L., Beckerleg, S., Kassem, F., Abu Jafar, A. M., Belmaker, I., Abu Saad, K., & Shoham-Vardi, I. (2000). Women's health custom made: building on the 40 days postpartum for Arab women. *Health Care Women International, 21*(6), 529-542. https://doi.org/10.1080/07399330050130313

Hunter, W. (n.d.). *It's not a seizure: Great baby fake-outs*. Baby Science. http://babyscience.info/its-not-a-seizure-great-baby-fake-outs/

Hunter, W. (2016, June 6). Scary baby symptoms (That are perfectly normal). *Parents*. http://www.parents.com/baby/health/scary-but-normal-baby-symptoms/

Infant vision: Birth to 24 months of age. (n.d.). American Optometric Association. Retrieved October 30, 2017, from https://www.aoa.org/patients-and-public/good-vision-throughout-life/childrens-vision/infant-vision-birth-to-24-months-of-age?sso=y

Jaafar, S. H., Ho, J. J., Jahanfar, S., & Angolkar, M. (2016, August 30). Effect of restricted pacifier use in breastfeeding term infants for increasing duration of breast-feeding. *Cochrane Database System Review*. https://www.ncbi.nlm.nih.gov/pubmed/22786506

James, A. (2009, October 18). *What your newborn baby looks like*. About Kids Health. http://www.aboutkidshealth.ca/En/ResourceCentres/PregnancyBabies/NewbornBabies/YourNewbornBabysBody/Pages/What-Your-Newborn-Baby-Looks-Like.aspx

Johnson, S., & Calfasso, J. (n.d.). *Umbilical hernia* (S. Kim, Ed.). Retrieved September 29, 2015, from https://www.healthline.com/health/umbilical-hernia#overview1

Jones, C. (2013, September 23). *Separating fact from fiction in the not-so-normal newborn nursery: Pacifiers and nipple confusion.* https://sciencebasedmedicine.org/separating-fact-from-fiction-in-the-not-so-normal-newborn-nursery-pacifiers-and-nipple-confusion/

Jones, C. (2019, January 11). *Breastfeeding improvement initiatives may increase risk of newborn falls.* The Fed Is Best Foundation. Retrieved December 28, 2022, from https://fedisbest.org/information-for-hospitals/pediatricians-views-on-the-baby-friendly-hospital-initiative/breastfeeding-improvement-initiatives-may-increase-risk-of-newborn-falls/

Jones, M. (2021, May 17). Preventing workplace violence in healthcare. *American Association of Critical-Care Nurses.* https://www.aacn.org/blog/preventing-workplace-violence-in-healthcare

Kair, L. R., Kenron, D., Etheredge, K., Jaffe, A. C., & Phillipi, C. A. (2013). Pacifier restriction and exclusive breastfeeding. *Pediatrics, 131*(4). http://pediatrics.aappublications.org/content/early/2013/03/12/peds.2012-2203

Kaneshiro, N. K. (n.d.). Fontanelles - bulging. In D. Zieve, B. Conaway, & A.D.A.M. Editorial Team (Eds.), *Medical encyclopedia: MedlinePlus.* https://medlineplus.gov/ency/article/003310.htm

Kaneshiro, N. K. (n.d.). Skin findings in newborns. In D. Zieve, I. Oglevie, & A.D.A.M. Editorial Team (Eds.), *Medical encyclopedia: MedlinePlus.* Retrieved November 19, 2015, from https://medlineplus.gov/ency/article/002301.htm

Kaneshiro, N. K. (2017). Hormonal effects in newborns. In D. Zieve & B. Conaway (Eds.), *Medical encyclopedia: MedlinePlus.* https://medlineplus.gov/ency/article/001911.htm

Karp, H. (2015, November 5). The 5 S's for soothing babies. *Happiest Baby.* https://www.happiestbaby.com/blogs/blog/the-5-s-s-for-soothing-babies

Katela, K. (2022, December 6). *As 'tripledemic' looms, here's how to keep your child safe* [White paper]. Yale Medicine. Retrieved January 2, 2023, from https://www.yalemedicine.org/news/tripledemic-guide-for-parents

Kelly, J. C. (2011). AAP sets guidelines for neonatal hypoglycemia. *Pediatrics,* (127), 575-579.

Ketchum, D. (2022). *Deploying a validated postnatal depression screening tool & guideline to improve evidence based screening for postpartum depression in ambulatory care* [Doctoral thesis, Boise State University]. Boise State University; Scholar Works. https://scholarworks.boisestate.edu/dnp/47/

Kibler, V. A., Hayes, R. M., Johnson, D. E., Anderson, L. W., Just, S. L., & Wells, N. L. (2012). Early postoperative ambulation: Back to basics [PDF]. *American Journal of Nursing, 112*(4). http://unmhospitalist.pbworks.com/w/file/fetch/66026896/Early%20Postoperative%20Ambulation%20Back%20to%20Basics%20A%20quality%20improvement%20project.pdf

Kozhimannil, K. B., Interrante, J. D., Tofte, A. N., & Admon, L. K. (2020). Severe maternal morbidity and mortality among indigenous women in the United States. *Obstetrics and Gynecology, 35*(2), 294-300. https://doi.org/10.1097/AOG.0000000000003647

Kuehn, B. M. (2017, August 24). *Newborn screening guidelines not followed by all hospitals*. https://www.medscape.com/viewarticle/884692

Kwek, K., & Yeo, G. S. (2006). Shoulder dystocia and injuries: Prevention and management. *Current Opinion in Obstetrics & Gynecology, 18*(2), 123-128. https://doi.org/10.1097/0000192976.38858.90

[LACTMED: Acetaminophen: Summary of use during lactation]. (n.d.). National Library of Medicine: National Institutes of Health: TOXNET. https://toxnet.nlm.nih.gov/cgi-bin/sis/search2/f?./temp/~Jw1wrB:1

[LACTMED: Diphenhydramine: Summary of use during lactation]. (n.d.). National Library of Medicine: National Institutes of Health: TOXNET. https://toxnet.nlm.nih.gov/cgi-bin/sis/search2/f?./temp/~dOqAeS:1

[LACTMED: Fentanyl: Summary of use during lactation]. (n.d.). National Library of Medicine: National Institutes of Health: TOXNET. https://toxnet.nlm.nih.gov/cgi-bin/sis/search2/f?./temp/~YqDwyz:1

[LACTMED: Hydrocodone: Summary of use during lactation]. (n.d.). National Library of Medicine: National Institutes of Health: TOXNET. https://toxnet.nlm.nih.gov/cgi-bin/sis/search2/f?./temp/~w4lOkh:1

[LACTMED: Ibuprofen: Summary of use during lactation]. (n.d.). National Library of Medicine: National Institutes of Health: TOXNET. https://toxnet.nlm.nih.gov/cgi-bin/sis/search2/f?./temp/~ugQnNL:1

[LACTMED: Morphine: Summary of use during lactation]. (n.d.). National Library of Medicine: National Institutes of Health: TOXNET. https://toxnet.nlm.nih.gov/cgi-bin/sis/search2/f?./temp/~kxPahY:4

[LACTMED: Oxycodone: Summary of use during lactation]. (n.d.). National Library of Medicine: National Institutes of Health: TOXNET. https://toxnet.nlm.nih.gov/cgi-bin/sis/search2/f?./temp/~Yh5Orp:1

Lee, K. (2015). Apnea of prematurity. In D. Zieve, I. Oglevie, & A.D.A.M. Editorial Team (Eds.), *Medical encyclopedia: MedlinePlus*. https://medlineplus.gov/ency/article/007227.htm

Lee, K. G. (n.d.). Bilirubin encephalopathy. In VeriMed Healthcare Network, D. Zieve, I. Oglivie, & A.D.A.M. Editorial Team (Eds.), *Medical encyclopedia: MedlinePlus*. Retrieved April 27, 2015, from https://medlineplus.gov/ency/article/007309.htm

Leighton, B. L., & Crock, L. W. (2017). Case series of successful postoperative pain management in buprenorphine maintenance therapy patients. *Anesthesia & Analgesia, 125*(5), 1779-1783. https://doi.org/10.1213/ANE.0000000000002498

Lessaris, K. J. (2016, January 2). Polycythemia of the newborn. In T. Rosenkrantz (Ed.), *Medscape*. https://emedicine.medscape.com/article/976319-overview

Livingston, G., & Thomas, D. (2019, December 16). Among 41 countries, only U.S. lacks paid parental leave [Fact sheet]. Retrieved February 21, 2023, from https://www.pewresearch.org/fact-tank/2019/12/16/u-s-lacks-mandated-paid-parental-leave/

Lockhart, T. (2017, May 8). *Circumoral cyanosis: Causes, symptoms, and how to treat it*. Doctors Health Press. https://www.doctorshealthpress.com/general-health-articles/circumoral-cyanosis-causes-treatment/

Ma, C. B. (2017). Tailbone trauma - aftercare. In D. Zieve, B. Conaway, & A.D.A.M. Editorial Team (Eds.), *Medical encyclopedia: MedlinePlus*. https://medlineplus.gov/ency/patientinstructions/000573.htm

MacDonald, L. (2016, May). *Becoming baby friendly: Rooming-in for patient centered care in the maternal setting*. Unpublished working paper, Honors college thesis. University of Massachusetts, Boston, MA.

Making the decision to breastfeed. (n.d.). Women's Health: U.S. Department of Health & Human Services. Retrieved May 3, 2017, from https://www.womenshealth.gov/breastfeeding/making-decision-breastfeed

Martinez-Vázquez, S., Hernández-Martínez, A., Rodríguez-Almagro, J., & Delgado-Rodríguez, M. (2022). Relationship between perceived obstetric violence and the risk of postpartum depression: An observational study. *Midwifery, 108*. https://doi.org/10.1016/j.midw.2022.103297

Mastitis. (2008). In *The Gale encyclopedia of medicine*.

Maternity care practices. (n.d.). Centers for Disease Control and Prevention. https://www.cdc.gov/breastfeeding/pdf/bf_guide_1.pdf

Mayo Clinic Staff. (n.d.). *Phenylketonuria (PKU)*. Retrieved October 17, 2017, from https://www.mayoclinic.org/diseases-conditions/phenylketonuria/basics/definition/CON-20026275

Mayo Clinic Staff. (2014, April 3). *Diseases and conditions: Infant jaundice*. https://www.mayoclinic.org/diseases-conditions/infant-jaundice/basics/causes/CON-20019637

Mayo Clinic Staff. (2014, November 27). *Diseases & conditions: Premature birth*. https://www.mayoclinic.org/diseases-conditions/premature-birth/basics/definition/CON-20020050

Mayo Clinic Staff. (2015, August). *Cesarean birth after care*. American Pregnancy Association. http://americanpregnancy.org/labor-and-birth/cesarean-aftercare/

Mayo Clinic Staff. (2015, October 15). *Diseases and conditions: Sacral dimple*. https://www.mayoclinic.org/diseases-conditions/sacral-dimple/basics/definition/CON-20025266

Mayo Clinic Staff. (2015, November 6). *Thermometer basics: Taking your child's temperature*. https://www.mayoclinic.org/healthy-lifestyle/infant-and-toddler-health/in-depth/thermometer/art-20047410?pg=2

Mayo Clinic Staff. (2015, November 25). *Lactation suppression: Can medication help?* Riverside. https://riversideonline.com/health_reference/Healthy-Baby/FAQ-20058016.cfm

Mayo Clinic Staff. (2017, July 12). *Sudden infant death syndrome (SIDS)*. https://www.mayoclinic.org/diseases-conditions/sudden-infant-death-syndrome/symptoms-causes/syc-20352800

Mayo Clinic Staff. (2017, August 22). *Undescended testicle*. https://www.mayoclinic.org/diseases-conditions/undescended-testicle/symptoms-causes/syc-20351995

McKee-Garrett, T. M. (n.d.). Assessment of the newborn infant. In L. E. Wiseman & M. S. Kim (Eds.), *UpToDate*. Retrieved July

21, 2017, from https://www.uptodate.com/contents/assessment-of-the-newborn-infant?source=search_result&search=eye%20color&selectedTitle=1-150

McKee-Garrett, T. M. (n.d.). Assessment of the newborn infant. In L. E. Wiseman & T. K. Duryea (Eds.), *UpToDate*. Retrieved July 21, 2017, from https://www.uptodate.com/contents/assessment-of-the-newborn-infant?source=search_result&search=umbilical%20hernia&selectedTitle=3-43

McKee-Garrett, T. M. (n.d.). Neonatal birth injuries. In L. E. Wiseman, W. Phillips, M. C. Patterson, & M. S. Kim (Eds.), *UpToDate*. Retrieved May 19, 2017, from https://www.uptodate.com/contents/neonatal-birth-injuries?source=search_result&search=petechiae%20neonate&selectedTitle=1-150

McLaughlin, M. R., O'Connor, N. R., & Ham, P. (2008). Newborn skin: Part II. birthmarks. *American Family Physician, 77*(1), 56-60.

Medical Advisory Committee. (n.d.). *Sexually transmitted diseases (STDs) and pregnancy*. American Pregnancy Association. Retrieved May 1, 2017, from http://americanpregnancy.org/pregnancy-complications/stds-and-pregnancy/

Medical Advisory Committee. (n.d.). *Your child's first test: The APGAR*. American Pregnancy Association. http://americanpregnancy.org/labor-and-birth/apgar-test/

Medical reasons for a c-section. (n.d.). Retrieved June, 2013, from https://www.marchofdimes.org/pregnancy/c-section-medical-reasons.aspx

Milk fever. (2009). In *Mosby's medical dictionary* (8th ed.).

Milk fever. (2012). In *Medical dictionary for the health professions and nursing*.

Miller-Keane encyclopedia and dictionary of medicine, nursing, and allied health (7th ed.). (2003).

Montag, S., & Palmer, L. S. (2011). Abnormalities in the penile curvature: Chordee and penile torsion. *The Scientific World Journal*, (11), 1470-1478. https://www.researchgate.net/publication/51536266_Abnormalities_of_Penile_Curvature_Chordee_and_Penile_Torsion

Moon, R. Y. (2011). SIDS and other sleep-related infant deaths: Expansion of recommendations for a safe infant sleeping environment. *Pediatrics, 128*(5), 1341-1367. http://pediatrics.aappublications.org/content/128/5/e1341.full

Moore, D. B., & Catlin, A. (2003). Lactation suppression: Forgotten aspect of care for the mother of a dying child. *Pediatric Nursing, 29*(5). https://www.medscape.com/viewarticle/464568

Morphine. (n.d.). Drugs.com. Retrieved December 27, 2017, from https://www.drugs.com/morphine.html

Morphine injection. (n.d.). Drugs.com. Retrieved December 27, 2017, from https://www.drugs.com/cons/morphine-injection.html

Neville, K. (2014, September/October). Besting breastfeeding bullies: A case for supporting, not shaming. *Food & Nutrition.* http://foodandnutrition.org/september-october-2014/besting-breastfeeding-bullies-case-supporting-not-shaming/

Newborn appearance. (n.d.). In *Stanford children's health.* http://www.stanfordchildrens.org/en/topic/default?id=newborn-appearance-90-P02691

Newborn appearance: What does a newborn look like? (n.d.). In L. C. Adler & D. Freeborn (Eds.), *Health encyclopedia: University of Rochester Medical Center.* https://www.urmc.rochester.edu/encyclopedia/content.aspx?ContentTypeID=90&ContentID=P02691

Nixon, H., & Leffert, L. (n.d.). Anesthesia for cesarean delivery. In D. L. Hepner & M. Crowley (Eds.), *UpToDate.* Retrieved July 26, 2017, from https://www.uptodate.com/contents/anesthesia-for-cesarean-delivery?source=see_link

O'Connor, N. R., McLaughlin, M. R., & Ham, P. (2008). Newborn skin: Part I. common rashes. *American Family Physicians, 77*(7), 47-52. http://www.aafp.org/afp/2008/0101/p47.html

Ondansetron. (n.d.). Drugs.com. Retrieved December 27, 2017, from https://www.drugs.com/ondansetron.html

Oral dextrose gel for treatment of newborn infants with low blood glucose levels [Review *Oral dextrose gel for treatment of newborn infants with low blood glucose levels,* by P. J. Weston, D. L. Harris, M. Battin, J. Brown, J. E. Hegarty, & J. E. Harding]. (2016). *Cochrane Database of Systematic Reviews.* https://doi.org/10.1002/14651858.CD011027.pub2.

Ostrower, S. T., & Bent, J. P., III. (2017, February 7). *Preauricular cysts, pits, and fissures* (A. D. Meyers, Ed.). Medscape. https://emedicine.medscape.com/article/845288-overview

Patient controlled analgesia. (n.d.). Drugs.com. Retrieved December 27, 2017, from https://www.drugs.com/cg/patient-controlled-analgesia.html

Penile torsion. (n.d.). In J. Donohoe (Ed.), *Cleveland clinic health library*. https://my.clevelandclinic.org/health/articles/penile-torsion

Phenergan. (n.d.). Drugs.com. https://www.drugs.com/phenergan.html

Phenergan. (n.d.). Drugs.com. Retrieved December 27, 2017, from https://www.drugs.com/phenergan.html

Phenylketonuria. (n.d.). National Institutes of Health: Genetics Home Reference. Retrieved October 24, 2017, from https://ghr.nlm.nih.gov/condition/phenylketonuria

Pielop, J. A. (n.d.). Benign skin and scalp lesions in the newborn and infant. In M. L. Levy, L. E. Wiseman, & R. Corona (Eds.), *UpToDate*. Retrieved July 31, 2017, from https://www.uptodate.com/contents/benign-skin-and-scalp-lesions-in-the-newborn-and-infant

Pielop, J. L. (n.d.). Benign skin and scalp lesions in the newborn and infant. In M. L. Levy & L. E. Wiseman (Eds.) & R. Corona (Author), *UpToDate*. Retrieved July 31, 2017, from https://www.uptodate.com/contents/benign-skin-and-scalp-lesions-in-the-newborn-and-infant

Pielop, J. L. (n.d.). Vascular lesions in the newborn. In M. L. Levy, L. E. Wiseman, & R. Corona (Eds.), *UpToDate*. Retrieved May 10, 2016, from https://www.uptodate.com/contents/vascular-lesions-in-the-newborn?source=see_link

PKU (Phenylketonuria) in your baby. (n.d.). Retrieved February, 2013, from https://www.marchofdimes.org/baby/phenylketonuria-in-your-baby.aspx

Pope, C. J., & Mazmanian, D. (2016, April 11). Breastfeeding and Postpartum Depression: An Overview and Methodological Recommendations for Future Research. *Depress Res Treat*. https://doi.org/10.1155/2016/4765310

Premature infant. (n.d.). In E. Gibson & U. Nawab (Eds.), *Merck manual: Professional version*. Retrieved January, 2015, from http://www.merckmanuals.com/professional/pediatrics/perinatal-problems/premature-infant

Pros & cons of co-sleeping. (n.d.). https://www.whattoexpect.com/first-year/cosleeping.aspx

Quinlan, J. D., & Murphy, N. J. (2015). Cesarean delivery: Counseling issues and complication management. *American Family Physician, 91*(3), 178-184. http://www.aafp.org/afp/2015/0201/p178.html

R, A. (2011, May 13). *Mottled skin in infants and babies: Causes and treatment*. Simple Remedies. http://www.simple-remedies.com/childrens-health/mottled-skin-in-infants.html

Reece, T. (2014). *When do babies' eyes change color?* http://www.parents.com/baby/development/physical/when-do-babies-eyes-change-color/

Rh incompatibility [Fact sheet]. (n.d.). Mount Sinai: Health Library. Retrieved February 20, 2023, from https://www.mountsinai.org/health-library/diseases-conditions/rh-incompatibility

Sachs, H. C. (2013). The transfer of drugs and therapeutics into human breast milk: An update on selected topics. *Pediatrics, 132*(3). https://doi.org/10.1542peds.2013-1985

Sacral dimple (pilonidal dimple). (n.d.). Internal Medicine and Pediatric Clinic. http://www.impcna.com/intranet/Nelson%20Pediatric/Newborn/SacralDimple%5B1%5D.pdf

Sauberan, J. B., Anderson, P. O., Lane, J. R., Rafie, S., Nguyen, N., Rossi, S. S., & Stellwagen, S. L. (2011). Breast milk hydrocodone and hydromorphone levels in mothers using hydrocodone for postpartum pain [Abstract]. *Obstetrics & Gynecology Journal, 117*(3), 611-617.

Save your life: Get care for these post-birth warning signs (Association of Women's Health, Obstetrics and Neonatal Nurses, Comp.) [Leaflet]. (2016). AWHONN. http://c.ymcdn.com/sites/www.awhonn.org/resource/resmgr/files/Post-Birth_Warning_signs_160.pdf

Segrave-Daly, B. J. (2020, November 18). I dropped my baby in a baby-friendly hospital while i was alone recovering from a cesarean section. *The Fed Is Best Foundation*. https://fedisbest.org/2020/11/i-dropped-my-baby-in-a-baby-friendly-hospital-while-i-was-alone-recovering-from-a-cesarean-section/

Severe maternal morbidity in the United States: a primer. (2021, October 28). Retrieved February 20, 2023, from https://www.commonwealthfund.org/publications/issue-briefs/2021/oct/severe-maternal-morbidity-united-states-primer#:~:text=Differences%20in%20severe%20maternal%20morbidity,between%20Black%20and%20white%20women.

Shu, J. (Ed.). (n.d.). *Movement: Birth to 3 months*. Healthy Children: American Academy of Pediatrics. Retrieved August 1, 2009, from https://www.healthychildren.org/English/ages-stages/baby/Pages/Movement-Birth-to-Three-Months.aspx

Siddiqui, M., Minhaj, M., Mueller, A., Tung, A., Scavone, B., Rana, S., & Shahul, S. (2017). Increased Perinatal Morbidity and Mortality Among Asian American and Pacific Islander Women in the United States. *Anesthesia & Analgesia, 24*(3). https://doi.org/10.1213/ANE.0000000000001778

Sinkey, R. G., Eschenbacher, M. A., Walsh, P. M., Doerger, R. G., Lambers, D. S., Sibai, B. M., & Habli, M. A. (2015). The GoMo study: a randomized clinical trial assessing neonatal pain with Gomco vs Mogen clamp circumcision [Abstract]. *American Journal of Obstetrics and Gynecology, 212*(5). https://doi.org/10.1016/j.ajog.2015.03.029

Smith, L. J. (n.d.). *Guidelines for rapid reduction of milk supply.* Bright Future Lactation Resource Centre. http://bflrc.com/ljs/breastfeeding/dryupfst.htm

Smith-Oka, V. (2022). Cutting Women: Unnecessary cesareans as iatrogenesis and obstetric violence. *Social Science & Medicine, 296.* doi.org/10.1016/j.socscimed.2022.114734

Sobol, J. (2015). Undescended testicle. In D. Zieve, I. Ogilvie, & A.D.A.M. Editorial Team (Eds.), *Medical encyclopedia.* https://medlineplus.gov/ency/article/000973.htm

Spain, J. E., Frey, H. A., Tuuli, M. G., Colvin, R., Macones, G. A., & Cahill, A. G. (2015). Neonatal morbidity associated with shoulder dystocia maneuvers [Abstract]. *American Journal of Obstetrics & Gynecology, 212*(3), 353-358. https://www.ncbi.nlm.nih.gov/pubmed/25291256

Stack, A. M. (n.d.). Etiology and evaluation of cyanosis in children. In S. J. Teach & J. F. Wiley (Eds.), *UpToDate.* Retrieved December 16, 2016, from https://www.uptodate.com/contents/etiology-and-evaluation-of-cyanosis-in-children

Stadol. (n.d.). Drugs.com. Retrieved December 27, 2017, from https://www.drugs.com/pro/stadol.html

STDs during pregnancy - CDC fact sheet [Leaflet]. (2016). https://www.cdc.gov/std/pregnancy/stdfact-pregnancy.htm

Stevens, S. (2012, August 14). *Evidence to support that 'rooming in' for mother and baby after birth could be beneficial.* https://medicalxpress.com/news/2012-09-evidence-rooming-mother-baby-birth.html

Stokowski, L. J. (2004). Hypospadias in the neonate. *Advances in Neonatal Care, 4*(4). https://www.medscape.com/viewarticle/489956_11

Thompson, E. G., & London, W. T. (n.d.). *Function of the liver.* https://www.webmd.com/hepatitis/function-of-the-liver

Tikkanen, R., Gunja, M. Z., FitzGerald, M., & Zephyrin, L. (2020, November 18). *Maternal Mortality and Maternity Care in the United States Compared to 10 Other Developed Countries* [Press release]. https://

www.commonwealthfund.org/publications/issue-briefs/2020/nov/maternal-mortality-maternity-care-us-compared-10-countries

Tomayochi, T. (2022, July 29). What you need to know about the latest parechovirus outbreak. *What you need to know about the latest parechovirus outbreak.* https://health.ucdavis.edu/news/headlines/what-you-need-to-know-about-the-latest-parechovirus-outbreak-/2022/07

Turner, B. (n.d.). *How to deal with swelling after pregnancy.* https://health.howstuffworks.com/pregnancy-and-parenting/pregnancy/postpartum-care/deal-with-swelling-after-pregnancy2.htm

Turner, B. (n.d.). *What causes swelling after pregnancy.* https://health.howstuffworks.com/pregnancy-and-parenting/pregnancy/postpartum-care/deal-with-swelling-after-pregnancy1.htm

Tuteur, A. (2014, September 5). Is the baby friendly hospital initiative really the baby deadly hospital initiative? *The Skeptical OB.* http://www.skepticalob.com/2014/09/is-the-baby-friendly-hospital-initiativ-really-the-baby-deadly-hospital-initiative.html

Van Der Waal, R., & Van Nistelrooij, I. (2022). Reimagining relationality for reproductive care: Understanding obstetric violence as "separation." *Nursing Ethics, 29*(5). https://doi.org/10.1177/09697330211051000

Victorian Government of Australia. The Centre for Culture, Ethnicity and Health (CEH) (Trans.). (2021, December). *Edinburgh Postnatal Depression Scale (EPDS)* [PDF]. https://www.healthtranslations.vic.gov.au/resources/edinburgh-postnatal-depression-scale-epds

What are the benefits of breastfeeding? (n.d.). In *Eunice Kennedy Shriver: National institute of child health and human development.* https://www.nichd.nih.gov/health/topics/breastfeeding/conditioninfo/Pages/benefits.aspx

What are undescended testicles (cryptorchidism)? (n.d.). Urology Care Foundation. http://www.urologyhealth.org/urologic-conditions/cryptorchidism

What is hypospadias? (n.d.). Urology Care Foundation. http://www.urologyhealth.org/urologic-conditions/hypospadias

When is a cesarean delivery necessary & what are the risks? (n.d.). In *Eunice Kennedy Shriver: National institute of child health and human development.* https://www.nichd.nih.gov/health/topics/obstetrics/conditioninfo/pages/risks.aspx

Whitlock, J. (n.d.). *What to do if you can't urinate after surgery* (R. N. Fogoros, Ed.). Retrieved July 7, 2017, from https://www.verywell.com/what-to-do-if-you-cant-urinate-after-surgery-3157318

Wong, R. J., & Bhutani, V. K. (n.d.). Patient education: Jaundice in newborn infants (Beyond the basics). In S. A. Abrams & M. S. Kim (Eds.), *UpToDate*. Retrieved April 28, 2017, from https://www.uptodate.com/contents/jaundice-in-newborn-infants-beyond-the-basics?source=see_link

World Health Organization, & UNICEF. (2009). Baby-Friendly hospital initiative: Revised, updated and expanded for integrated care. In *World Health Organization*. http://www.who.int/nutrition/publications/infantfeeding/bfhi_trainingcourse/en/

Your baby's eyes. (n.d.). Bausch and Lomb. http://www.bausch.com/vision-and-age/infant-eyes/eye-development

Yuen, M., Hall, O. J., Masters, G. A., Nephew, B. C., Carr, C., Leung, K., Griffin, A., McIntyre, L., Byatt, N., & Moore Simas, T. A. (2022). The effects of breastfeeding on maternal mental health: A systematic review. *Journal of Women's Health, 31*(6), 787-807. https://doi.org/10.1089/jwh.2021.0504

Zofran. (n.d.). Drugs.com. Retrieved December 27, 2017, from https://www.drugs.com/zofran.html

NOW IT'S YOUR TURN

Discover the EXACT 3-step blueprint you need to become a bestselling author in as little as 3 months.

Self-Publishing School helped me, and now I want them to help you with this FREE resource to begin outlining your book!

Even if you're busy, bad at writing, or don't know where to start, you CAN write a bestseller and build your best life.

With tools and experience across a variety of niches and professions, Self-Publishing School is the only resource you need to take your book to the finish line!

DON'T WAIT

Say "YES" to becoming a bestseller:

https://self-publishingschool.com/friend/

Follow the steps on the page to get a FREE resource to get started on your book and unlock a discount to get started with Self-Publishing School

Made in the USA
Monee, IL
01 October 2023